The EVERYTHING® American Government Book

Dear Reader:

Ever since grade school, I've had a passion for American government. I admired politicians and elected officials the way some people admire rock stars and athletes. I fiendishly pored over book after book on the subject in search of the nuances and subtleties that help define our system of government. I sought out teachers and mentors who added special insight into the process. I even watched C-Span every day to view it up close. I continue to do so today.

While the exuberance of my youth may have worn off, I hope some of the excitement and passion come through in the writing, and that readers experience the same sense of wonderment and exploration that I have along the way.

Nowhere does it say that history, government, and politics must be boring and tedious. More than anything, my goal is to make American government understandable, relatable, and fun. I would love nothing more than for readers to take away a greater appreciation for American government, and to share it with family, friends, colleagues, and acquaintances. If I had a marketing slogan, it would simply be "Government Fever: Catch It!"

Nick Ragone

The EVERYTHING® Series

Editorial

Publishing Director	Gary M. Krebs
Managing Editor	Kate McBride
Copy Chief	Laura MacLaughlin
Acquisitions Editor	Eric M. Hall
Development Editor	Julie Gutin
Production Editor	Jamie Wielgus

Production

Production Director	Susan Beale
Production Manager	Michelle Roy Kelly
Series Designers	Daria Perreault
	Colleen Cunningham
Cover Design	Paul Beatrice
	Frank Rivera
Layout and Graphics	Colleen Cunningham
	Rachael Eiben
	Michelle Roy Kelly
	John Paulhus
	Daria Perreault
	Erin Ring
Series Cover Artist	Barry Littmann

Visit the entire Everything® Series at www.everything.com

THE
EVERYTHING®
AMERICAN GOVERNMENT BOOK

From the Constitution to present-day
elections, all you need to understand
our democratic system

by Nick Ragone

Adams Media
Avon, Massachusetts

*To my beautiful wife, Tyan, without whom
this could not have been possible*

An Everything® Series Book.
Everything® and everything.com® are registered trademarks of F+W Publications, Inc.

Published by Adams Media, an F+W Publications Company
57 Littlefield Street, Avon, MA 02322 U.S.A.
www.adamsmedia.com

ISBN: 1-59337-055-5
Printed in the United States of America.

J I H G F E D C B A

Library of Congress Cataloging-in-Publication Data
Ragone, Nick.
The everything American government book : from the Constitution to
present-day elections, all you need to understand our democratic system /
by Nick Ragone.
p.   cm.
(An everything series book)
ISBN 1-59337-055-5
1. United States—Politics and government.
2. Democracy—United States.
I. Title. II. Series: Everything series.

JK31.R34 2004
320.473—dc22

2003026250

*This book is available at quantity discounts for bulk purchases.
For information, call 1-800-872-5627.*

Contents

Acknowledgments

Like every endeavor of my life, this book was the result of many helping hands. A million thanks to Barb Doyen, a wonderful agent and even better friend. Her enthusiasm for this project was infectious. Same for editor Eric Hall, whose encouragement, insight, and guidance made for an infinitely better book. I hope this will be the first of many collaborations. Robert Lakind, a wonderful writer in his own right, had a special eye for detail, poring over each draft as though grading a term paper. I look forward to returning the favor someday. Sharon Nieuwenhuis and Shannon Webb provided valuable feedback. The Rutgers University library staff made research enjoyable and easy. And a special thanks to my father, Frank T. Ragone, for being there every step of the way. It's been that way for as long as I can remember.

Top Ten Things You Should Know
About American Government

1. Only Congress can declare war.

2. The Bill of Rights is composed of the first ten amendments to the Constitution.

3. The Senate confirms presidential appointments.

4. The number of members of the House of Representatives is fixed at 435.

5. Only one president—James Garfield—was elected directly from the House of Representatives.

6. The vice president casts the tie-breaking vote in the Senate.

7. The Speaker of the House is the highest-ranking Congressional officer specified in the Constitution.

8. Congress can override a presidential veto with a two-thirds vote.

9. The attorney general is the highest-ranking law enforcement official in the United States.

10. The Supreme Court begins a new term on the first Monday in October.

Introduction

▶FOR SOME OF US, learning about American government in grade school and high school was an enthralling experience. For most, however, it was just one more subject to be dreaded. Fortunately, *The Everything® American Government Book* can make the experience easy and enjoyable—as simple as watching the History Channel or reading a newspaper. You'll be amazed at how American government comes to life in the pages ahead. And it might even get your youngsters to turn off the television and turn on to reading.

Understanding how our system of government works is a critical part of being a responsible citizen. Knowing the *hows* and *whys* of American government carries more importance than just being able to improve your score on the game show *Jeopardy*! It's about being an informed participant in the world's oldest constitutional democracy—a noble experiment brought to life by our Founding Fathers more than two centuries ago.

In many respects, it has been a remarkable privilege for Americans to bear witness to one of the most successful endeavors of all mankind. It is easy to forget or overlook the genius and inspiration that breathed life into the American experiment. Sometimes it helps to be reminded.

And yet with that privilege come responsibilities. As one former Speaker of the House once put it, living in a democracy isn't easy; it requires willing members to be actively engaged in all facets of civic life. In our system of governance, there is no higher virtue than participation and no greater vice than apathy. Unfortunately, apathy has gotten the better of participation in recent years.

Let *The Everything® American Government Book* serve as an easy-to-use reference guide to understanding American government—from the Bill of Rights to the presidential elections and everything in between—and the responsibilities that come with being an American citizen. If you have questions about how the electoral college works, where the presidential primaries begin, or the services that local government provides, just pick up this book and the answers are at your fingertips. It also provides practical information, such as how to register to vote, run for office, contact elected officials, and seek government solutions. Understanding our government has never been this easy.

And if you're seeking an even deeper appreciation of our system of government, let *The Everything® American Government Book* serve as a companion on your quest for knowledge, a journey that ideally will last a lifetime. Perhaps it will spur some readers to take a trip to Washington, D.C., or their state's capital to observe the wheels of government in motion. The pilgrimage will be well worth the while. There is something quite wondrous about seeing the majesty of the White House, the halls of Congress, and the Supreme Court up close, and realizing that they belong to us. The monuments of our Republic are simply awe-inspiring.

Like everything touched by human hands, our system of government is flawed. Thomas Jefferson all but confessed this in a letter to a friend more than two hundred years ago, when he wrote, "With all the imperfections of our present government, it is without comparison the best existing, or that ever did exist." As you'll see, that statement is just as true today as it was 200 years ago.

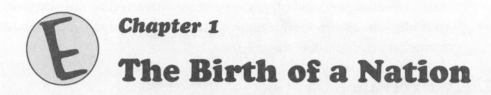

Chapter 1
The Birth of a Nation

The American government is an institution born of reason and reflection. At its foundation lie three historic documents: the Declaration of Independence, the Constitution, and the Bill of Rights. While political leaders, movements, interpretations, and ideas have come and gone the past 200 years, the underlying principles of American government have remained the same.

Settling the New World

The story of American government dates back to the earliest settlement of North America. Our grade-school textbooks taught us that the first settlers were religious separatists who came to America to escape the Church of England. Some did seek religious freedom; others sought a new beginning; and still others were simply attracted to the adventure of it all. A few were even fortune seekers. None had any intention of changing the world—but they did.

Early Arrivals

The earliest English settlement took place at Roanoke Island, North Carolina. Established by Sir Walter Raleigh in the mid to late 1580s, the Roanoke Island colony is best remembered for its mysterious and sudden demise. The British government tried again, setting up a trading outpost at Jamestown, Virginia, in 1607. Although the colony managed to survive for more than ninety years, it had to contend with harsh conditions and hostile Indians. Jamestown did leave an important legacy, however: The colonists adopted a representative assembly to govern their affairs, which was an important precedent that would be observed by later colonies.

FACT

For the first 150 years of settlement on the North American continent, the king and English Parliament showed little interest in the nuances of colonial government. The Crown viewed the colonies as nothing more than a vast market for English goods and provider of an endless supply of natural resources. Government took a back seat to commerce.

The year 1620 saw the establishment of a colony in New England, when the Puritans crossed the Atlantic and landed at Plymouth, Massachusetts. The Crown did not charter these pilgrims; rather, they were fleeing England in search of greater religious freedom and tolerance.

Before touching land, forty-one men on board the *Mayflower* signed the Mayflower Compact—a social contract that bound them to obey the authority of whatever government was established on land. Though the compact wasn't a constitution, it did have a profound impact on future generations of colonists, because it established the precedent that any governing authority in the New World requires the consent of the people. This was a unique and powerful notion that would spread throughout the colonies.

The Colonies Flourish

By 1732, all of the original thirteen colonies were established. By this time, the colonies had already developed a strong tradition of limited government and local rule. Though technically governed from London, the colonies enjoyed an enormous amount of autonomy. In fact, all thirteen had popularly elected legislatures that passed laws, levied taxes, and set policy, and each also had a formal governing document that resembled a constitution. For instance, Connecticut had the Fundamental Orders, Pennsylvania passed the Frame of Government, and Massachusetts adopted the Body of Liberties.

Given its vast distance from the New World, and its abiding interest in commerce with the colonies, Britain found the system of home rule equally agreeable. It was a comfortable fit on both sides of the Atlantic.

Prelude to a Revolution

Relations between the colonies and Britain remained smooth through the mid 1750s, until the French and Indian War. Although ultimately victorious, the tremendous cost of waging this seven-year war left England virtually bankrupt. Parliament decided to replenish Britain's treasury by taxing the colonies; something it hadn't done before.

Beginning in 1763, the British Parliament began imposing a series of taxes and demands on the colonies, including the Sugar Act, the Townshend Acts, and the Quartering Act. The most controversial measure was the Stamp Act of 1765, which raised a tax on all printed materials—everything from newspapers and legal documents to consumer products like playing cards. The colonies rallied around the idea of "no taxation without representation" and began to boycott British goods, effectively forcing the British Parliament to repeal the tax. For the first time, the colonies had acted in unison to thwart Britain's will. This was an important first step toward gaining independence.

Things came to a boiling point in 1773, when a group of patriots called the Sons of Liberty boarded three British ships and dumped 342 chests of tea into Boston Harbor. In response to what was called the Boston Tea Party, King George III quarantined Boston Harbor and seized control of Boston's government.

ALERT!

Many people ascribe the following line to the Constitution: "We hold these truths to be self-evident, that all men are created equal, that they are endowed by their Creator with certain unalienable Rights, that among these are Life, Liberty and the pursuit of Happiness." Actually, it appears in the Declaration of Independence.

The Struggle for Independence

Alarmed by the developments in Massachusetts, the colonies convened the First Continental Congress in Philadelphia on September 4, 1774. Independence and revolution were not on the agenda. The primary action was the adoption of a Declaration of Rights and Grievances, which reiterated the colonists' opposition to taxes and reasserted their right to home rule. The delegates also agreed to boycott British goods and raise their own troops. Ultimately, their goal was to reclaim colonial autonomy—not independence.

By the time the delegates gathered for the Second Continental Congress in the spring of 1775, fighting had already begun between the colonists and the British army. Skirmishes had taken place at Lexington and Concord in Massachusetts, and the port of Boston was under British occupation. The Congress appointed George Washington commander in chief of the ragtag militia that had formed outside of Boston, even though there was no formal declaration of war against England.

With the colonists evenly divided between British loyalists and revolutionaries, heated debate engulfed the thirteen colonies. Virginian Thomas

Paine brilliantly articulated the revolutionary cause in his pamphlet *Common Sense*, which sold more than 120,000 copies in the early months of 1776. "It is infinitely wiser and safer, to form a constitution of our own in a cool deliberate manner, while we have it in our power, than to trust such an interesting event to time and chance," wrote Paine. It was a sentiment that was sweeping the colonies.

QUESTION?

Do you know when the Declaration of Independence was signed? Although the Declaration of Independence was formally adopted on July 4, the delegates to the Second Continental Congress didn't actually sign the document until August 2.

The Declaration of Independence

In the spring of 1776, the Second Congress set out to formally declare its independence from Britain. A young Virginian named Thomas Jefferson was assigned the task of drafting the document, which he presented to the full Congress in late June. After debate and revision, the Congress adopted Jefferson's Declaration of Independence, and with that step embarked on one of the most momentous experiments in all humankind. There would be no turning back.

The Declaration of Independence accomplished three things:

1. It laid out a new governing principle—specifically, that all persons are created equal with certain unalienable rights, and that governments derive their power from the consent of the governed.
2. It set forth a specific list of grievances against King George III.
3. It formally declared war against Britain.

Winning the War

The Declaration of Independence made it clear to Britain that the colonies were fighting for their sovereignty. King George III and the British Parliament expressed little concern, and with good reason: few believed that a disorganized militia of peasants and farmers could prevail over the greatest army in the world.

For much of the war, the colonists suffered one defeat after another, overwhelmed by the better-trained, better-equipped, better-funded, and better-fed British army. On more than one occasion, it took everything George Washington could muster to keep the Continental Army from disbanding. But the revolutionary spirit gained momentum as the war progressed. With victories at places like Cowpens, South Carolina; Monmouth, New Jersey; and Saratoga, New York, the tide turned for the Continental Army. On October 19, 1781, George Washington defeated British General Charles Cornwallis at Yorktown, Virginia, forcing England to sue for peace. After six long years, the war was finally over.

Articles of Confederation

Declaring independence from Britain was one thing; creating a new government was quite another. With the backdrop of war, the colonists hammered out the Articles of Confederation in only sixteen months (from July 1776 to November of the following year). It took longer to ratify: South Carolina was the first to sign in February 1778; Maryland was the last in March of 1781. During its short existence, the Articles would account for few successes and many failures.

FACT

George Washington was so dismayed by the Articles of Confederation that he referred to it as "a half-starved limping government, that appears to be always moving upon crutches and tottering at every step."

A Flawed Document

As a governing document, the Articles of Confederation was flawed from the start. With the memory of British oppression still fresh, the colonists—particularly outspoken revolutionaries like Sam Adams, Patrick Henry, and John Hancock—were wary of creating a strong central government. Most preferred a loose confederation of states, with the national government subordinate to them. In effect, they were trying to reproduce a system of local rule that prevailed prior to the French and Indian War.

The organizing principle of the Articles was a unicameral (single-body) legislature with limited authority. Each state had one vote in this Congress, and there was no independent executive or judiciary branch. Instead, the Congress appointed temporary officers to do this work. Major pieces of legislation, such as raising revenues or amending the Articles, required a unanimous vote, which meant that any one state held veto power over the national government. When the Congress was out of session—which was frequent—a conference of delegates from each state acted in its stead.

An uprising in western Massachusetts led by a bankrupt farmer named Daniel Shays finally convinced political leaders that the Articles of Confederation was ineffective. Shays's Rebellion was put down in the autumn of 1786, and it spurred political leaders to convene the Constitutional Convention the following year.

The Articles of Confederation lacked the power to perform the most basic tasks, such as regulating interstate commerce, establishing a national currency, taxing the people directly, enforcing treaties, raising revenues, or compelling the states to contribute monies to the national government. As a consequence, the country was an economic wreck throughout its tenure. The Articles even struggled to maintain tranquility among the states. Toward the end of the war, things got so bad that the Congress was forced to sell off western lands just to pay for the militia. For all intents and purposes, the national government existed at the mercy of the states—a recipe for failure.

A Few Important Achievements

While the Articles of Confederation was unquestionably a failure, it did make an important contribution to the development of our nation. The Articles served to create a kind of "transition" government between the Revolutionary War and the birth of the Republic as the country went through a "cooling off" period, with revolutionary zeal giving way to tempered reason. Leaders learned from its shortcomings, and used the experience to create the Constitution. And it even had a few outright successes, such as the Land Ordinance of 1785 and the Northwest Ordinance of 1787, two major pieces of legislation that helped settle the West.

But perhaps most important, the Articles of Confederation represents an important milestone in the history of Western democracies. For the first time, citizens used reason and logic to create a new form of government. In fact, they created something radically different from anything that had previously existed. It was a bold and dramatic first step, and although it didn't succeed, it proved that a government of consent could be achieved through peaceful means. And it also gave our country its name: The United States of America.

Drafting the Constitution

Even with the hard-fought victory over Britain, the survival of the young nation was still in doubt. The economy remained in shambles, there was rampant civil unrest, states were bickering with each other, and the nation lacked the ability to defend itself against foreign powers. It became apparent to the Founding Fathers that the Articles would have to be dramatically altered or replaced if the new nation was to survive.

In September of 1786, representatives from five states gathered in Annapolis, Maryland, to discuss amending the Articles of Confederation. Not long after convening, however, the group realized it would require delegates from all thirteen states to give the matter proper attention, so they decided to meet again in Philadelphia the following year.

Fifty-five delegates from twelve states (Rhode Island refused to attend) arrived in Philadelphia on May 25, 1787, with the purpose of creating a new and better government. The convention lasted the entire summer and was conducted in secret, as participants sought an honest exchange of ideas and compromise. As the first order of business, the delegates unanimously voted George Washington convention chair. It would be the only unanimous agreement all summer.

Virginia and New Jersey Plans

Shortly after the convention convened, Virginians James Madison and Edmund Randolph, two of the most well respected attendees, submitted a constitutional proposal called the Virginia Plan, which was a radical departure from the Articles of Confederation. At the heart of the Virginia plan was a bicameral (two-chamber) legislature with the lower house chosen by the people and the upper house chosen by the lower house. The plan also called for a national executive and judiciary, both of which were to be selected by the legislature. The Virginia Plan was a bold attempt at creating a strong central government.

FACT

Delegates suffered through brutal working conditions in the East Room at the Pennsylvania State House. With secrecy at a premium, these distinguished Americans were forced to deliberate with closed windows for the duration of the summer—one of the hottest on record. The only reprieve from the suffocating heat was an occasional after-hours deliberation at the Indian Queen, a popular local tavern.

While delegates from the large states supported the Virginia Plan, representatives from the smaller states cried foul as it became apparent that the larger states would dominate the national legislature (the number of legislative representatives would be determined by population). Other delegates feared that such a strong central government would snuff out states' rights and restrict individual liberty.

After weeks of heated debate, William Patterson of New Jersey hastily submitted an alternative document dubbed the New Jersey Plan. The New Jersey Plan wasn't so much a new proposal as it was a modification of the Articles of Confederation. It called for a unicameral legislature with equal representation for each state regardless of population, a weak two-person executive branch, and a single judiciary body. Small-state delegates and weak-government proponents rallied around the New Jersey Plan, while big-state members stood firmly opposed.

The Great Compromise

Delegates were at a stalemate over the two proposals. In late July, Roger Sherman of Connecticut broke the impasse with a compromise known as the Connecticut Plan. Sherman's compromise was mostly a patchwork of both proposals. It adopted the bicameral legislature approach of the Virginia Plan (with its population-based lower chamber), and the independent upper chamber (with equal representation) of the New Jersey Plan. Small-state delegates were satisfied with the equal representation of the upper chamber (Senate), while big-state representatives took solace in the population-based lower chamber (House). A Great Compromise had been reached.

With the framework of the Constitution in place, the delegates found common ground on the remaining issues. After rancorous debate, it was decided that the slave trade would remain legal until 1808—a twenty-one-year "winding down" period—and that escaped slaves would be returned to their owners. It was believed that slavery would eventually wind down of its own volition.

Another issue related to slavery was how to count slaves for the census. Southerners wanted people of color counted equally in determining representation in Congress (because most slaves resided in the South), while northerners argued that they shouldn't be counted at all. The delegates eventually agreed on the "three-fifths" compromise, which stated that slaves would be counted as three-fifths of a free person. This decision, combined with the failure to abolish slavery, marks the greatest shortcoming of the Constitution.

FACT

The Constitution of the United States is the oldest written constitution still in use, and one of the shortest, coming in at approximately 7,000 words. The original Constitution is on display at the National Archives in Washington, D.C., along with the Declaration of Independence and the Bill of Rights.

The delegates also came to agreement in selecting the chief executive. Many were opposed to having the president elected by the people, who were viewed as uneducated and uniformed. Others were adamant that the president should be chosen directly by the people. To solve the problem, the delegates came up with the Electoral College, which called for a separate body of "electors"—selected by each state's legislature—to ultimately vote for the president.

On September 17, 1787, thirty-nine of the remaining forty-two delegates signed the Constitution (some of the original fifty-five left early). The only remaining question was, would it be ratified?

The Process of Ratification

Ratification of the newly created Constitution was not a sure thing. There was a real concern that the document granted too much power to the federal government and would ultimately lead to aristocratic tyranny. Sensing the struggle that lay ahead, the framers wisely stated that the Constitution need only be approved by nine out of thirteen states. They also stipulated that the states would not vote on ratification through their state legislatures—which the Founders feared would have great misgivings about the new central government—but rather through a special elective convention. Were it not for these two crucial provisions, the Constitution might not have been ratified at all.

Federalists and Antifederalists

Opinions regarding the Constitution were divided into two camps: The Federalists and antifederalists. The Federalists believed in a strong central government that shared powers with the states, and therefore they supported the Constitution. The antifederalists were suspicious of this new central government and preferred direct democracy and local rule. In the fall of 1787, each side began publishing essays in support of its position, and today these writings represent some of the most important (and most studied) discussions on American government and political theory.

The Federalists were led by James Madison, Alexander Hamilton, and John Jay, who together wrote *The Federalist Papers*. Two essays in particular—James Madison's Federalist No. 10 and Federalist No. 51—are cited as the most persuasive in support of the Constitution, and are mandatory reading in college history classes around the country. The antifederalists were led by patriots such as Patrick Henry, John Hancock, George Mason, future president James Monroe, and Revolutionary War hero Sam Adams. Even Thomas Jefferson had misgivings about a Constitution that didn't include a Bill of Rights. The antifederalists rebutted the *Federalist Papers* with their own set of essays published under the pseudonyms Montezuma and Philadelphiensis.

The antifederalists were particularly concerned that the Constitution did not include a Bill of Rights, which they considered essential in safeguarding against an overbearing central government and protecting individual freedoms and liberty.

Race to the Finish Line

Beginning in the winter of 1787, state conventions began the process of ratification. The Constitution was officially ratified on June 21, 1788, when New Hampshire narrowly adopted it with a 57–46 vote. However, it wasn't until late July that it became clear the new union was destined to survive, after Virginia and New York, the two largest states at the time, approved the document. The following is the order of ratification:

1. Delaware, December 7, 1787
2. Pennsylvania, December 12, 1787
3. New Jersey, December 18, 1787
4. Georgia, January 2, 1788
5. Connecticut, January 9, 1788
6. Massachusetts, February 6, 1788
7. Maryland, April 28, 1788
8. South Carolina, May 23, 1788
9. New Hampshire, June 21, 1788
10. Virginia, June 25, 1788
11. New York, July 26, 1788
12. North Carolina, November 21, 1789
13. Rhode Island, May 29, 1790

And with that, the United States of America got a fresh start.

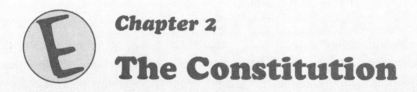

Chapter 2

The Constitution

The structure of the Constitution is straightforward and simple. It establishes the three branches of government—legislative, executive, and judicial—and creates the system of "checks and balances" that defines American government. That way, each branch has certain checks over the others so that no one branch dominates. In this chapter, we'll take a closer look at the Constitution and how it shapes our system of government.

The Preamble

"We the People of the United States, in Order to form a more perfect Union, establish Justice, insure domestic Tranquility, provide for the common defence, promote the general Welfare, and secure the Blessings of Liberty to ourselves and our Posterity, do ordain and establish this Constitution for the United States of America."

With those words, the framers embarked on one of the greatest experiments in recorded history—to create a nation in which the governed confer legitimacy to the government and consent to its rule. The preamble is probably the single most recognizable phrase from the Constitution. It accomplishes two goals: it defines the purpose of the Constitution and reiterates that ultimate authority rests with the people, not the government.

Article I: Legislative Branch

Article I is the longest of the seven articles that compose the Constitution. The framers established the Congress in Article I, even before establishing the presidency (Article II), because they believed that the legislative branch should be pre-eminent in American government. Article I consists of ten sections, some of which are further subdivided by clauses.

The framers left it up to the states to determine who may vote for members of Congress. Prior to the Civil War, most states restricted voting to white male property owners over the age of twenty-one. Over time, the property requirement was dropped. African-Americans, other minorities, and women also were granted voting rights.

Creating the House and Senate

Article I, section 1 of the Constitution establishes the Congress as the first branch of government with one sentence. Section 2 establishes the

House of Representatives and contains five clauses. Clauses 1 and 2 lay out the qualifications for serving in the House of Representatives, and the process for House elections.

As we learned in Chapter 1, a state's representation in the House is based on its population size. The Constitution guarantees that each state will have at least one representative, and it originally called for one representative for every 30,000 citizens. That number has increased to 600,000 citizens per representative over the years. Today, the number of representatives is capped at 435. Section 2 also states that when a vacancy occurs in the House, the state's governor must call a special election to fill it. Clause 5 gives the House—and only the House—the power to impeach elected officials. The framers considered impeachment to be one of the most potent checks in American government. They believed that it should only be used sparingly, and with the consent of the people.

ALERT!

Many people don't really know what it means to "impeach." Impeachment is an accusation of wrongdoing brought against a federal official with the intent of removing him from office. In order to be removed, however, the impeached person must be convicted by the Senate.

Section 3 establishes the United States Senate. Originally, the Constitution called for senators to be chosen by their respective state legislatures. The framers did this because they wanted the Senate to be insulated from politics—a place where issues could be deliberated freely without the specter of electoral politics. They also gave senators six-year terms instead of two-year, which they thought would further remove them from the popular passions of the day.

Section 3 also establishes qualification for office, Senate leadership, the role of the vice president, impeachment trials, and the penalty for impeachment conviction. Under clause 7 of section 3, the only penalty for impeachment is removal from office. It does state, however, that the impeached individual may still be tried in both criminal and civil courts.

Provisions for Running the Show

The next three sections establish the procedures for operating both the House and the Senate. Some of the more interesting provisions include the following:

- Congress must assemble at least once a year. When travel was difficult during the early years of the Republic, Congress did convene only once a year. In fact, most members held full-time jobs while Congress was out of session.
- Both chambers may refuse to seat a member. Although this is rarely done, it has occurred on occasion. After scandal-ridden Representative Adam Clayton Powell was elected to his twelfth term in 1968, Congress refused to seat him—his seat remained unoccupied.
- Both chambers must publish a journal of their proceedings after each session.
- Neither chamber can recess for more than three days without the consent of the other chamber.
- Congressional salaries are paid by the Department of Treasury, not by the respective states. The framers wanted all members to be paid equally, and did not want to give states undue influence over their representatives. Members of the first Congress received $6 for every day in session!
- Members of Congress cannot be arrested or sued for things said during speeches and debates made in the Capitol Building. This provision was included to encourage free and open debate.
- Members of Congress cannot simultaneously hold another federal government position. This provision was included to avoid any violations of the separation of powers clause.

The Powers of Congress

Most scholars consider sections 7 through 10 of Article I as the most important in the Constitution, because it outlined the Congress's powers and limitations. Section 8 is the longest of the Constitution with its eighteen clauses. Three in particular are considered the most important:

1. Commerce Clause. Clause 3 gives the Congress the power to regulate interstate commerce and trade with foreign nations. Over the years, the commerce clause has expanded to give Congress the ability to more or less regulate the national economy. Recently, there has been an attempt by the courts to "roll back" the power of the commerce clause in keeping with the framers' original intent.

2. Declaring War. Clause 11 gives Congress—not the president—the power to declare war. The framers did not trust the president to declare war; they feared that the power could easily be abused by a would-be dictator or tyrant. Since the Korean War, Congress and the president have struggled to find a balance between the right of the Congress to declare war and the role of the president as commander in chief.

3. The Elastic Clause. Clause 18 of section 8 gives Congress the power to make all "necessary and proper" laws that would help execute the enumerated powers of the Constitution. Many scholars consider this the single most important provision of the Constitution—the clause that makes it a "living document."

The framers explicitly denied certain powers to both Congress and the states. Section 9 prohibits Congress from passing any law that inflicts punishment on an individual without a trial or provides punishment for acts that weren't illegal when the act was committed. It also prohibits Congress from taxing commerce between the states.

FACT

One of the more obscure—and interesting—provisions in the Constitution is clause 8 of section 9, which prohibits the federal government (as well as the states) from granting a title of nobility, such as duke or duchess, to citizens and noncitizens.

Article II: Executive Branch

The second article of the Constitution establishes the executive branch and defines the powers of the presidency. This article is divided into four sections.

Section 1

Section 1 of Article II establishes the office of the presidency, and the method for selecting the president—the Electoral College. The College is a group of people known as "electors" who select the president of the United States. The framers devised this system because they had little confidence in ordinary citizens' ability to choose the right president, and they believed that the states should have weighted influence relative to population size.

The Electoral College is composed of electors who equal the number of representatives and senators from a state. For instance, the state of Alaska—with its two senators and one House member—has a total of three electors in the Electoral College. When citizens vote for a presidential candidate, they are actually voting for the electors from that state. In order to become president, a candidate must receive 270 votes in the Electoral College. If neither candidate receives the requisite 270 electoral votes, then the House of Representatives determines the president. This first occurred in 1824, when John Quincy Adams was selected president by the House of Representatives after Andrew Jackson failed to receive a majority of the Electoral College votes. Jackson's supporters cried foul, and used the "stolen" election of 1824 as a rallying point for their 1828 victory.

QUESTION?

How does each state choose electors for the Electoral College? Every state except Nebraska and Maine has a "winner takes all" system, meaning that the presidential candidate who wins the popular vote receives all the delegates. In Maine and Nebraska, electors are apportioned by Congressional district—the candidate who wins the popular vote in a Congressional district receives that district's electoral vote.

In section 1, the framers gave Congress the power to determine when presidential elections are held and when the Electoral College meets. Congress set the Tuesday after the first Monday in November in every fourth year as the presidential election day, and the Monday after the second Wednesday in December for the meeting of the Electoral College. Finally, section 1 established that the president's salary cannot be diminished during his term in office and that he cannot receive other forms of payment while in office.

Section 2

Unlike section 8 of Article I, which uses eighteen clauses to enumerate the powers of Congress, section 2 of Article II accomplishes the task of establishing the power of the presidency in only three clauses. In particular, the clauses cover the following duties and limitations:

1. **Commander in Chief.** Clause 1 states, "The President shall be Commander in Chief of the Army and Navy of the United States, and of the Militia of the several States." The framers wanted all military authority to ultimately reside in civilian control, but they wisely divided war-making between the president and Congress. The president is commander in chief, but only Congress can formally declare war.

2. **Treaties and Appointments.** As we'll learn in Chapter 9, the power to make treaties and appointments has been one of the president's most acted-upon constitutional powers. When drafting the Constitution, the framers believed that this would be the president's main power.

3. **Filling Vacancies.** When Congress is not in session, the president has the power to make temporary appointments without Senate approval. Known as recess appointments, these temporary appointments expire at the end of the Congressional term. Every president since Washington has made recess appointments—some more controversial than others. Recess appointments are most commonly used when the Senate refuses to take up a presidential nominee.

The Last Two Sections of Article II

Section 3 requires the president to give Congress information regarding the State of the Union, and section 4 prescribes impeachment for all civil officers who commit high crimes or misdemeanors.

Many of the powers and duties that the president enjoys today are not written in the Constitution, but are the result of precedent, court decisions, and the expanded role of government. At times throughout history, the expansion of the president's powers has created tension between the executive and legislative branches.

Article III: Judicial Branch

Article III establishes the judicial branch of government and the federal court system: "The judicial power of the United States shall be vested in one supreme Court, and in such inferior Courts as the Congress may from time to time ordain and establish." In accordance with this statement, Congress created the lower court system (Judiciary Act of 1789). The framers also provided that federal judges would serve lifelong terms and that their pay could not be diminished. They wanted the judiciary to be impartial and immune from political and other pressures. With that being the case, federal judges can only be removed by impeachment and conviction. This remedy has been used sparingly; only thirteen judges have been impeached and removed from office.

A notable provision of Article III is the definition and punishment for treason. Treason is defined as "giving aid and comfort" to the enemy or levying war against the United States. The framers left it to Congress to decide the punishment for treason, which Congress in turn has defined as a minimum of five years in prison and a maximum of death.

QUESTION?

How many civilians have been executed for treason or espionage?
In 1953, Julius and Ethel Rosenberg became the only American civilians to be executed for treason after they were convicted of providing atomic weapon secrets to the Soviet Union.

Article IV: Relations among the States

Article IV of the Constitution establishes the relationship among the states, and is an important point of distinction from the Articles of Confederation. Under the Articles, the states were in "confederation" with each other, meaning that they were largely independent. Because this system was largely a failure, the framers were determined to find a balance between a strong central government and the powers of the states.

What they came up with was federalism—a system of government in which authority is shared by the federal government and various state governments. The framers settled on this system because it satisfied those delegates who believed a strong central government was necessary to create a union as well as those who wanted to preserve state autonomy.

The framers enumerated several key doctrines in Article IV that helped construct the federal model of government:

- **Full Faith and Credit Clause.** This clause mandates that the states respect each other's laws, legal decisions, and records, such as driver's license, marriage proceedings, divorce records, and the like. In recent years, there has been much speculation about whether the full faith and credit clause would mandate that same-sex marriages in one state be recognized in all fifty states.
- **Privileges and Immunities Clause.** This clause establishes that a state can't treat nonresidents any differently than it treats its own residents.
- **Extradition Clause.** Accused persons who flee to another state must be returned to the state where the crime was committed.
- **Admission of States.** Section 3 provides that only Congress can admit a new state into the Union. This provision held greater importance in the nineteenth century, when admission to the Union occurred on a regular basis.
- **Republican Form of Government.** Section 4 establishes three important doctrines. First, states must elect their government officials. Second, the federal government is bound to protect the states from foreign invasion. And third, the state governments can call upon the federal government to quell domestic violence within their states.

Article V: Amendments

The Constitution can be amended in one of two ways. The first (and more common) approach requires a two-thirds vote of each chamber of Congress, followed by ratification by three-fourths of all the state legislatures. The second approach requires two-thirds of the state legislatures to call for a constitutional convention. This method has never been tried.

Every section of the Constitution is subject to amendment except one: States must have equal representation in the United States Senate. This provision was a central tenet of the great compromise.

ALERT!

There was a second provision of the Constitution that was also exempt from amendment. Under section 9 of Article I, Congress was prohibited from outlawing the international slave trade prior to 1808. After 1808, Congress outlawed the importation of slaves, although slavery itself wasn't abolished until the Civil War.

Article VI: National Supremacy

This article establishes the supremacy of the Constitution. Referred to as the supremacy clause, it declares that all federal laws take precedence over concurrent state laws. Put another way, any local or state law that contradicts federal law is considered unconstitutional. National laws that are parallel to state laws are said to "pre-empt" state law, or take precedence over it.

Article VI also requires every federal and state official to pledge—with an oath—to support and uphold the Constitution of the United States, and bans religion as a qualification to hold any federal or state office.

FACT

The Constitution ends with the seventh Article, which simply states, "The Ratification of the Conventions of nine States, shall be sufficient for the Establishment of this Constitution between the States so ratifying the Same."

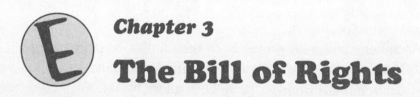

Chapter 3

The Bill of Rights

The Bill of Rights has come to symbolize the ideal that forms the basis of the American system of government: Freedom. Freedom to speak out against the government; freedom to assemble peaceably; freedom to worship; freedom from government intrusion. While some Americans would have difficulty in pointing to the Constitution as the source of our system of checks and balances, far fewer would have trouble identifying the Bill of Rights as the repository of our basic freedoms.

How the Bill Was Born

Contrary to common belief, the Bill of Rights did not introduce the concept of inalienable freedoms from government power. In fact, the early settlers and colonists began defining liberties shortly after setting foot in the New World.

Maryland passed the Toleration Act of 1649, becoming the first colony to codify religious liberty. The others soon followed suit. A decade earlier, Massachusetts had adopted the Body of Liberties, a rudimentary bill of rights that (although it was silent on religious freedoms) guaranteed the right to assemble peaceably, the right to a jury trial in civil cases, the equal protection of laws, and compensation for private property taken for public purposes, among other things. William Penn took it one step further, creating a long list of enumerated rights in Pennsylvania's first Constitution, which was adopted in 1682.

State Constitutions

Following the Declaration of Independence, the states began adopting new state constitutions. The first of these efforts, the Virginia Constitution of 1776, actually begins with a sixteen-point Declaration of Rights that restrained all three branches of government—executive, legislative, and judicial. It was the first to proclaim that all men are created equal, and that all power derives from the people.

Pennsylvania's Bill of Rights introduced the separation of church and state, the right to counsel in criminal cases, the right to bear arms, and the right to travel. Delaware's Bill of Rights was the first to prohibit the quartering of troops in homes during peacetime, while Maryland's outlawed bills of attainder.

QUESTION?

What is a bill of attainder?
A bill of attainder is a legislative act that finds a person guilty of a crime without conducting a trial. This was fairly common in the colonial era, and one of the biggest grievances of the colonists. Eliminating bills of attainder is one of the cornerstones of our legal system.

Massachusetts's Bill of Rights made an important contribution in out-lawing all unreasonable searches and seizures, but more important was the method by which it was created. Unlike the other states, which created their bills of rights through the normal legislative process, Massachusetts was the first to call a special constitutional convention. By doing this, it established the precedent that the Bill of Rights could only be altered by constitutional convention—an important safeguard against a whimsical legislature.

Creating the Bill of Rights

The Constitution that was signed in Philadelphia in September of 1787 did not contain a bill of rights. Throughout the convention, the issue was barely raised at all, save Virginian George Mason's last-minute suggestion that the Constitution be prefaced by such a bill in order to "give quiet" to citizens back home. The matter was hardly debated, and a motion to adopt a bill of rights was defeated unanimously.

However, as the states began deliberating the adoption of the newly created Constitution, the delegates quickly realized their political blunder in not including a bill of rights. Antifederalists used the lack of a bill of rights to rally the public against the Constitution. In response, James Madison and his fellow Federalists promised that the new Congress would create a bill of rights as its first order of business.

The Bill of Rights was not the first federal document to safeguard personal freedoms and liberty. One of the first acts of Congress was to pass the Northwest Ordinance of 1787, which established the process for territories to become states. The Ordinance contained a bill of rights that guaranteed settlers habeas corpus (the right to go before a judge to determine if imprisonment is lawful), trial by jury, just compensation for taken property, and the right to bail.

True to his word, Madison took up the issue of a bill of rights in the summer of 1789. Borrowing from state bills of rights and other public writings, Madison proposed seventeen amendments to the Constitution, which the House quickly passed. The Senate pruned the list, and the Bill of Rights was submitted to the states for ratification. On December 15, 1791, Virginia became the eleventh state to ratify ten amendments, and with that the United States Constitution had a Bill of Rights.

Freedom of Expression

It's no coincidence that the First Amendment appears at the top of the list. The framers believed that free speech, free religious expression, and a free press were critical to democracy, and an essential component of liberty. The First Amendment provides some of our most cherished freedoms.

Freedom of Religion

The First Amendment begins with the following: "Congress shall make no law respecting an establishment of religion, or prohibiting the free exercise thereof." During colonial times, several colonies had official churches, which citizens were required to attend. In fact, a few of the colonies were quite intolerant of minority religions. However, Madison, Jefferson, and other Founding Fathers believed that there should be complete separation between church and state.

The First Amendment does two things: It prohibits the government from creating an "official" religion (establishment clause), and prevents the government from prohibiting the practice of any religion (free exercise clause). Over the years, the Supreme Court has interpreted the establishment clause to mean that the federal and state governments cannot set up a church, give preference to one religion over another, participate in the affairs of religious organizations, or punish individuals because of their religious beliefs. The issue of prayer in public schools is an example of the difficult application of the First Amendment to everyday scenarios, because some people argue it violates the establishment clause.

On the other hand, the free exercise clause prevents the government from restricting religious practices. Broadly speaking, the government cannot ban religious practices or interfere with citizens' religious beliefs. This, too, can sometimes lead to murky public policy decisions. The courts have ruled that children cannot refuse certain types of medical vaccinations, even if it goes against their religious beliefs, arguing that it would jeopardize public safety. In 1993, Congress passed the Religious Freedom Restoration Act, which requires federal, state, and local governments to accommodate religious conduct in the least restrictive manner possible.

FACT

In the summer of 2003, Alabama Supreme Court Chief Justice Roy Moore created a national stir when he refused a federal court order to remove a 5,300-pound stone engraving of the Ten Commandments from a state judicial building. (Later, Moore was removed from the bench by a Court of the Judiciary.) It wasn't Moore's first brush with controversy; eight years earlier, the American Civil Liberties Union (ACLU) had sued him for posting the Ten Commandments in his courtroom.

Freedom of the Press

At the time of the framing of the Constitution, freedom of the press referred to newspapers and pamphlets. Today, it applies to multiple media—television, radio, Internet, magazines, e-mail, billboards, and so on. The framers believed that a free press was essential to good government, and that the press, in effect, acted as a "super-check" on all three branches of government.

Over the years, the Supreme Court has interpreted freedom of the press broadly, putting few restrictions on the media. In 1971, the Supreme Court denied President Nixon an injunction against the *New York Times* from publishing a classified report (which it had obtained from a disgruntled former Defense Department employee) that detailed the role of the United States in the Vietnam War. The court ruled that such an injunction would violate the First Amendment.

Freedom of Speech

The right to free speech has been a balancing act between legitimate expression and public safety. Is there an absolute right to free speech, or may the government curtail certain types of speech and expression? In a landmark Supreme Court case in 1919, legendary justice Oliver Wendell Holmes created the "clear and present danger test" for free speech. The doctrine allows the government to curtail or limit speech if it can demonstrate that the speech represents a clear and present danger to public safety. To make his point, Holmes used the example of shouting "fire" in a public theater when in fact there was no fire. Such speech would not be protected under the clear and present danger test.

The courts have been unwilling to extend constitutional protection to speech that is considered slanderous or obscene. Defining and regulating obscene speech has been particularly difficult for the courts, as Supreme Court Justice Potter Stewart all but admitted when he wrote in a 1964 decision that, although he couldn't define obscenity, "I know it when I see it."

The Right to Bear Arms

The Second Amendment ranks among the most contentious provisions in the Constitution. It simply states: "A well regulated Militia, being necessary to the security of a free State, the right of the people to keep and bear Arms, shall not be infringed." The question remains: Does that mean individuals have an inviolable right to possess a gun, or does it simply mean that states have the right to create an armed militia?

The Third Amendment, which prohibits government quartering of soldiers in private homes, can be viewed as a corollary to the Second Amendment. Madison included it because during the Revolutionary War, British soldiers frequently commandeered citizens' homes against their will. The framers did not want the states or federal government doing the same.

Gun owners and their powerful lobbying group, the National Rifle Association (NRA), contend that citizens have an absolute right to bear arms. Many states and the federal government have enacted laws restricting gun ownership, which the courts have upheld. The courts have reasoned that the framers intended for the Second Amendment to allow states to continue having armed militias (remember, state militias won the Revolutionary War), and not to give individuals an inviolable right to a gun.

Criminal Rights Amendments

The drafters of the Bill of Rights believed that constitutional protection against arbitrary prosecution was a critical check on government power. The Fourth, Fifth, Sixth, and Eighth Amendments safeguard individuals from abusive practices in the criminal process and limit the government's ability to prosecute unjustly. Many scholars consider these amendments to be the most important provisions of the Bill of Rights.

No Illegal Searches or Seizures

The Fourth Amendment guarantees "the right of the people to be secure in their persons, houses, papers, and effects, against unreasonable searches and seizures" without a properly authorized warrant. The Supreme Court has interpreted the Fourth Amendment to mean that evidence obtained illegally (or without a warrant) by law enforcement officials is excluded from trial. This is not an absolute rule, however. The exception to the exclusionary rule is when law enforcement officials make a "good faith" effort to follow established procedures. In those situations, the evidence is admissible. This is a fluid area of case law, and has been subject to numerous modifications over the years.

The Right Against Self-Incrimination

Most Americans are familiar with the Fifth Amendment from movies and popular culture, in which "I plead the Fifth" is a commonly used phrase. The Fifth Amendment is the longest in the Bill of Rights. It establishes the following:

- **No "Double Jeopardy" Trials:** A person cannot be tried twice for the same crime.
- **The Right Against Self-Incrimination:** A person cannot be forced to testify against himself or herself in a criminal trial. Only when a

person is granted immunity from prosecution can an individual be compelled to testify against himself.

- **The Right to a Grand Jury:** A person cannot be held for a crime punishable by death without a grand jury indictment.

ALERT!

In the landmark 1961 Supreme Court case *Miranda v. Arizona*, the court created the notion of "Miranda Rights" from the Fifth Amendment right against self-incrimination. Under Miranda Rights, law enforcement officials must inform suspects of their constitutional right to ask for an attorney and to remain silent. In recent years, the Supreme Court has weakened *Miranda* protections.

The Right to Counsel and Jury Trial

The Sixth Amendment gives criminal defendants the right to a speedy jury trial and the right to counsel (the right to have an attorney represent the defendant). The right to an attorney has evolved over the years. In 1932, the Supreme Court held that the right to an attorney applied only to capital offenses, which are cases with the threat of the death penalty. In 1963, the Court widened the right to counsel to include felony arrests—cases in which the threat of imprisonment exceeds one year. And later, the Court broadened it again to include any case that held a possible prison term. (It's important to note that there is no right to an attorney in civil cases.) The court will appoint an attorney if a criminal defendant cannot afford one.

The right to a jury trial includes the right to be tried before a representative jury. For decades, several southern states excluded African-Americans and women from jury pools, a practice that is now deemed unconstitutional.

No Cruel and Unusual Punishment

The Eighth Amendment consists of only sixteen words: "Excessive bail shall not be required, nor excessive fines imposed, nor cruel and unusual punishments inflicted." Although the death penalty has never been held by the Supreme Court to constitute cruel and unusual punishment, certain methods of execution have been, such as public hanging and torture. The Supreme Court has expanded the Eighth Amendment to include a prohibition against using torture and other forceful measures to obtain confessions from criminal suspects.

The Supreme Court's interpretation of the Eighth Amendment has also given rise to the practice of separating the sentencing stage from the conviction in capital cases. Once a felon is convicted of a capital crime, the sentencing phase begins, and the jury hears evidence from the prosecution and defense on whether the death penalty should be imposed.

FACT

The Seventh Amendment establishes that "in suits at common law, where the value in controversy shall exceed twenty dollars, the right of a trial by jury shall be preserved." At the time, the twenty-dollar threshold was quite high; today, every civil case tried in federal court has a jury unless both parties stipulate otherwise.

Protecting Rights

Both the Ninth and Tenth Amendments essentially serve as a reminder that any rights not specifically enumerated are reserved to the people and the states, respectively.

Some of the most controversial decisions in Supreme Court history emanate from the Ninth Amendment, including the landmark abortion case *Roe v. Wade*, and *Griswold v. Connecticut*, in which the Supreme Court overturned a Connecticut state law that outlawed the use of contraception. The Court reasoned in those decisions and others that the Ninth Amendment included a fundamental right to privacy—"penumbral rights"—that could not be violated. The Supreme Court has used the Ninth Amendment penumbral rights to broadly protect private behavior from government intrusion, although it has done so cautiously and slowly.

The Tenth Amendment declares that "the powers not delegated to the United States by the Constitution, nor prohibited by it to the States, are reserved to the States respectively, or to the people."

Other Amendments to the Constitution

In addition to the Bill of Rights, the United States Constitution has been amended seventeen times. The first additional amendment was made in 1795 and the last in 1992. Only one amendment to the Constitution has been repealed—the eighteenth, which prohibited the production, sale, or transportation of alcohol.

Like the Bill of Rights, over the years some amendments have loomed larger in importance than others:

- **Thirteenth Amendment.** Ratified in December of 1865, it freed all slaves and abolished slavery in the United States and its territories. Former slaves were given the same rights as other citizens.

- **Fourteenth Amendment.** Ratified in 1868, the Fourteenth Amendment is both the longest and most frequently cited amendment in constitutional law. Initially passed to protect the rights of former slaves, over time the Fourteenth Amendment has evolved to mean that all citizens are subject to due process and equal protection of the laws.

- **Fifteenth Amendment.** Ratified in 1870, it states that "the right of citizens of the United States to vote shall not be denied or abridged by the United States or by any State on account of race, color, or previous condition of servitude." It wasn't until the landmark Civil Rights Act of 1964, however, that true voting rights were established for all Americans.

- **Sixteenth Amendment.** Ratified in 1913, it overturned an 1894 Supreme Court decision that held income taxes to be unconstitutional. Essentially, this amendment allows Congress to tax income without apportioning the revenues evenly among the states.

- **Nineteenth Amendment.** Ratified just prior to the 1920 presidential election, it gave women the right to vote in state and federal elections. The amendment was first proposed in 1878, and came before Congress eight times before finally winning passage. A few states— Wyoming, Idaho, Utah, and Colorado—allowed women to vote prior to the Nineteenth Amendment, but the majority did not.

- **Twenty-second Amendment.** Ratified in 1951, it prohibited presidents from serving more than two elected terms. It also stipulates that if a president succeeds to office after the halfway point of his predecessor's term, he can serve two more elected terms (for a total of ten years in office). This amendment was a direct response to Franklin Roosevelt's four terms in office, which many legislators considered excessive and somewhat reckless.

- **Twenty-fifth Amendment.** Ratified in 1967, it established that the president can appoint a vice president (subject to a majority vote of Congress) when the office becomes vacant. Prior to that, the office remained vacant for the entire term.
- **Twenty-sixth Amendment.** Ratified in 1971, it established that citizens who are eighteen years of age or older cannot be denied the right to vote in federal or state elections by virtue of age. This amendment was largely a response to discontent stemming from the Vietnam War, during which thousands of teenagers died on the battlefield.

Chapter 4

The House of Representatives

The American Congress is made up of two houses—the House of Representatives and the Senate. In this system, the House is the governing body that is closest to the people. It's where the majority sets the agenda and passions run high. When it comes to understanding public policy issues, one of the best ways to take the pulse of the American people is to observe the House of Representatives. Whether it's health care insurance or increasing the minimum wage, popular issues do not reach critical mass until taken up in the House.

The People's House

The House of Representatives is often referred to as "The People's House" because its members represent the smallest unit of the population. The typical House district encompasses approximately 600,000 people. Moreover, with re-election every two years, members tend to spend a great deal of time in the district tending to their constituents.

It is often the case that constituents in need turn to their representative for assistance, whether in finding a lost Social Security check, helping a son or daughter get into a military academy, or navigating the federal bureaucracy. Not surprisingly, most members specialize in constituency casework, with the good ones having elevated it to an art form. Over the course of their careers, many members will come to know thousands of their constituents by name—a surefire way to guarantee a long tenure in the House!

FACT

The first woman elected to Congress was Jeanette Rankin, a Republican who captured Wyoming's lone House seat in 1916. An avowed pacifist, Rankin attempted to run for the Senate the following year but was defeated in the primary. In 1940, she was voted back to the House, where she cast the only vote in Congress against the declaration of war on Japan. Rankin was easily defeated for re-election the following year.

This is by design. The two-year terms, smaller districts, and direct election by the people were intended to make the House a populist institution where minority interests give way to majority passions. In fact, until the passage of the Seventeenth Amendment, which called for direct election of U.S. senators, the House of Representatives was the only branch of the federal government elected directly by the people.

Take Me to Your Leader

Without strict leadership and discipline, little would get accomplished in a body with 435 disparate members, so leadership positions play a critical role in the function and operation of the House of Representatives.

Congressional leadership is organized by party. Congressional leaders serve an important function within the institution (as parliamentarians) as well as "outside" the House in their efforts to recruit candidates, advocate policy positions in the media, raise money, and provide long-term political and policy strategy.

Speaker of the House

The Speaker of the House is the most powerful and visible member of the House of Representatives. It is the only House leadership position specifically accounted for in the Constitution. The Speaker stands third in line in presidential succession.

The Speaker is nominated by a majority of his party's caucus or membership in the House (the nomination is usually unanimous) at the beginning of each two-year session of Congress, and is formally elected by a straight-party vote of the entire House of Representatives. Rarely do members of the minority party cast a vote for the opposing party's Speaker designee.

QUESTION?

Must the Speaker of the House be a member of the House of Representatives?
The Constitution does not specifically provide that the Speaker of the House be a member of Congress, although nobody outside of the chamber has ever held the position.

The Speaker derives much of his power from the sheer force of his personality and the knowledge of House procedures. In addition, the Speaker has the institutional powers to do the following:

- Determine committee assignments
- Preside over the House
- Decide on points of order and interpret the rules
- Refer legislation to the appropriate committees
- Set the agenda and schedule legislative action
- Coordinate policy agenda with Senate leadership

Depending on party affiliation, a strong Speaker can be the best friend or worst enemy of the White House when it comes to enacting the president's legislative agenda. Democratic Speaker Tom Foley was an effective foil to President George H. W. Bush; he was widely credited with forcing the president to renege on his "no new taxes" pledge. Similarly, Republican Newt Gingrich was a formidable adversary to President Clinton, particularly on issues such as welfare reform, tax cuts, and balancing the budget. As they did with committee chairmanships, the House Republicans have limited the Speaker's position to four terms.

Majority and Minority Leaders

The majority leader is the principal deputy to the Speaker of the House, and the floor leader of the majority party. He is elected by a secret ballot of his party's caucus at the beginning of each two-year session of Congress. His primary function is to foster unity and cohesion among the majority members, and assist the Speaker in setting the agenda, scheduling debate, and monitoring the legislative process. Often, the majority leader is considered next in line to serve as Speaker of the House, although this is not always the case.

Although usually conducted in secret behind closed doors, House leadership races can be fierce and acrimonious contests. In 2003, Harold Ford of Tennessee, considered by many a rising star within the Democratic Party, upset party elders with his insurgency campaign for minority leader. Because Ford was only thirty-two years old, some considered his candidacy premature.

The minority leader is the leader of the opposition party in the House. His function is similar to that of majority leader—to maintain unity within the ranks. Often, the minority leader will work closely with the Speaker and majority leader on scheduling floor debate, recognizing members who wish to speak on the House floor, and determining the rules for particular pieces of legislation, although he doesn't have institutional powers to do any of these. The minority leader will sometimes use procedural maneuvers and delaying tactics to "gum up" the legislative process in an effort to win concessions, make a point, seek compromise, or simply gain the attention of his counterparts.

Whips

Both the majority and minority leadership rely on "whips"—deputies who are responsible for maintaining party loyalty and "counting heads" on key votes. Whips are also elected by secret ballot, and are notorious for exerting pressure on their members to vote the party position. Both the majority and minority whips recruit deputy whips to assist in this process.

FACT

In 2003, Nancy Pelosi became the first woman to attain the highest Congressional leadership position of her party when she was voted minority leader by the House Democrats. Pelosi replaced Dick Gephardt of Missouri, who stepped down after failing to produce a Democratic majority during the previous midterm elections.

House by Committee

Although not specified in the Constitution, committees are where the substantive and legislative work of Congress takes place. Given the enormous complexity and diversity of issues that members confront each session, committees have evolved into specialized divisions of labor where members can concentrate on particular areas of expertise. As a general rule, each House member serves on two standing committees, although members of the powerful Appropriations, Rules, and Ways and Means committees serve only on those committees. Most House committees are divided into five subcommittees that focus on more specific areas.

Types of Committees

There are four primary types of committees in the House of Representatives.

1. **Standing Committees.** These are the permanent bodies of Congress where virtually all of the legislative action takes place. Standing committees are by far the most important structures in Congress. The following are the nineteen standing committees of the 108th Congress:

- Agriculture
- Appropriations
- Armed Services
- Banking and Financial Services
- Budget
- Commerce
- Education and the Workforce
- Government Reform
- House Administration
- International Relations
- Judiciary
- Resources
- Rules
- Science and Technology
- Small Business
- Standards of Official Conduct
- Transportation and Infrastructure
- Veterans Affairs
- Ways and Means

2. **Select or Special Committees.** These committees are temporary panels created from time to time to study or investigate a particular problem or issue. They have a narrow focus and are usually disbanded at the end of the Congressional session in which they were created. These committees produce reports, not legislation. Several years ago, the 105th Congress convened a special committee to examine the issue of aging. Congresses also employed select committees to investigate the Iran-Contra and Watergate scandals.

3. **Joint Committees.** These committees are composed of members from both the House of Representatives and Senate. Typically, they deal with administrative matters pertaining to Congress. Joint committees can be either permanent or temporary, and are most likely to produce recommendations, not legislation.

4. **Conference Committees.** These committees are also composed of House and Senate members, but they have the express purpose of standardizing the exact language of concurrent pieces of legislation

that the two chambers have passed. You'll learn more about conference committees in Chapter 7.

Joining a Committee

For members of Congress, committee assignments rank among the most important aspects of their job. The Speaker of the House and the minority leader determine assignments for their respective party members in conjunction with their steering committee, which is convened for that specific purpose.

Committees vary in importance. Some committees, such as Ways and Means, Banking and Financial Services, Rules, and Budget, are considered prized appointments. Others, such as Standards of Official Conduct and House Administration, are less coveted posts. Oftentimes, committee assignments can determine the career trajectory and expertise of a member.

There are several factors that go into committee assignments. The most important is seniority—the longer a member has served in Congress, the greater his or her chances of receiving a plum assignment. Some members receive committee assignments based on particular knowledge or expertise, while others are assigned based on the needs of his or her district (midwestern members often serve on the Agriculture Committee, for instance). It's not unusual for members to receive a desired committee post as a reward for party loyalty or fundraising prowess, or for ideological reasons.

Committee Leaders

The most powerful member of any committee is the chairperson. The chair hires majority staff, appoints subcommittee members and leaders, and allocates the committee and subcommittee budgets. At one time, it was said that chairpersons dominated their committees like feudal lords, ruling with an iron fist. Recent reforms, however, have curbed their powers.

After taking power in 1994, the Republicans adopted term limits for their committee chairpersons, restricting their members to only three terms as a chairperson on a given committee. This limitation does not prohibit term-limited Republicans from serving as chairperson on another committee, and does not apply to House Democrats.

Rules Rule

The large size and populist composition of the House of Representatives require that its activity be governed by a strict set of formal rules. The House rules that matter most are those that deal with legislative debate, determining the amount of time a bill can be debated on the floor and the types of amendments that can be offered. At the request of the reporting committee's chairperson, the Rules Committee typically grants one of three rules that govern floor debate and the amendments process for a given piece of legislation:

1. An open rule allows for any amendments to be offered, as long as they are relevant to the subject of the bill.
2. A closed rule prohibits any amendments from being offered.
3. A modified rule allows amendments to some parts of the bill.

With the rise of partisanship over the past few years, the Rules Committee has begun to write more complex or "creative" rules in an effort to exert greater control over floor action. With names like the King-of-the-Hill Rule, the Multiple-Step Rule, the Self-Executing Rule, and the Anticipatory Rule, these are mostly used to keep unfriendly amendments from sinking a bill. More often than not, the type of rule a bill receives will determine the likelihood of its passage.

Cliques and Caucuses

Outside of the formal leadership structure, rank-and-file members of both parties can play an important role in shaping policy and legislation through participation in caucuses, coalitions, clubs, and alliances. These are informal groups of members who band together over common ideological, regional, industry-related, or ethnic interests. Most but not all caucuses are bipartisan, and many caucuses are composed of members from both chambers and both parties.

FACT

The first Congressional caucus was formed in 1959, and since that time the number has proliferated to more than 100 in the House of Representatives alone. Virtually every region, interest group, ethnicity, and cause has its own caucus.

The two most recognized and influential caucuses in Congress are the Congressional Black Caucus and the Blue Dog Democrats. Both groups wield considerable power over the House Democrats, although usually at opposite ends of the political spectrum. The Blue Dog Democrats are a group of fiscally conservative Democrats who frequently vote with the Republicans on economic matters, while the Congressional Black Caucus is almost always at odds with the opposition. In 2002, the Congressional Black Caucus played a pivotal role in ousting Senate Majority Leader Trent Lott from his leadership post after the Mississippi Republican made racially insensitive remarks.

So You Want to Be a Member?

Given the intense political climate of recent years, it's sometimes difficult to imagine why anyone would consider running for Congress. These days, just about every aspect of a candidate's life is fair game for public scrutiny and commentary.

Even so, hundreds of candidates run for Congress every two years. Some seek the position as a steppingstone to higher office; others do it in order to effect change in a specific policy area; others are compelled by a sense of civic duty.

Eligibility Requirements

The Constitution lays out three requirements for gaining entry to the U.S. House of Representatives:

1. You must be at least twenty-five years old at the time of inauguration.
2. You must be a resident of the state in which your district resides.
3. You must have been a U.S. citizen for seven years prior to inauguration.

Of course, those are just the technical qualifications for becoming a member of Congress. Most successful Congressional candidates are long-standing and respected members of their communities. They tend to be upper-income or wealthy professionals who are active in civic and local organizations and have some political experience, whether it's on the state or local level. Very few novices are elected to the House of Representatives.

Incumbency Protection

Winning a seat in the U.S. House of Representatives is one of the most difficult chores in all of politics. On the other hand, incumbents (those running for re-election) almost never lose. In fact, since World War II, House members have enjoyed a whopping 92 percent re-election rate, which is nearly 20 percent higher than their Senate counterparts. During the 2000 Congressional elections, all but six incumbents were victorious!

There are two primary reasons. For one thing, incumbents enjoy much greater access to the media and are better funded than their challengers. Moreover, sitting members can accumulate political goodwill in their districts by doing constituent casework, bringing home "pork-barrel" spending projects (projects that benefit local industry or constituents), sending out mail that highlights their successes, and conducting town hall meetings.

Chapter 5
The Senate

The U.S. Senate is a unique institution in American government. Unlike the lower chamber, the Senate was born neither of popular sovereignty nor majority principles. In fact, it was conceived for quite the opposite purpose. The framers wanted one chamber of the legislature to remain insulated from the popular passions of the day, so that members could deliberate and debate the great issues without fear of reprisals from voters.

Cooling Off the House

It is said that George Washington, in explaining the role of the Senate to Thomas Jefferson, compared the upper chamber to a saucer: Just as hot coffee is poured into a saucer to cool it off, the passions of the House of Representatives will be cooled in the Senate. Apocryphal or not, the analogy captures the essence of the upper chamber's mission.

Until 1913, senators were selected by their state legislatures and not by the people. This distance from the people allowed the Senate to establish procedures that would safeguard minority rights in a way that the House could not. In fact, a handful of senators—and in some cases just one— have the ability to bring the body to a standstill through delaying tactics and unlimited debate. No other institution in American government so fiercely guards minority rights.

The Constitution mandates that one-third of the Senate be selected every two years. In order to properly stagger the terms to meet this requirement, the first Senate divided its membership into three "classes," with senators drawing lots to determine which members would have to stand for reappointment two and four years later. This decision was the first official act of the Senate.

As a chamber, the United States Senate experienced its "golden years" during the nineteenth century as it debated the great issues of the day—slavery, secession, and reconstruction—and enjoyed unprecedented sway over a series of weak presidents. It was a time of great orators, great issues, and great influence.

But since the ascension of the presidency as the first branch of government, which began with Theodore Roosevelt, the Senate has lost some of its pre-eminence. It is less elitist and more populist today, but retains some important vestiges of its noble origins.

The Privileges of Membership

The Senate enjoys two constitutional prerogatives that set it apart from the House of Representatives. It alone has the authority to advise and consent on the president's appointments and treaties, as well as to conduct impeachment trials for federal officials. Both powers are exercised sparingly, but with dramatic impact.

The Power to Advise and Consent

The "advise and consent" provision in the Constitution is the Senate's most powerful check on the president. Over the years, it has been a steady source of friction between the upper chamber and the White House, and at times has put a severe strain on the relationship.

FACT

Since 1789, the Senate has rejected 21 treaties, the most notable being the Treaty of Versailles, which it voted against in 1919 and 1920. As a consequence, the United States did not join the League of Nations, which was the precursor to the United Nations. This was a huge defeat and embarrassment for President Woodrow Wilson, who had helped create the League following World War I.

During each session of Congress, the Senate approves thousands of presidential appointments—ambassadors, federal judges, Supreme Court justices, cabinet members, and other executive branch officials. Over the course of a single term, a president can make up to 35,000 military and civilian appointments that require Senate confirmation.

In recent years, the confirmation process for presidential nominations has become more contentious. For a long time, the Senate focused solely on the qualifications and competency of presidential appointments when considering approval, with the result being that very few nominees were rejected. But with the rise in partisan tension and the growing trend toward divided government, the confirmation process has become more politicized. Such was the situation for Judge Robert Bork, who was nominated to the Supreme Court and rejected by the Senate because his viewpoints were considered by some to be out of the mainstream. A couple of years later, Justice Clarence Thomas narrowly avoided a similar fate in one of the most vitriolic and divisive confirmation hearings in history. In many ways, the confirmation power has become the most potent political weapon the Senate wields against the president.

For most appointments, the Senate follows an unwritten practice known as "Senatorial courtesy," whereby the senators from the nominee's state have great influence over the final vote. Should a senator be opposed to a nominee from his home state, chances are the rest of the Senate will follow suit. Often, the president will consult with the home state senators before making a nomination.

Trial by Senate

While the House of Representatives has the sole ability to impeach federal officials, the Senate has exclusive domain over trial and conviction. Impeachment trials have been held only sixteen times in Senate history, with the result being seven convictions, seven acquittals, and two officials stepping down before the proceedings concluded. All seven convicted officials were federal judges. No president has ever been removed from office. Richard Nixon would have been the first president convicted by the Senate had he not resigned in August of 1974.

In 1805, the Senate established the precedent that impeachment would not be used for political retribution when it acquitted Supreme Court Justice Samuel Chase, an outspoken Federalist and vocal critic of the Jefferson administration. Had Chase been convicted, it would have set the disturbing precedent that officials could be removed simply because of their political beliefs, and would have dramatically altered the nature of government and politics.

Nearly 200 years later, a similar controversy was revisited when President Clinton was impeached for allegedly perjuring himself before a grand jury during the Paula Jones deposition. Given the Constitution's vague language about what constitutes an impeachable offense, there was fierce disagreement over the propriety of Clinton's impeachment and trial.

Most scholars and commentators took the position that conviction and removal should be reserved for indictable crimes only, while some took a broader interpretation and sought to use it as a political weapon. The narrow viewpoint won the day, as President Clinton was easily acquitted of both counts.

Who Runs This Place?

The nature and style of leadership in the Senate is dramatically different than that of the lower chamber. As you learned in Chapter 4, the House requires a rigid hierarchy of leaders and deputy leaders enforcing strict discipline to get anything accomplished. The Senate takes the opposite approach. With only 100 members, leadership can be more collegial and informal. Members are on a first-name basis with their colleagues, and they're accustomed to working together on unanimous consent and other agreements.

Floor Leaders

Although the Constitution provides that the vice president shall serve as the Senate president, it's mostly a symbolic title. The only time the vice president presides over the Senate is to cast the occasional tie-breaking vote.

During his eight years as vice president, Al Gore cast four tie-breaking votes, the most notable being the one that passed President Clinton's 1993 budget. John Adams holds the record for breaking the most ties, casting 29 votes while serving as vice president under George Washington.

When the vice president is absent, which is usually the case, the Senate President pro tempore (also known as the pro tem) presides over the chamber. The pro tem position is typically held by the member of the majority party with the longest continuous service in the Senate. Like the role of the vice president, it is mostly a ceremonial position. However, it does carry one important function: The pro tempore is fourth in line to the presidency behind the vice president and the Speaker of the House.

Real leadership in the Senate is provided by the majority and minority leaders elected by their party's caucus, along with whips, who serve as their deputies. Given the shortage of formal rules, and the ability of the minority to obstruct floor action, the two leaders are forced to work more closely together than their House counterparts.

The most important power the leaders enjoy is the right of first recognition, meaning they are allowed to speak first during floor debate. It gives leaders the ability to outflank their adversaries by shaping the debate, offering amendments, and making other motions to reconsider.

In addition, leaders control the scheduling of floor debates, help determine committee assignments, select conference committee members, work closely with committee chairpersons to set legislative priorities, and act as one of the party's chief spokespersons. When the majority leader is a member of the president's party, he acts as the legislative point man for the White House, and is expected to mobilize support for the president's agenda. The opposition leader is expected to thwart the president's agenda, more so than the House opposition leader, who has few tools at his disposal to derail the majority.

Through the years, majority leaders have adopted varying styles of leadership to accomplish their goals. Lyndon Johnson was legendary for his unique skills of persuasion, often referred to as the "LBJ treatment." Robert Byrd is considered the finest parliamentarian in Senate history, and Bob Dole is unrivaled in the art of compromise and conciliation.

Committee Chairmen

The Senate first established standing committees shortly after the War of 1812. At first, committee chairmen were appointed by the vice president. Then, in 1846, party leaders began making the selection. Today, committee chairmen are elected by a majority of their caucuses, although their election is in keeping with the seniority system. Typically, the majority member with the longest tenure on a committee is automatically elevated to chairman, subject to caucus approval.

Currently, the Senate has seventeen standing committees (two fewer than the House):

- Agriculture, Nutrition, and Forestry
- Appropriations
- Armed Services
- Banking, Housing, and Urban Affairs
- Budget
- Commerce, Science, and Transportation
- Energy and Natural Resources
- Environment and Public Works
- Finance
- Foreign Relations
- Governmental Affairs
- Health, Education, Labor, and Pensions
- Indian Affairs
- Judiciary
- Rules and Administration
- Small Business
- Veterans' Affairs

These committees are ranked in importance by class: Class A (the most important), Class B, and Class C. Chairmanship of the Judiciary, Budget, and Foreign Relations committees are particularly coveted posts.

FACT

When the Republicans took control of the Senate in 1995, one of the first orders of business was to reduce committee staff by 20 percent—a drastic and unprecedented move. According to Democratic senator Robert Byrd of West Virginia, the staff reductions "affected the ability of Members to adequately address issues of national importance which arise in Congress every day."

Subject to Debate

The Senate's tradition of unlimited debate dates back to the first Congress, when a handful of senators used stalling tactics to defeat a proposal to move the capital from New York City to Philadelphia. Since then, the practice of unlimited debate has been one of the most cherished rights in the Senate, and is the most distinguishing characteristic that sets it apart from the House of Representatives.

What's a Filibuster?

When unlimited debate is used to defeat a bill, it is called a *filibuster*. Popularized by Jimmy Stewart in the movie *Mr. Smith Goes to Washington*, filibustering typically involves endless speech on the Senate floor by a member or members, and may also include a series of delaying tactics such as calling for consecutive roll calls, raising points of order, and offering nongermane (not relevant) amendments.

Filibustering is a highly effective mechanism for senators to defeat legislation or win concessions on nonrelated issues, especially if employed late in the session when there is insufficient time to break it. If timed correctly, the mere threat of a filibuster can be an effective negotiating tool. In some cases, senators will block legislation simply by asking their party leaders not to schedule the matter. This is called a *hold*, and using the hold is a custom honored by Senate leaders. In the last few years, the use of holds has been modified and curtailed.

In 1917, at the urging of President Woodrow Wilson, the Senate amended its rules to provide a means for cutting off debate. Rule 22 (or *cloture,* as it is known) is invoked when three-fifths of the members present vote in favor of ending debate. Once cloture is adopted, senators have thirty hours of remaining debate before a final vote is taken.

ALERT!

The late Senator Strom Thurmond of South Carolina holds the record for the longest solo filibuster. He spoke for twenty-four hours and eighteen minutes against the Civil Rights Act of 1957. Throughout the late 1950s and early '60s, southern Democrats repeatedly filibustered a series of civil rights initiatives until cloture was finally invoked and the historic Civil Rights Act of 1964 became law.

Unanimous Consent Agreements

One way the Senate avoids the cycle of endless filibusters and cloture is through unanimous consent agreements. These are agreements that the majority and minority leaders make regarding the length of debate, the number and types of amendments that can be offered, and the time of final vote for a particular piece of legislation. As its name suggests, a unanimous consent agreement requires the full consent of every senator present—one "nay" vote kills the agreement. Most Senate business is conducted according to unanimous consent agreements.

Joining the Club

As you've learned, the Senate has undergone a radical transformation in the way its members are selected. For the first 130 years, senators were appointed by their respective state legislatures.

Changing the Rules

The selection process was troubled from the beginning, rife with inconsistencies, corruption, backroom deal-making, and ultimately, mistrust from the public. Starting with Oregon in 1907, states began scrapping the selection process and replacing it with direct elections. Sensing that the tide had turned, the Congress followed suit. The Seventeenth Amendment to the Constitution, which changed the process of selecting senators, was ratified in 1917. The amendment did not, however, alter the formal qualifications established in the Constitution for becoming a member. Senators still must be thirty years of age or older and a United States citizen for nine years prior to election, and they must be residents of the state they represent.

Money, Money, Money

Although anyone who meets the age, citizenship, and residency requirements can run for the United States Senate, the most important requirement is money—and lots of it. The average senatorial candidate spends $5 million during each campaign in hopes of achieving victory.

Over the past decade, there has been a surge in the number of wealthy individuals who have sought Senate seats, and approximately one-third of the chamber is now composed of millionaires. Outside of the superwealthy who can finance their own campaigns, most members spend anywhere from a quarter to a third of their time raising money for re-election. Members and challengers from states like California, New York, and Texas, where media is expensive, can spend upward of $25 million to win or retain a seat—a truly staggering sum of money.

Presidential Dreaming

There's an often-told joke in Washington about how every time a senator looks in the mirror, he sees a president staring back. Perhaps that's a bit of an exaggeration, but it contains a kernel of truth. At one time or another, most senators have visions of occupying the White House.

Even so, it's rarely a direct route. Though many have tried, only two sitting senators have been elected president: Warren G. Harding and John F. Kennedy. In total, fifteen presidents have been members of the Senate at some point in their careers, with six (the ones listed in bold) having served as vice president:

1. James Monroe
2. John Quincy Adams
3. Andrew Jackson
4. **Martin Van Buren**
5. William Henry Harrison
6. **John Tyler**
7. Franklin Pierce
8. James Buchanan
9. **Andrew Johnson**
10. Benjamin Harrison
11. Warren G. Harding
12. **Harry S. Truman**
13. John F. Kennedy
14. **Lyndon B. Johnson**
15. **Richard M. Nixon**

While ten senators became presidents in the nineteenth century, only five did so in the twentieth century. In recent years, the governor's mansion has replaced the Senate as the most reliable path to the White House. Voters seem to be placing less emphasis on legislative experience and more on executive experience, which the Senate does not provide. Ⓔ

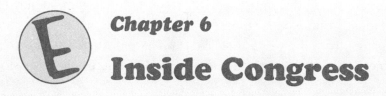

Chapter 6

Inside Congress

I n Chapters 4 and 5 you were introduced to the two chambers of Congress—the House of Representatives and the Senate. In this chapter, we'll take a closer look inside both chambers to better understand the duties of representatives and senators, their many responsibilities, and how they work together as well as with other branches of our government.

Congress Is in Session

Congress is in session throughout the year, with several scheduled recesses. Under normal circumstances, the House of Representatives is in session from Tuesday through Thursday, with members back in the district the remainder of the time. The Senate, on the other hand, is typically in session the entire week; thus most senators travel home less frequently than do their House counterparts (unless it's an election year). Senators and representatives from the western states, Hawaii, and Alaska usually return to their districts only once or twice a month while Congress is in session.

What Members Do

While Congress is in session, a typical day for a member may include up to a dozen activities:

- Attending committee and subcommittee meetings and hearings
- Meeting with staff and other members to discuss pending legislation
- Participating in floor debate and voting on legislation
- Meeting with constituents and overseeing casework
- Caucusing with party members to devise legislative strategies
- Meeting with other government officials, interest groups, and lobbyists to discuss pending legislation
- Managing the staff and office operations
- Making media appearances to advance a piece of legislation or advocate a policy position

All of those are just the normal activities of the business day. After-hours duties may include attending fundraisers and other political events, preparing for the next day's activities, making phone calls to contributors and supporters back home, and traveling to other districts in support of party colleagues.

The pace doesn't slow down much back home. Most members spend their weekends in the district participating in town hall meetings, meeting with constituents, holding office hours, making public appearances, and attending political events. Between work and travel, there is little time for anything else. As former Congressman Fred Grandy of Iowa put it, "Congress is a good job for someone with no family, no life of their own, no desire to do anything but get up, go to work, and live and die by their own press releases."

FACT

With so many things to do and places to be, casting votes can sometimes present a challenge for members of Congress. Fortunately, members are alerted by a special pager when a roll call is imminent, and have fifteen minutes to race back to the Capitol building to record their vote. Some members are fastidious about never missing a vote, while others are more lax in their approach.

The Congressman's Roles

Congressmen serve in many capacities as they discharge the various duties of their office. All of their responsibilities may be seen as fitting into four primary roles: legislator, constituent servant, representative, and educator.

Legislator

This is the most important role for any member of Congress. Representatives and senators cast thousands of votes each session. Most votes are on procedural matters, some are on legislative issues, and a few are on appointments and confirmations. Tax cuts, health care reform, and entitlement spending are just a few of the issues that members vote on every year, with financial implications running in the trillions of dollars. When it comes time for re-election, most members—especially senators—are judged on their voting record by the electorate.

Constituent Servant

This is a less high-profile and glamorous role than lawmaking, but for House members in particular it can be equally as important come re-election time. Members are expected to intervene on behalf of their constit-uents to help solve problems, promote local businesses and commerce, bring money and projects back to the district, and explain the meaning of legislation to affected interest groups. House members tend to pay closer attention to constituent casework than do their upper chamber counterparts.

FACT

Former senator Al D'Amato of New York earned the nickname "Senator Pothole" for his mastery of constituent casework. In a state known for producing liberal senators, the conservative three-term senator was twice re-elected on the strength of his ability to solve constituent problems and bring projects back to New York State.

Representative

Much as it sounds, this role pertains to the congressmen's duty to understand and represent the views of their constituents in Washington—one of the cornerstones of a republican government. Members usually adopt one of two approaches when discharging their representative duty. Some (most often senators) take a broader or "trustee" view of representation, meaning that they put the interests of the country before the narrow needs of their district or state. This is sometimes referred to as "voting your conscience." Other members (most often representatives) believe that their votes should mirror the views of their constituents, even if it's in conflict with their own beliefs. This is sometimes referred to as the "instructed-delegate" approach to representation. Most members will vary their approach depending on the issue.

Educator

Finally, members have a duty to educate the public about the issues that are before the Congress. They typically keep their constituents informed through newsletters, office hours in the district, town hall meetings, direct mail, and media appearances. Some of the more savvy members will use committee or subcommittee hearings as a way to galvanize public opinion and "educate" the electorate to their particular (often partisan) point of view.

Making Decisions

Political scientists have long theorized about why senators and representatives decide to vote a particular way on a piece of legislation. While there is no hard-and-fast rule that governs the decision-making process, there are several considerations that most members factor into the equation.

Party Affiliation

A majority of the votes that take place in Congress occur along straight party lines, meaning that an overwhelming number of Republicans vote one way, and a majority of Democrats the other way. This should come as no surprise, considering that the primary function of Congressional leaders and whips is to enforce party discipline during votes. As a result, party affiliation is the best indicator of a member's vote.

Constituency

In some cases, members will take into account the views of their constituents. This is especially true if it's a high-profile or polarizing issue such as gun control, abortion, tax cuts, or sending troops abroad. It's not unusual for members to vote against their own beliefs if they're in conflict with their constituents' viewpoints.

However, sometimes the opposite occurs, as was the case with Democratic Representative Marjorie Margolies-Mezvinsky, who represented a swing district in Pennsylvania. Margolies-Mezvinsky cast the deciding vote in favor of President Clinton's 1994 budget plan (which increased taxes), and was subsequently voted out of office by her conservative constituents.

Presidential Pressure

Although members of Congress pride themselves on their independence from the executive branch, presidential persuasion weighs heavily on key Congressional votes. Historically, when the president has an announced position on an issue, he prevails on about 75 percent of the Congressional votes. Leading up to the 2002 midterm elections, many southern and midwestern Democrats facing re-election voted for President George W. Bush's agenda at the "behest" of the White House, even though the party leadership was opposed to his agenda.

As a general rule, the more popular the president, the more "persuadable" the Congress. President Lyndon Johnson was particularly adept at using presidential pressure (some would call it arm-twisting) to gain support from Congressional Democrats for his Great Society programs, civil rights initiative, and the war in Vietnam. Johnson had mastered the art of "subtle persuasion" while serving as majority leader of the Senate.

Vote Trading

Sometimes lawmakers will strike deals with other members to cast a vote a certain way in return for the same consideration on a future vote. Most vote trading takes place on low-profile and procedural matters—it rarely occurs on highly public issues. Vote trading is particularly common when a member is trying to take a spending project back to his or her district.

QUESTION?

What is logrolling?
Logrolling is the process of vote trading as it relates to omnibus pork-barrel spending projects. This occurs when narrow interest groups band together on public works, subsidy, tariff and trade, or taxation legislation so that each constituency gets something from the bill. Participating members will then vote for the entire package, regardless of the provisions, as long as their narrow interest is included.

Ideology

In the rarest of cases, members will vote according to deeply held ideological or philosophical beliefs about the role of government. Sometimes ideological voting is consistent with straight party voting. At other times, depending on the issue, ideological voting splits across party lines. This often is the case with First Amendment, abortion, and gun control legislation.

Working with Others

The Congress interacts with the other branches and institutions of government on a regular basis. Three relationships in particular—the president, the courts, and the bureaucracy—help define the various powers and roles of Congress.

The President

Since the inception of the Republic, the relationship between the Congress and the president has been a complex one. There has always been a natural tension between the two as each has struggled to gain dominance over the other.

As you learned in Chapter 2, this is by the design. The Founding Fathers believed that the best way to avoid oppressive and unjust rule was by making it difficult for government to act at all. They also believed that the real threat of tyranny lies with the president, not the Congress. Thus, they provided for a strong Congress with many enumerated powers, and a relatively weak president with few specific powers.

Over the years, the balance of power has shifted between the two, with both branches enjoying pre-eminence at one time or another. The Congress held the upper hand for most of the nineteenth century as it overshadowed a succession of caretaker presidents, but since the presidency of Theodore Roosevelt, the White House has been the first branch of government. Its ascension was further spurred by four events: the Great Depression, World War II, the cold war, and the war on terrorism.

All through this, the relationship between the Congress and the president has alternated between cooperation and confrontation. Presidents with clear electoral mandates, such as Franklin Roosevelt, Lyndon Johnson, and Ronald Reagan, have enjoyed relatively smooth relations with Congress during their first terms, and used their broad popularity to achieve sweeping legislative successes—the New Deal, the Great Society, and a series of tax cuts dubbed "Reaganomics," respectively.

Other presidents, like Richard Nixon, Jimmy Carter, and George H. W. Bush, either squandered their goodwill or lost the confidence of the people, and as a result were unable to accomplish much on the legislative front without bending to the will of Congress. It's no coincidence that Carter and George H. W. Bush were only one-term presidents.

FACT

During his first term, President Reagan was able to push sweeping tax reform through a Democratically controlled Congress by winning over a group of southern Democrats nicknamed the "Boll Weevils." Reagan wisely barnstormed through swing states where he received a majority of the vote and appealed directly to voters to pressure their representatives to support his tax plan.

The Courts

The Founding Fathers also vested Congress with broad authority to establish the federal court system. The Senate, in particular, was given the power to confirm judicial appointments. With that being the case, the Congress has been instrumental in shaping both the infrastructure of the court system and its ideological makeup.

The Congress also can influence the courts in more subtle ways. In the case of lawsuits brought against federal agencies, the courts will often interpret the "legislative intent" of the members in order to better understand the meaning of the federal statute at issue. Knowing this, legislators in both chambers have increasingly begun to leave vast paper trails explaining the meaning and intent of legislation passed by the Congress. In most cases, this legislative intent is mostly partisan spinning, and it tends to bear little resemblance to the actual intention of the statute. Nonetheless, courts are obliged to consider Congress's meaning when the plain language of the statute is unclear or ambiguous.

The Bureaucracy

One of the most important activities of Congress is overseeing the federal bureaucracy. It's up to Congress to ensure that the laws it passed are being properly administered and enforced. Members can hold committee and subcommittee hearings, conduct investigations, and subpoena documents to make this determination. Should something be amiss, Congress can force the bureaucracy into compliance by reducing the size of agency budgets or refusing to vote on key appointments. Members rely upon the General Accounting Office (GAO) to help determine whether agencies are following the letter of the law.

Both the Congress and the president share responsibilities when it comes to the fourth branch of government—its bureaucracy. The Congress has the power to establish and disband departments, agencies, commissions, and quasi-governmental corporations, while the president staffs, administers, and sets policy direction. Ministering to the bureaucracy is a frequent source of turf battles between the two branches.

The Role of Staff

Office and personal staff play a vital role in the function and operation of Congress. With members being pulled in a dozen different directions on any given day, staffers will often act as the "eyes and ears" for their bosses, doing everything from answering phones and reading mail to tending to constituent casework, monitoring legislative affairs, attending committee and subcommittee meetings, scheduling events, and communicating with the press.

More Is Better

Over the past thirty years, the size of Congressional staff has grown dramatically (at taxpayer expense). Currently, more than 10,000 staffers work in the district and Capitol offices of the members. The average Senate office employs thirty-five staff members, with the average House office employing half that number. Senators from the populous states receive a greater percentage of staff than those from less populous states, while House members all receive the same number of staff.

FACT

In addition to personal, office, and committee staffs, members of Congress have access to the expertise and knowledge of professional staffers at the Congressional Research Service (CRS), the Congressional Budget Office (CBO), and the General Accounting Office (GAO), among others. These agencies were created for the express purpose of providing information to members of the House and Senate.

House Versus Senate

As you learned in the previous two chapters, the House and Senate are two distinct chambers. Although both bodies compose a single bicameral legislature, each serves a different purpose. We've learned that these institutional differences stem from several things: the size of the bodies, the powers prescribed to each in the Constitution, the use of rules, and the leadership structure. Over the course of two centuries, other differences have evolved as well.

The Prestige Factor

During the early years of the Republic, service in the House was considered more prestigious than the Senate. The disparity in size between the two chambers wasn't nearly as large as it is today, and only House members were elected directly by the people (senators were chosen by their state legislature). In fact, it wasn't unusual for senators to give up their seats in order to run for the House. Moreover, unlike the present, most of the important debates of the early nineteenth century took place in the lower chamber, where the great orators and debaters of the day served. This was so much the case that President John Quincy Adams, upon losing his bid for re-election in 1828, returned to Massachusetts and subsequently won a seat in the House of Representatives. He served there until his death.

The balance of prestige between the chambers has shifted over the years, owing to the change to direct election of senators, which began in

1913, and the growth of the House to its current size of 435. These days, it's very common for representatives to "graduate" to the Senate (almost a third of the current Senate has served in the House), while it's unheard of for a senator to seek a House seat. For politicians with national ambitions, the Senate has served as a viable steppingstone to the presidency and vice presidency.

QUESTION?

Do you know how many former senators have served as vice president since World War II?
Seven: Alben Barkley (Harry Truman), Richard Nixon (Dwight Eisenhower), Lyndon Johnson (John F. Kennedy), Hubert Humphrey (Lyndon Johnson), Walter Mondale (Jimmy Carter), Dan Quayle (George H.W. Bush), and Al Gore (Bill Clinton). During that same time, only two representatives were even nominated for the second spot by either of the major parties: Tom Miller in 1964 (Barry Goldwater), and Geraldine Ferraro in 1984 (Walter Mondale).

Media Attention

For most House members not in a leadership position, getting the attention of the media is a full-time (and usually fruitless) task. Most reporters and broadcasters have little interest in covering the daily toiling of a representative unless it involves scandal or a gaffe.

Senators, on the other hand, are regulars on the six o'clock news and Sunday talk shows, particularly those from the larger states like California and New York, where they're thrust into the national spotlight simply by holding office. Even small-state and junior senators have little trouble getting media coverage on a regular basis.

This ability to garner media attention gives senators a national platform from which to advocate policy, raise money, increase their awareness among the electorate, and lay the groundwork for a presidential campaign (should that be his or her ambition). Ⓔ

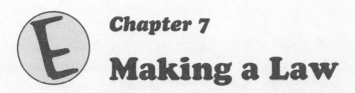

Chapter 7

Making a Law

Have you ever wondered where our laws come from—who determines the amount of taxes we pay, the quality of our drinking water, the size of our Social Security check, or the laws and regulations governing our financial institutions? Most of us give it little thought because the process seems distant and complicated. The fact of the matter is, the way in which a self-governing people create their laws is perhaps the most critical function of any government. We all share a stake in the outcome, and we should all be familiar with the process.

A Nation of Laws

The United States is a nation of laws. On a local, state, and national level, tens of thousands of laws are passed each year. Some are fairly innocuous, such as laws commemorating certain dates and events, while others have a profound impact on our daily lives. They can be broad or narrow, well known or obscure. Some have been around for decades, and others a few years.

Each year, thousands of bills are introduced in both chambers of Congress. Of these, only a fraction—a couple hundred at most—will make it to the president's desk for signature and become law. The rest are either quietly forgotten or rejected outright. The process of lawmaking is the central focus of the legislative branch, and its single most important duty.

Most of the legislation that is taken up by Congress involves mandatory issues: appropriations bills (those that determine which programs receive money) and authorization bills (those that allocate the amount of money for programs). Some matters are revisited every few years, such as increases in the minimum wage and revisions to the federal tax code. Other matters may be visited once every few decades. Incoming presidents typically have one or two high-profile pieces of legislation that make up the thrust of the domestic agenda, and those are typically given priority by the Congress.

Much of the mandatory legislation comes in the form of "omnibus" bills, or comprehensive packages of bills. These mega-bills typically cover a broad range of issues, and in the past would have been voted on as separate bills. For reasons of political expediency, both chambers are increasingly using these omnibus bills to accomplish much of the legislative work.

It's important to keep in mind that the framers of the Constitution purposely established a framework whereby lawmaking would be difficult. Their biggest fear was creating an overreaching federal government that would usurp the authority of state and local governments. To guard against this, the framers created a lawmaking process that includes many opportunities for dissenters to derail legislation. As a consequence, only measures with broad appeal are able to survive this legislative gauntlet to become law.

Introducing Legislation

The first step to lawmaking is introducing a bill. Only a member of Congress can actually sponsor a bill, although inspiration for legislation can come from many different sources—the president, a lobbyist or interest group, a concerned citizen, or a constituency group in the district. Occasionally, members of the minority party will introduce legislation that they know has little chance of passing for the simple purpose of framing a policy position or scoring political points with the electorate.

Sometimes a member will draw from personal experience. Such was the case for former senator Strom Thurmond, who sponsored a bill requiring liquor companies to include warning labels in their print and broadcast advertising after his daughter was killed by a drunk driver. Former Senate majority leader Bob Dole helped establish National Men's Health Week after being diagnosed with prostate cancer.

In most cases, the names of the sponsoring legislators are used as the informal name of the legislation, such as Gramm-Rudman-Hollings (for the Balanced Budget and Emergency Deficit Control Act of 1985), Sarbanes-Oxley (for the Public Company Accounting Reform and Investor Protection Act of 2002), and perhaps most famously, McCain-Feingold (for the Bipartisan Campaign Reform Act of 2001).

ALERT!

In rare instances, an entire federal program will be named after the sponsoring representative or senator. For instance, the Basic Educational Opportunity Grant Program (a program that offers financial aid to college students) was renamed Pell Grants after Rhode Island senator Claiborne Pell.

Building Support

As former House majority leader Dick Armey put it, anyone can introduce a piece of legislation—the real challenge is to make something happen with it. An overwhelming majority of the bills introduced in Congress never even make it out of committee, let alone get enacted into law.

Often, the sponsoring legislator will seek out fellow lawmakers to cosponsor his or her legislation as a way to demonstrate a broad base of support. Members send out "dear colleague" letters to inform fellow legislators of the contents of their bills, and solicit support and cosponsors. It's not unusual for a bill to have upward of 100 cosponsors.

On particularly high-profile bills, lawmakers will sometimes seek out members of the opposite party to cosponsor their legislation. Senate Republicans did just that in 2001, when Democrat Zell Miller of Georgia cosponsored President George W. Bush's landmark tax reform bill, which was ultimately enacted into law. President Bush used a similar tactic with Democratic senator Ted Kennedy to help pass the education reform bill that same year.

Drafting Legislation

Although only members of Congress can introduce legislation, anyone can draft it. Most of the time, Congressional staff drafts legislation, though it's not uncommon for interest groups, activists, or the executive branch to put the words on paper. Many members take advantage of the attorneys and expert drafters at the nonpartisan Office of Legislative Counsel to help craft bills and amendments. Over the years, the length of bills has dramatically increased, while the number of bills has sharply decreased.

Committee Referral

Once a bill has been introduced and drafted, it is assigned a number and referred to the appropriate committee for review. The proper committee is determined by the content of the bill; the committee most relevant to the subject matter receives jurisdiction.

In cases in which the subject matter is broad and encompasses several different areas, the legislation may be assigned to several committees for review. Securing a favorable committee for review—one that is likely to act on the legislation—can play a decisive role in the success or failure of the bill.

In very rare instances, the Speaker may bypass committee assignment altogether and send a bill directly to the House floor for review and vote. This is usually done when the Speaker wants to force a vote on a particularly controversial issue that is certain to embarrass the minority party.

FACT

In 2000, Democratic Representative Lynn Woolsey of California introduced HR 4892, a bill that called for the revocation of the federal charter of the Boy Scouts of America because the group does not admit homosexual members. Sensing a chance to gain political advantage, the Republican leadership bypassed committee assignment and sent the bill directly to the floor for a vote. The measure was defeated 361–12.

Committee Consideration

The large majority of bills that are assigned to a committee languish without receiving any consideration and are quickly forgotten. For the few bills that are acted upon, the committee chairman will usually assign it to a subcommittee for further consideration. Subcommittees are where the bulk of legislative crafting takes place.

The Importance of Hearings

If the subcommittee decides to act, the first thing it does is hold hearings. Every year, Congressional committees and subcommittees hold thousands of hearings, with some receiving more attention than others. Hearings are held for several reasons:

- To explore the need for legislation
- To allow members to make their point of view known

- To build support and create a record for the legislation
- To attract media attention to the issue
- To give the chairman a forum to increase public exposure

The ranking members of the subcommittee call witnesses to testify on the pending legislation. This can include anyone from the sponsor of the bill to lobbyists, experts, other federal officials, ordinary citizens affected by the legislation, and even celebrities.

In most instances, the format doesn't vary much. Witnesses read a prepared statement, and then each member is given an allotment of time (usually five minutes) to ask the witness questions. If the subcommittee chairman is opposed to the bill but doesn't want to publicly come out against it, he may hold an endless number of hearings as a way of slowly killing it without arousing suspicion among the public.

FACT

Television star Michael J. Fox has frequently testified on Capitol Hill in support of greater funding for Parkinson's disease, an ailment from which he suffers. Other celebrity testifiers include Christopher Reeve (spinal cord paralysis), Julia Roberts (Rett Syndrome), and Mary Tyler Moore (stem cell research).

Committees and subcommittees are required by law to publish their hearing schedule a week in advance in local papers so that witnesses, the press, and the public are given appropriate time to prepare. While most hearings take place on Capitol Hill, sometimes committees conduct hearings in parts of the country where area residents will be particularly affected by the proposed legislation. It's not unusual for agriculture hearings to take place in midwestern states and for dairy-related hearings to be held in Wisconsin.

The Markup Phase

Once hearings have been completed, the bill enters the markup phase. During markup, subcommittee members debate the language of the bill, offer amendments, and vote on a final bill.

After markup, the bill is referred to the entire committee, where several things can occur. The committee may accept the recommendation, send it back to the subcommittee for further work, or conduct hearings and markups of its own. Usually, the committee accepts the findings of the subcommittee. Except for issues related to national security, committee and subcommittee markups must be conducted in public.

Public markups were part of the "sunshine" laws that resulted from a series of post-Watergate Congressional reforms. Some members of Congress contend that public scrutiny of markups has made the legislative process more difficult because most members are unwilling to negotiate bill provisions in public. As a result, many committees have "pre-markup" sessions prior to the public markups.

Report Submission

Once the bill has been written, the committee staff submits a report to all the members, explaining the contents of the bill. The committee report usually describes the purpose of the bill, contains the arguments for and against it, summarizes the hearings' findings, explains how the bill may impact existing law, and includes a perspective from affected executive branch agencies. According to House and Senate rules, a majority of committee members must be present for a bill to be voted out of committee.

With a growing number of bills running into the thousands of pages (and written in confusing legalese), the report has become an invaluable tool for members to evaluate a piece of legislation. The courts and regulatory agencies that have to interpret and implement the law also rely on the committee report to better understand the scope and meaning of the legislation. Committee members who oppose the final legislation are given the opportunity to file a supplemental report stating their views.

Scheduling Debate

Bills that are reported out of committee face one last obstacle before making it to the floor for debate and a vote: the calendar. Both the House and the Senate have specific calendars to determine the order in which bills are taken up by the entire chamber. In the House there are four different calendars, depending on the type of legislation:

1. The Union Calendar is reserved for bills that either raise or spend money.
2. The House Calendar is reserved for important public bills that do not deal with money.
3. The Private Calendar (or Consent Calendar) is reserved for noncontroversial items. (Here the formal rules are dispensed with so that items can be passed quickly.)
4. The Corrections Calendar is reserved for repealing frivolous or outdated laws and regulations that are still on the books.

FACT

House Republicans created the Corrections Calendar six months after taking control of the chamber in 1995. The Speaker of the House alone determines which bills are placed on the Corrections Calendar, although the bill must have been favorably reported from a committee first. Bills on the Corrections Calendar must receive a three-fifths majority (261 votes) to become law.

The Senate has only two calendars:

1. The Executive Calendar is used to schedule confirmation proceedings for treaties and executive branch nominations.
2. The Legislative Calendar is used to schedule all other matters, such as bills and resolutions. Its largest section is called General Orders.

In the House, the Rules Committee controls the calendar; in the Senate, the majority and minority leaders set the schedule together.

Floor Action

Floor action—rules and agreements, amendment and debate, and final vote—represents the homestretch of the legislative process. More so in the Senate than in the House, this is the most decisive step in determining the shape and fate of the bill.

Adoption of the Rule

The House Rules Committee plays an important role in the legislative process: It announces the rules that govern the floor action of a bill. Like the other committees in Congress, the Rules Committee sometimes conducts hearings and calls witnesses when formulating a rule for a particular piece of legislation. The witnesses are usually members of the committee that is writing the bill.

In order for a House rule to take effect, it must be adopted by a majority of the chamber. If it fails to receive the requisite 218 votes, the Rules Committee can either turn to another rule or let the bill die in committee. Before the vote takes place, the Speaker usually allots one hour of debate between the majority and minority members of the Rules Committee, with the ranking members acting as floor managers (you'll learn more about floor managers in the next section).

Once in a while, either a standing committee will refuse to report on a bill, or it will not be granted a rule from the Rules Committee. In those situations, members can file a discharge petition to discharge the bill from committee and bring it directly to the floor. The rarely used discharge petition can be filed by any member, and requires a majority of signatures. In cases in which a member is secretly opposed to a particular piece of legislation, but hesitant to vote against it for fear of rousing public anger, he can vote against the rule (and thus defeat the bill) without being on the record as having voted against the bill.

As you have learned, the Senate usually dispenses with its formal rules in favor of unanimous consent agreements, which the majority and minority leaders craft before scheduling a piece of legislation. Unanimous consent agreements allow the Senate to debate and amend legislation without the fear of a filibuster derailing the process.

The use of unanimous consent agreements has been on the rise in recent years.

Debate and Amendments

Once a bill receives its rule, it goes to the floor for debate and amendment. In both the Senate and the House, floor managers—usually the chairman and ranking minority member of the committee that wrote the bill—are appointed to "quarterback" this process. The majority floor manager tries to shepherd the bill to final passage, while the minority floor manager tries to defeat it. The floor managers usually speak first during debate, and then parcel out the remaining time to members of their teams.

ALERT!

In most situations, floor debate is divided along partisan lines, with Republicans advocating one side and Democrats the other. On issues that split across party lines, however, such as the North American Free Trade Agreement (NAFTA), the floor managers will work with members of the opposite party to advance their cause.

The debate and amendment process plays different roles in the two chambers. In the House, debate is almost always perfunctory, meaning that rarely does one side influence the outcome of the vote. It mostly serves as an opportunity for members to make their viewpoints known to the public, and in some cases grandstand on the issue.

In the Senate, however, legislation takes its shape on the floor. Senators take advantage of the unlimited debate and amendments to add and subtract provisions, negotiate concessions, and alter language of the final bill. In the upper chamber, members tend to legislate from the floor rather than in committee—a dramatic departure from the process in the House.

Time to Take a Vote

As soon as debate has ended, the bill comes to a final vote. Since 1973, members have used an electronic device that looks like a credit card at one of three dozen voting stations on the chamber floor to record their vote. They have one of three options to select from: Yes, No, or Present. Present is used when a member doesn't want to be on record against a particular bill, but he doesn't want to support it either. Members have fifteen minutes to vote, and an electronic bulletin board near the press gallery keeps a running tally of "yeas" and "nays."

Agreement Between the House and Senate

Before a bill can be forwarded to the president, the House and Senate versions must be identical. Most of the time, this is not an issue, because the two chambers usually coordinate the wording of the legislation throughout the process. About a quarter of the time, however, the House and Senate bills contain different provisions. On these occasions, a conference committee is needed to reconcile the gaps.

FACT

In both bodies, members from the committee that wrote the bill tend to look favorably upon conference committees because it allows them an opportunity to reinsert their findings into the final bill. It's important to note, however, that new provisions can't be added and old provisions can't be removed during the conference committee.

During conference committees, representatives from both chambers work to iron out the language differences between the two bills. The chairman and ranking minority member of the committee with jurisdiction select the conferees from their respective chambers. The number of conferees depends on the size and complexity of the two bills. The ratio of Republicans and Democrats chosen as conferees usually mirrors the ratio between the two parties in the House and Senate.

Once the conferees have come to agreement over a compromise bill, it is presented to and voted on by both chambers. On the rare occasions when one or both bodies reject the new bill, another conference can be convened, or the bill can be shelved. If the bill is passed by both chambers, it is sent to the president.

Presidential Prerogative

The final leg of the legislative journey is the White House, where the president can either sign the bill into law or veto it. (You can learn more about the veto power in Chapter 9.) But even if the president rejects the legislation, Congress still has one final recourse—it can override the president's veto with a two-thirds vote of both chambers. This process, however, is extremely difficult and rare, so much so that less than 5 percent of all presidential vetoes have been overridden. In fact, Congress had been in existence for fifty-three years before it successfully overrode its first veto, overturning President John Tyler's rejection of a tariff bill.

In 1996, the Senate fell nine votes short (after the House had surpassed the two-thirds threshold) of overturning President Clinton's veto of a bill that would have banned third-trimester abortions, one of the most contentious override battles in recent times. Nevertheless, the ability to override a veto remains one of Congress's most important checks over the presidency.

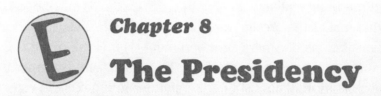

Chapter 8

The Presidency

It's arguably the most powerful office in the world, and the most coveted job in America. Although the Constitution established the Congress as the first branch of government, the presidency has supplanted it as the focal point of our system over the course of 200 years. This remarkable transformation did not happen overnight, nor was it the product of just one event. As we'll see, a combination of personalities and events has reshaped the office into the modern presidency of today.

A Special Office

The presidency stands apart for many reasons. The presidency and the vice presidency are the only nationally elected offices, which means that the president enjoys a mandate unlike any other in American politics. It's also the only term-limited position among the three branches of government. And the president serves as both chief executive and head of state.

But what makes the presidency truly special—what sets it apart from the other institutions of American government—is that the office is greater than the sum of its constitutional parts. The person who occupies the White House is more than just the commander in chief, chief executive, chief legislator, chief diplomat, and head of state. The president represents America abroad, and the aspirations of Americans at home. World economic markets react to his actions and utterances. He is the leader of the free world and commander of the lone superpower. The president speaks to the people and embodies our values. He alone can comfort a nation in mourning, lead us during times of crisis, and rally us to war and peace. And only the president can command the nation's attention with a single speech or comment.

Americans have always enjoyed a special relationship with our presidents. Every four years, we choose between two people to occupy the highest office in the land. We ask a lot of them as candidates, and demand even more of them as presidents. We place in them our trust, and hope that it is rewarded. Whether we voted for the president or not, we expect him to be the president of all the people.

The First American President

The father of our country understood that every action he took while president would establish a precedent for future officeholders, and he kept that in mind throughout his eight years in the White House. He wanted to make certain that future presidents acted with humility and respected the separation of powers among the three branches of government.

Perhaps Washington's most important precedent was to walk away from the office after two terms. It's hard to imagine it now, but at the time it was an extraordinary notion for the head of a nation-state to voluntarily turn over the seat of government to someone else and retire. Washington believed two terms was appropriate, and that precedent was followed until Franklin Roosevelt won a third term in 1940.

FACT

As George Washington's vice president, John Adams spent a good deal of time trying to figure out how the president should be formally addressed. He was in favor of an elegant title, and proposed "His Highness the President, Protector of the Liberties of the United States" to the Senate. Thankfully, Washington settled on "Mr. President." Adams also wondered aloud how the vice president should be addressed, to which one senator acidly remarked, "His Rotundity."

Washington also believed that the president should seek the best available minds for his cabinet, even if they didn't agree on every issue. His cabinet included Thomas Jefferson, Alexander Hamilton, and Edmund Randolph, three giants of the day who held different political philosophies.

Throughout the nineteenth century and into the twentieth, cabinet officers enjoyed a great deal of autonomy over their departments, and had an important role in the decision-making and implementation of executive power. During the last fifty years, however, the cabinet—save a few extraordinary individuals—has been reduced primarily to an advisory position, and has lost much of its influence.

George Washington shaped the office in other ways as well:

- He successfully asserted the right to remove his cabinet officers without Senate approval.
- He established the president's supremacy in organizing the executive branch.
- He used the veto power very sparingly, believing it was important not to usurp the will of the people.
- He asserted presidential control during times of emergency when he nationalized state militias to put down the Whiskey Rebellion.

- He made a point of touring all corners of the country so that the American people could meet the president.

Evolution of the Presidency

More than any other branch of government, the presidency has undergone a remarkable transformation during the past 200 years. Though the framers did not provide the presidency with many powers, and George Washington tried to keep it that way, the balance of power between the presidency and Congress began to shift over the decades.

The Era of the Caretaker Presidents

The nineteenth century was the era of great legislators, not presidents. The initial wave of founding father presidents (Washington, Adams, Jefferson, and Madison) quickly gave way to a collection of relatively weak and forgettable officeholders.

FACT

The group of presidents often referred to as the caretaker presidents includes Martin Van Buren, William Henry Harrison, John Tyler, James K. Polk, Zachary Taylor, Franklin Pierce, James Buchanan, Rutherford B. Hayes, James Garfield, Chester Arthur, Grover Cleveland, and Millard Fillmore, whom many historians consider the most unmemorable president of the era.

The presidency was looked upon mostly as a source of federal patronage jobs, and a platform from which to fight the Indians. In fact, the president spent much of his time actually interviewing and appointing thousands of federal workers, which included mail carriers, census officials, and patent reviewers. The dominant issues of the day—slavery and states' rights—were debated in Congress. In fact, it wasn't uncommon for the great legislators, including Henry Clay, John Calhoun, Daniel Webster, and Stephen Douglas, to enjoy greater celebrity and popularity than did the president. However, two presidents from this era do stand out: Andrew Jackson and Abraham Lincoln.

Andrew Jackson

"Old Hickory" believed that the presidency should be the dominant force in American government. He asserted the right of the president to replace any federal officeholder without consulting Congress, and wasn't shy about putting his cronies in key government positions (thus creating the patronage system). He stood up to the members of Congress who opposed tariffs, and threatened to use the military to enforce federal law.

Abraham Lincoln

Regarded by many as our greatest president, Lincoln's election led to the secession of the Confederate states from the Union. Faced with the greatest crisis the country had encountered up to that point (and arguably since), Lincoln understood that only the president could keep the country together. Citing the implied emergency powers of the Constitution, he freed the slaves, suspended civil liberties, and imposed marshal law, even though he lacked the explicit authority to do so. His most important act, however, may have been his decision to hold the election of 1864 during the midst of the Civil War, even though he probably could have suspended it.

The Modern Presidency

The modern presidency bears little resemblance to its nineteenth-century antecedent. As the federal government has grown in size and influence, so has the presidency. Since the beginning of the twentieth century, the president has been the dominant force in American government and politics. This seemingly irreversible trend was pioneered by some of the twentieth century's most prominent presidents.

Teddy Roosevelt

Theodore Roosevelt established the notion of the "bully pulpit"—using the prestige and reach of the White House to rally the American people to certain ideas and legislation. Roosevelt took an activist approach to both domestic and international affairs. He believed that America should pursue an expansionist foreign policy and a populist domestic policy. During his presidency, Roosevelt proved that the White House could be a platform for extraordinary change.

Franklin Roosevelt

FDR responded to the challenge of the Great Depression with the New Deal, a series of landmark laws that transformed the role of the federal government and solidified the presidency as the epicenter of American government. During his thirteen years in office, Roosevelt dramatically expanded the powers of the presidency to combat the Great Depression and wage war against Germany and Japan. By the end of World War II, the presidency was a much stronger office than the one that Roosevelt had inherited.

The Cold War Presidents

The cold war between the United States and the Soviet Union may have done more to enhance the powers of the presidency than any single event during the twentieth century. America's role in the world became the primary preoccupation of the president, and consequently spurred an unprecedented growth of the executive branch and presidential powers. While the Congress remained instrumental in domestic affairs, it acquiesced to the president on matters of foreign policy and war powers.

With the dissolution of the Soviet Union in the early 1990s and the end of the cold war, the Congress began to reassert itself, particularly following the 1994 midterm elections. But with the terrorist attacks of September 11 and the ongoing war against terrorism, the president has a renewed mandate on both domestic security and international issues.

A Day in the Life of a President

The presidency is a 24/7 occupation. Regardless of whether he's enjoying a weekend at Camp David, spending some quiet time in the residential quarters, or simply vacationing, the president is always the president of the United States. He can be pressed into action at a moment's notice. At no time is he free from the duties of the job.

The president's daily routine is usually packed with meetings, events, briefings, speeches, and public ceremonies. His time and schedule are highly regimented and closely guarded by his chief of staff. The activities of a typical day may include:

- Receiving security briefings from heads of the Federal Bureau of Investigation, Central Intelligence Agency, National Security Administration, and the Department of Homeland Security
- Making phone calls to other heads of state
- Meeting with members of Congress
- Meeting with governors and other state officials
- Meeting with cabinet officials and other executive agency personnel
- Having lunch with the vice president
- Attending public events and ceremonies
- Discussing policy with advisors and staff
- Speaking with the media
- Making public remarks from the White House
- Signing bills and executive orders into law
- Attending fundraisers or other political events
- Traveling on behalf of candidates

QUESTION?

Which president holds the record for most foreign travel?
President Clinton so far has spent the most days abroad, tallying 229 days on the road while visiting 133 countries during his eight years in office. His foreign travel peaked during his impeachment year of 1998, when he spent forty-five days overseas. President Nixon's foreign travel also peaked during his impeachment year of 1974, when he visited ten countries over twenty-two days.

During the past fifty years, presidential travel—both domestic and international—has increased sharply. The president typically spends two months of every year in domestic travel, and another twenty days outside of the country. Travel at home is used primarily to boost the president's standing in certain regions of the country, and usually peaks around the midterm elections. The president travels overseas to meet with foreign heads of state, attend conferences and summits with world leaders, and rally the American troops during times of conflict.

Styles of Leadership

Each president who occupies the White House brings his own style of leadership to the position. Political scientists have theorized that leadership style is an indicator of how a president will organize his administration and approach the job.

Delegators

Presidents Franklin D. Roosevelt and Ronald Reagan are considered to be the classic examples of delegators. Both brought a broad, bold vision of the role of government to the White House, and each relied heavily upon staff, executive agencies, and cabinet heads to implement their policies. Not coincidentally, both were largely successful in advancing their agendas, though at opposite ends of the political spectrum. In the first two years of his presidency, George W. Bush had exhibited many of the leadership traits of Reagan and Roosevelt.

Micromanagers

Presidents Lyndon B. Johnson and Jimmy Carter were known as micromanagers. As a former Senate majority leader, Johnson took an unusually active role in Congressional affairs, and was fond of monitoring the minutiae of the legislative process. He took a similar approach to managing the Vietnam War, picking many of the bombing targets himself during late-night strategy sessions with his generals.

Although Jimmy Carter campaigned as an outsider to the political system (having served one term as the governor of Georgia), he quickly developed a reputation as a "policy wonk" and micromanager. He was faulted for lacking the grand vision of previous presidents, and for obsessing over the administrative details of the office at the expense of seeing the big picture. It was reported that Carter once took time to resolve a scheduling dispute between staffers over the use of the White House tennis courts.

Charismatic Leaders

Presidents John F. Kennedy and Bill Clinton are regarded as charismatic leaders—extraordinary communicators who used the media to project an image of youth, vitality, and action. Both presidents drew heavily from academia to fill high-profile positions and were persuasive advocates for their agendas.

FACT

Richard Nixon's leadership style has been described as "keeping his own counsel." The thirty-seventh president had few advisors that he trusted, and rarely sought out dissenting opinions or advice from others. It is believed that Nixon's mistrust of virtually everyone around him contributed to his downfall following the Watergate break-in.

Who Runs?

Running for president of the United States is an awesome undertaking. In the words of one political analyst, it requires someone with a big enough ego to think that he should be president of the United States, and the humility to appreciate the responsibilities of the office. There are three strict constitutional requirements for becoming president: The candidate must have been born in the United States, have been a resident of the country for the fourteen years prior, and be at least thirty-five years old. (You can learn more about presidential elections in Chapter 19.)

Different Paths

Presidents come in all different stripes. Some, such as John Quincy Adams, Benjamin Harrison, and George W. Bush, were born into political dynasties, while others, such as Abraham Lincoln, Ronald Reagan, and Bill Clinton, come from humble beginnings. Many were military heroes, while others have no military experience at all. A few were groomed for the office their entire lives, but for most the opportunity arose later in their careers.

Just as the office has evolved over the past 200 years, so has the typical route to the White House. Throughout the nineteenth century, a large majority of presidents (and candidates who lost the elections) were either generals or senators. Only a few were governors, and even fewer were businessmen. The past 100 years have seen a dramatic reversal: Dwight D. Eisenhower has been the only general to serve as president, and governors have outnumbered senators six to two.

ALERT!

Some believe that another military man, Colin Powell, would have been elected president had he run in 1996 or 2000. Throughout his career as chairman of the Joint Chiefs of Staff and secretary of state, the former five-star general has consistently polled as the most popular public servant in America. Powell holds the distinction of being the highest-ranking African-American ever to serve in both the military and the executive branch.

During the 1990s, billionaire H. Ross Perot self-financed two bids for the presidency. While he finished a distant third both times, his 1992 campaign yielded him the highest vote total of any third-party candidate in eighty years. With the cost of presidential campaigns spiraling out of control, it can be expected that wealthier individuals will finance third-party campaigns in the future.

Presidential Succession

The wording of the Constitution is somewhat ambiguous when it comes to the subject of replacing the president. All it says is, "In Case of the Removal of the President from Office, or of his Death, Resignation, or Inability to discharge the Powers and Duties of the said Office, the Same shall devolve on the Vice President."

When William Henry Harrison became the first president to die in office, in 1841, no one was sure whether Vice President John Tyler would become president, or whether he would simply be entrusted with discharging the duties of the presidential office. Many in Congress considered Tyler to be the "acting president," although Tyler himself behaved as though he were the president. Tyler's approach won the day, and he established the precedent that the vice president was to be elevated to president upon the president's death or removal from office.

QUESTION?

Which president served the briefest term?
William Henry Harrison was the first president to die in office, and remains the president with the shortest tenure, serving only thirty-one days. The story goes that Harrison caught a severe case of pneumonia while delivering a three-hour inaugural speech in freezing weather without a hat. A half century later, his grandson Benjamin would become the twenty-third president.

What happens if both the president and vice president die at the same time? The Presidential Succession Act of 1947, passed by President Harry S. Truman, established the order of succession should both officials die, resign, or become incapacitated. The Speaker of the House is next in line, followed by the president pro tempore of the Senate. After that, it falls to the cabinet officers according to the order in which their departments were created:

1. Secretary of State
2. Secretary of the Treasury
3. Secretary of Defense
4. Attorney General
5. Secretary of the Interior
6. Secretary of Agriculture
7. Secretary of Commerce
8. Secretary of Labor
9. Secretary of Health and Human Services
10. Secretary of Housing and Urban Development

11. Secretary of Transportation
12. Secretary of Energy
13. Secretary of Education
14. Secretary of Veterans Affairs
15. Secretary of Homeland Security

FACT

Former Secretary of State Alexander Haig caused a bit of a stir when, in the moments following the 1981 shooting of President Ronald Reagan, he declared at a press briefing that "I am in charge here," leaving some to believe that he was invoking the Presidential Succession Act of 1947. At the time of Haig's pronouncement, Vice President George H. W. Bush was flying back to the White House on Air Force Two.

The First Lady

Although there is no mention of the role of first lady in the Constitution, it has developed into an important position in American government. After all, perhaps no other person carries as much influence with the president as his spouse.

First Ladies and Their Causes

Whereas first ladies were once confined to simply setting the social calendar and hosting White House receptions, today they work on issues of public policy and advance agendas based on their own interests. Recent first ladies have adopted the following causes:

- Jacqueline Kennedy devoted herself to restoring the White House and establishing the White House Historical Association.
- Lady Bird Johnson continued Jacqueline Kennedy's work, creating the First Ladies Commission for a More Beautiful Capital.
- Pat Nixon enhanced the White House art collection and was a strong proponent of volunteerism.

- Betty Ford was closely identified with her fight against drug and alcohol abuse, and founded the Betty Ford clinic.
- Rosalynn Carter worked with the mentally ill, and served as the honorary chairwoman of the President's Commission on Mental Health.
- Nancy Reagan started the "Just Say No" campaign, an anti-drug and anti-alcohol program targeted at young Americans.
- Barbara Bush focused on adult literacy and elderly care.
- Hillary Rodham Clinton took an active role in public policy, serving as chairwoman of the National Commission on Health Care Reform. She was also an advocate for children, and author of the bestselling book *It Takes a Village.*
- Laura Bush, like her mother-in-law, has promoted literacy. She also played an important role in comforting parents and children across the country in the weeks and months following the terrorist attacks of September 11.

Three Who Stood Out

Of the thirty-eight women who have occupied the White House as first ladies, three in particular have stood out for their achievements, and have helped shape the role.

Eleanor Roosevelt

Eleanor Roosevelt revolutionized the role of first lady, transforming it from hostess to public policy advocate. Eleanor was a tireless advocate for the poor and underprivileged, reaching out to millions through barnstorming tours, a weekly newspaper column, press conferences, and frequent radio interviews. After leaving the White House, Eleanor Roosevelt carried on her husband's legacy of social activism, and also served as the United States ambassador to the United Nations.

Jacqueline Kennedy

Perhaps more than any first lady before or since, Jacqueline Kennedy is responsible for restoring the beauty and elegance of the White House. Her interest in the arts, culture, and the history of the

White House captured the imagination of the country, and added to the youthful and energetic image of her husband's administration. Jacqueline Kennedy won the admiration of the world for her strength and courage following the assassination of President Kennedy.

Hillary Rodham Clinton

Eleanor Roosevelt began the transformation of the role of first lady, and Hillary Rodham Clinton completed it, elevating the role of public policy advocate to the primary responsibility of the first lady. Like Eleanor Roosevelt, her public service did not end after leaving the White House. As the junior senator from New York, she is the only first lady to hold elected office. Hillary Clinton blazed a new path while first lady, and continues to do so in the U.S. Senate. There are some who believe that she might even run for president someday. Ⓔ

Chapter 9

Powers of the President

The president derives his authority from the formal and inherent powers of the office. As you have already learned, the Constitution provides fewer explicit powers to the president than it does to the Congress. Nevertheless, the presidency has evolved into an enormous position. The duties and responsibilities of the president can be divided into seven categories: chief executive, head of state, commander in chief, chief diplomat, legislator in chief, party leader, and comforter in chief.

Chief Executive

As chief executive, the president has the authority to enforce the laws of the country. He derives these powers from the phrase "he shall take Care that the Laws be faithfully executed" in section 3 of Article II in the Constitution. The president has at his disposal the entire executive branch (almost 3 million workers) to help carry out the laws of the land.

The president's chief executive powers include administering the law, covered in Chapter 13; taking care of finances, covered in Chapter 15; and enforcing the law, covered in Chapter 13. Additionally, the president has the power of appointments and pardons.

Making Appointments

While the president exercises the power to make judicial and executive branch appointments, the Senate must approve his nominees. This process has grown increasingly contentious over the past few decades, particularly in the case of cabinet and Supreme Court appointments.

Out of the 3 million federal jobs, most are held by civil servants who are hired, but approximately 6,000 are appointed by the executive branch. These appointments include cabinet and subcabinet members, ambassadors, members of the Senior Executive Service, and special aides in "Schedule C" positions. Approximately one-fifth of the president's appointments are for State Department positions, even though that department is one of the smaller bureaucracies.

While a majority of the executive branch appointments are made on the basis of merit, some are given to reward party loyalists, and others are made for purely political reasons. Most presidents treat ambassadorships as nothing more than thank-you appointments to prominent campaign and party donors. In the Reagan White House, a $100,000 party contribution was usually good for an overseas post.

For cabinet and other high-profile appointments, the president usually takes into consideration those nominees who will shore up their support with certain interest groups. President Clinton won praise from supporters for appointing a record number of women and minorities to his cabinet, in keeping with a campaign promise to make his cabinet "look more like

America." President George W. Bush appointed Mel Martinez, a Cuban refugee and former chairman of Orange County, Florida, to head the Department of Housing and Urban Development. In part, he made this appointment to solidify his standing among Hispanics and Floridians—two key interest groups in his bid for re-election.

FACT

Appointments have been the source of much presidential angst. As Thomas Jefferson was fond of saying, "Every time I make an appointment, I create nine enemies and one ingrate," a lament often repeated by many presidents. Dwight Eisenhower once remarked that his single worst decision as president was appointing William Brennan to the Supreme Court.

Granting Pardons

The Constitution gives the president the power to "grant Reprieves and Pardons for Offences against the United States, except in Cases of Impeachment." The ability to grant pardons and reprieves is one of the few constitutional powers of the presidency that does not require any assent from the Congress. In 1925, the Congress tried to restrict the president's pardon authority, but the Supreme Court rejected it as unconstitutional.

A reprieve is an action whereby the president can reduce the severity or length of a felon's sentence, but it does not erase the conviction. A pardon, on the other hand, wipes out both the guilt and sentence, and completely restores all civil rights to the offender (such as the right to vote and hold a passport). Pardons are much broader than reprieves, and are more commonly used.

Pardons and reprieves are most commonly granted as a corrective action—to reverse a wrongful or politically motivated conviction. Sometimes, pardons and reprieves are used to grant political amnesty to particular groups of Americans. George Washington was the first to do this, pardoning the participants of the Whiskey Rebellion shortly after using military force to arrest them. Following the Civil War, Abraham Lincoln and Andrew Johnson pardoned numerous Confederate soldiers and political leaders, and President Carter pardoned draftees who refused to join the military in protest of the Vietnam War.

Perhaps the most famous act of clemency was Gerald Ford's pardon of Richard Nixon following Nixon's resignation from office in 1974. Trying to put the Watergate scandal behind the nation, Ford granted his predecessor a full and unconditional pardon, which removed the possibility of Nixon being prosecuted in a criminal court for his involvement in any Watergate crimes. Ford was roundly criticized for the decision (many believed that Nixon should be held responsible for any crimes), and it most likely contributed to his loss to Jimmy Carter in 1976.

FACT

President Clinton created a firestorm of controversy that resulted in a Congressional investigation when he pardoned 140 individuals on his last day in office. Included in that group was billionaire financier Marc Rich, an American fugitive living in Europe, and several individuals who had close ties to "first brother" Roger Clinton and to Hugh Rodham, the president's brother-in-law.

Head of State

In addition to being the chief executive, the president also serves as the head of state. Most nations split the head of state and chief executive powers between two or more individuals. In countries like Great Britain, Sweden, Denmark, and Belgium, the king or queen serves as the head of state, while an elected prime minister or president discharges the chief executive functions. Other countries, such as France, Italy, and Germany, have an elected head of state (usually a president) who works alongside an elected chief executive (usually a prime minster). In the United States, the president serves both of these functions—a rarity among Western democracies.

As the head of state, the president fulfills certain ceremonial and symbolic obligations, such as throwing out the first pitch to open a new baseball season, greeting foreign dignitaries with formal White House dinners, lighting the national Christmas tree, dedicating monuments and landmarks, and so on. It has become customary for the president to invite championship athletes and teams to the White House for a public reception. There is no constitutional basis for this ceremonial aspect of the presidency—it has simply evolved as a part of the office over the years.

The president is a symbol of our government and the nation. He represents the majesty and dignity of the office both at home and abroad, and provides our national voice. His gestures—no matter how big or small—carry special meaning and importance. It was reported that the sale of hats dropped dramatically following John F. Kennedy's inauguration, because the president broke with tradition and failed to don one during the parade. When Jimmy Carter turned the White House thermostat down to sixty-five degrees in the winter to save energy, the nation followed suit.

George Washington used the head-of-state aspect of the presidency to help legitimize the office and the federal government itself. He paid particularly close attention to the seemingly trivial details of protocol and the pomp and circumstance of the office because he knew it would establish important precedents for future officeholders.

Commander in Chief

Over the years, presidents have exercised more authority in their role as commander in chief than in any other facet of the job. It's without question the most important responsibility of the office. As commander in chief, the president has the ability to commit American troops to battle. It is the most difficult decision a president can make, and is always handled with great care and reflection.

Declaring War

The framers of the Constitution were careful not to vest too much military power in the presidency for fear of creating an abusive and unjust government, or even a military dictatorship. Therefore, the Constitution gives the Congress the authority to declare war, raise an army, and fund wars, while it gives the president the power to manage and execute military action. The framers did not want the president to have the ability to both declare and execute wars without Congressional involvement.

For the most part, nineteenth-century presidents adhered to the Constitution when it came to decisions of war, consulting Congress on military actions and committing troops only with formal declarations of war. Preceding both World War I and World War II, however, the Congress delegated by statute to the president increased authority to fight wars. The onset of the cold war with the Soviet Union resulted in even greater military authority for the president, as the Congress believed that he was best able to combat the growing menace of communism and the threat of nuclear war.

The Korean War was the first large-scale war for which the president did not seek prior Congressional approval. Harry Truman cited the commander-in-chief authority as well as a United Nations resolution authorizing the use of force as justification for sending troops into battle without a formal declaration of war. Ten years later, President Lyndon Johnson relied on this precedent to send troops to Vietnam—another undeclared war.

FACT

In August of 1964, the Congress passed the Tonkin Gulf Resolution, a joint resolution that authorized President Lyndon Johnson to use military force in Vietnam. The resolution resulted from the purported attack on the naval destroyer USS *Maddox* by two North Vietnamese gunboats. A Congressional investigation in 1968 revealed that the Johnson administration had mostly fabricated the incident as a pretext to war.

In response to the Vietnam War, the Congress passed the War Powers Act in 1973 over President Richard Nixon's veto. With this act, the Congress tried to reign in the president's ability to make war, setting out a specific set of conditions under which he could commit troops without prior Congressional authorization. Even though the Supreme Court has struck down parts of the act as unconstitutional, it has been somewhat successful in forcing presidents to seek Congressional approval before sending troops into harm's way. President George H. W. Bush received Congressional authorization to use military force in the first Gulf War, as did President George W. Bush prior to Operation Iraqi Freedom.

Military Commander

As part of his commander-in-chief function, the president is in charge of the armed forces—he is the first general and admiral. Presidents have approached the military commander function differently. Depending on their background, some have taken a more hands-on approach, while others have left all the decision-making up to their generals. In 1794, George Washington nearly took charge of the militia that put down the Whiskey Rebellion. During the Civil War, Abraham Lincoln was deeply involved in strategy, troop movements, and battle plans, and on occasion even gave direct orders to his field generals. President Wilson left the battlefield strategy to the military during World War I, as did President Franklin Roosevelt (for the most part) in World War II. Lyndon Johnson was famous for selecting specific bombing targets in Vietnam. In Operation Iraqi Freedom, President George W. Bush approved the overall military strategy, but did not involve himself in any tactical decisions.

ALERT!

Wherever the president goes, a military aide follows him carrying "the football"—a briefcase containing all the codes and documents necessary to order a nuclear launch. The president is the only person with the power to authorize a nuclear launch. President Kennedy created "the football" following the Cuban missile crisis.

Chief Diplomat

The president has a broad mandate when it comes to international diplomacy. The Constitution gives him the authority to make treaties (with the advice and consent of the Senate) and recognize foreign governments. He can also enter into executive agreements with other heads of state.

Signing a Treaty

The president needs the consent of two-thirds of the Senate in order to enter into a foreign treaty. Some presidents have interpreted this to mean that the Senate should be consulted on all aspects of treaty negotiations, while others have viewed Senate approval as a rubber stamp.

Regardless of interpretation, the president is the one who drives the treaty process. He alone decides which treaties to pursue. He selects the negotiators, devises the negotiating strategy, and lobbies the Senate for approval. He can even reject a treaty that the Senate has approved if he doesn't like the changes made to it. A treaty is not officially recognized until the president signs it into law.

Although the president needs the Senate's consent to ratify a treaty, he does not need it to terminate one. The Constitution is silent on this issue, but the Supreme Court has held that the president alone should have the power to terminate treaties. In 2002, President George W. Bush terminated the Anti-Ballistic Missile (ABM) treaty with Russia, drawing criticism from some Democrats for not seeking Congressional input first.

Executive Agreements

An executive agreement is a pact between the United States and a foreign government that falls short of being a treaty, but binds the two countries to a mutual action such as arms reduction, trade agreements, military commitments, and territory annexation. An executive agreement is a powerful foreign policy tool because it does not require Senate approval and because it gives the president the flexibility to negotiate international agreements quickly and in secret—two important considerations when dealing with sensitive and timely matters.

The biggest difference between treaties and executive agreements is that treaties are binding on all future presidents, while executive agreements must be reauthorized by each succeeding administration. Executive agreements have grown increasingly popular over the past five decades. In total, there have been close to 10,000 executive agreements, compared to 1,500 treaties.

President John Tyler used an executive agreement to annex Texas in 1845. Tyler feared that the Senate would not approve annexation through a treaty, and he wanted to move quickly before another country laid claim to the Lone Star state. Following Tyler's precedent, President William McKinley annexed Hawaii as a territory through an executive agreement in 1898.

Diplomatic Recognition

Although it's not an explicit power in the Constitution, the president also has the sole authority to recognize a foreign government. This power stems from the president's ability to receive and send ambassadors. Formal recognition of a foreign government is required before treaties, executive agreements, and other diplomatic actions can take place. The simple act of receiving a foreign diplomat is enough to officially recognize his or her government. In determining whether or not to recognize a particular foreign government, presidents typically take into account that country's record on human rights, its ability to govern its people, the moral character of the regime, and its willingness to abide by international law.

In some cases, presidents have used the recognition power to make a political statement. President Andrew Jackson recognized the independent country of Texas in 1836 because he knew it would provoke Mexico into a war with the United States. Harry Truman recognized the newly created state of Israel in 1946 as a way to support the fledgling country. In 1978, Jimmy Carter recognized the Palestinian authority in Israeli-occupied territories in an effort to jump-start the peace process. President Clinton severed relations with Afghanistan after the Taliban seized power, and President George W. Bush reinstated it after the provisional government of Hamid Karzai took control.

Legislator in Chief

The president plays a dominant role in the legislative process. He proposes legislation, works closely with Congressional leadership on scheduling and strategy, and frequently lobbies members on key votes. When the president is of the same party as the Congressional majority, his legislative agenda is given top priority.

State of the Union Address

The Constitution requires that the president "from time to time give to the Congress information of the State of the Union, and recommend to their Consideration such Measures as he shall judge necessary and expedient."

This annual State of the Union address has developed into the president's most powerful tool to shape the legislative agenda. For most of the nineteenth century, presidents discharged this responsibility with a letter to Congress. Beginning with Woodrow Wilson, however, the president began delivering the State of the Union address in person. It is now given in late January to a packed session of Congress (including the Supreme Court justices and cabinet officials). The nationally televised address allows the president to lay out a comprehensive legislative agenda for the coming session of Congress. Most of the time, the president enjoys a spike in popularity following the speech, and tries to takes advantage of it by quickly introducing his legislative agenda in Congress.

Veto Power

The Constitution vests with the president the power to veto—or reject—any legislation passed by the Congress. This power is a valuable political tool because it allows the president to influence and shape legislation simply by raising the specter of a veto.

Presidents tend to exercise the veto power judiciously. Using it too often can give the appearance of being out of touch with the American people, or behaving like an obstructionist. Franklin Roosevelt vetoed 635 bills during his thirteen years in office, far and away the most of any president. Seven presidents, including Thomas Jefferson and John Adams, didn't veto any legislation at all.

As you learned in Chapter 7, the Congress can override a presidential veto with a two-thirds majority of both chambers, although this rarely occurs. Less than 5 percent of all vetoes are overridden.

FACT

In 1996, Congress gave the president the line-item veto—a special type of veto that allowed the president to strike certain provisions out of a bill while signing the remainder into law. However, the Supreme Court later declared it unconstitutional.

Party Leader

As the nation's highest elected officeholder, the president wields considerable influence over his political party. He sets party policy, defines the legislative agenda, establishes the tone for political dialogue, and serves as the party's chief spokesperson. The political fate of his party is inextricably linked to the president's fortune.

The president's most important party function is fundraising. Every year, the president raises hundreds of millions of dollars for the party and fellow officeholders at the state and national level. Cabinet members and high-profile White House officials assist in the fundraising, particularly during election seasons. During the 1990s, many Republicans, consumer advocate groups, and even some in the press criticized President Clinton for his aggressive use of the White House for party fundraising. They believed that Clinton's White House coffees and Lincoln bedroom sleepovers were an inappropriate use of the White House, although prior administrations had used it in a similar fashion.

In addition to fundraising, the president also has the following responsibilities as the leader of his party:

• He selects the national committee chairperson.
• He writes the party policy platform at the nominating convention.
• He influences party members in Congress with promises of fundraising support and projects for their district.
• He campaigns for candidates.

FACT

Most presidents stay clear of Congressional and gubernatorial primaries. During the midterm elections of 2002, however, President George W. Bush and his chief strategist Karl Rove handpicked and backed candidates they believed would be the strongest in key Congressional and Senatorial races. The strategy was successful, as Republicans retook the Senate and gained seats in the House.

Comforter in Chief

The "comforter-in-chief" aspect is one of the most important roles of the modern presidency, even though it is nowhere to be found in the Constitution, and was never envisioned by the framers. In fact, sometimes a president makes his deepest connection with the American people during times of crisis and tragedy.

This role stems from the uniqueness of the office: only the president can command the nation's undivided attention. In times of emergencies, crises, and tragedies, we turn to the president for comfort, guidance, and perspective. With the advent of television and mass communication, this aspect of the presidency has taken on even more importance.

President Clinton was particularly adept at comforting the nation. Even his critics complimented his handling of the Oklahoma City bombing, where he publicly wept with and reassured the victims and their families. President George W. Bush was equally up to the task following the terrorist attacks of September 11, as he simultaneously led us in mourning, soothed our fears, and steeled our resolve for the war on terrorism. First Lady Laura Bush was dubbed "the first comforter" for her handling of the aftermath of the terrorist attacks. Ⓔ

Chapter 10

The Vice Presidency

The vice presidency is a peculiar office. It has virtually no constitutional authority, and has often been relegated to an afterthought by the president. Yet the person who occupies it is only a heartbeat away from assuming the presidency. For the first 150 years, the vice president played almost no role in American government. Since World War II, however, the vice presidency has assumed greater responsibilities, and very recently has blossomed into the second most powerful position in Washington.

The Early Years

The vice presidency was given little consideration by the framers of the Constitution. Some of them were opposed to having the position at all, so as a compromise it was made into a weak office, made possible by a last-minute insertion into the Constitution and given just one explicit duty—to preside over the Senate.

Mess of the 1800 Election

The country's first constitutional crisis occurred during the election of 1800, when Thomas Jefferson and Aaron Burr received the same number of presidential votes in the Electoral College. What made it particularly troublesome was that Burr was Jefferson's running mate!

How did a presidential and vice presidential candidate tie for the nation's top office? Well, the Constitution set up a system in which there was no separate vote for president and vice president. Members of the Electoral College were allowed to submit two votes, but they could not indicate which vote was for president and which was for vice president. The candidate receiving the most votes was elected president, and the runner-up was made vice president. The framers created this odd system because they wanted the vice president to be the second most qualified person in the country (essentially the loser of the presidential election), and in the first two elections it worked.

FACT

As the presidential election was being contested in the House of Representatives, Alexander Hamilton worked behind the scenes to deny Aaron Burr a victory. Hamilton detested Burr, and thought he was unfit for the office. Burr blamed Hamilton for his defeat, and four years later (while serving as vice president) challenged Hamilton to a duel, during which he shot and killed him.

What the system didn't anticipate were political parties and running mates. In the election of 1800, Jefferson and his running mate Burr both received 73 electoral votes, while Jefferson's opponent John Adams received only 65. By constitutional mandate, the election was then thrown to the House of Representatives, where on the thirty-sixth ballot Jefferson finally edged out his vice presidential running mate.

As a result of the mess of 1800, the Twelfth Amendment was passed, which called for separate ballots for the election of the president and vice president. Thus, instead of the second most qualified person obtaining the office of vice president (the presidential loser), the president's running mate would become the vice president. A few years later, Congress tried to abolish the vice presidency altogether, but the measure was narrowly defeated in the Senate.

The Veeps History Forgot

The Twelfth Amendment ushered in an era of forgettable—and sometimes regrettable—vice presidents. Few men of national stature were interested in the powerless office, and as a result a rash of vastly underqualified candidates filled the void. Garret Hobart was a New Jersey state legislator when he was tapped as William McKinley's vice president. Chester Arthur, who became president after James Garfield was assassinated, had been a customs collector for the port of New York prior to becoming vice president.

For the seven-year stretch from 1850 to 1857 there was effectively no vice president of the United States. Millard Fillmore became president following the death of Zachary Taylor in 1850, leaving the vice presidency vacant for the remainder of the term. In 1853, newly elected vice president William Rufus King succumbed to tuberculosis only a month into his term, leaving the office unoccupied for the remainder of Franklin Pierce's presidency.

Some nineteenth-century vice presidents had interesting ways of passing the time while in office. Richard Johnson spent much of the Martin Van Buren administration tending bar at his saloon. Ulysses S. Grant's second vice president, Henry Wilson, used the time to pen a three-volume history of slavery. William Rufus King decided to do nothing at all, skipping Franklin Pierce's inaugural to receive medical treatment for tuberculosis in Cuba. He died a month later in his native Alabama without ever serving a day in the office.

The Modern Vice Presidency

The transformation of the vice presidency has coincided with the rapid expansion of the federal government and the powers of the presidency. Franklin Roosevelt's sudden death in 1945 and Harry Truman's unpreparedness to succeed him put political leaders of the day on notice that the vice presidency needed to take on more importance. This became even more urgent with the onset of the cold war only a few years later.

The presidency of Dwight Eisenhower marked a turning point for the vice presidency. "I personally believe the Vice President of the United States should never be a nonentity. I believe he should be used. I believe he should have a very useful job," Ike once remarked at a press conference.

Eisenhower lived up to those words, giving his number-two man Richard Nixon a more prominent role than any previous vice president. Nixon served as the party spokesperson and political troubleshooter, and was active in foreign affairs. He traveled to fifty-eight nations—far and away the most of any vice president to that time—and conducted several sensitive diplomatic missions on Ike's behalf. Twice when Eisenhower fell ill for long stretches of time, the vice president surprised many with his reassuring presence. Nixon's signature moment as Ike's sidekick occurred in 1959, when he faced off with Soviet Premier Nikita Khrushchev in an impromptu debate while the two toured the American National Exhibition in Moscow. The moment was captured live on television, and in an instant elevated the status and prestige of the vice presidency.

Lyndon Johnson picked up on Nixon's role as goodwill ambassador to the world, globetrotting to meet with foreign heads of state on dozens of occasions. As a former Senate majority leader, he played a part in devising the Kennedy administration's legislative strategy—particularly for the Civil Rights bill—and was also given broad responsibilities with the newly created National Aeronautics and Space Administration (NASA). Johnson's time as vice president prepared him well for assuming the presidency following President Kennedy's assassination in November of 1963.

FACT

After serving in the shadows of Ronald Reagan for eight years, Vice President George H. W. Bush faced the daunting task of winning the presidency on his own. One prominent news magazine wrote that his biggest obstacle was overcoming the "wimp" factor. Many felt that he succeeded in doing so. Bush became the second sitting vice president to be elected president.

Spiro Agnew's tenure as Richard Nixon's vice president represented something of a setback for the office. Nixon had plucked the one-term governor from relative obscurity in 1968, but never really developed a role for him. Agnew is best remembered for his scathing attacks against the news media and the "elite establishment," and for resigning the office in disgrace after pleading nolo contendere to the charge of income tax evasion.

The Option of Co-Presidency

For a brief time in the summer of 1980, there was talk of creating a "dream" Republican presidential ticket of Ronald Reagan and Gerald Ford, with the former president serving as Reagan's vice president. Reagan was attracted to the idea of having Ford's experience at his disposal, and Ford envisioned a kind of "co-presidency" in which power would be shared. The two camps couldn't come to an agreement, however, and talks of the co-presidency were scuttled.

Al Gore and Dick Cheney

Since the early 1990s, the vice presidency has taken another leap forward in stature and importance. During that time, it has completed the transition from an office of ridicule to one of the most powerful positions in Washington. Former president Bill Clinton and President George W. Bush are largely responsible for this final metamorphosis, having given their vice presidents more responsibility than did any previous administration.

Vice President As Successor

The vice president's most important duty—or, as some would argue, its sole reason for existence—is to succeed the president in the case of death, resignation, or incapacitation. As Woodrow Wilson's often quoted vice president Thomas Marshall put it, "The only business of the Vice President is to ring the White House bell every morning and ask what is the state of health of the President." Though a slight exaggeration, it captures the essence of the office succinctly.

The Successors

In our nation's history, nine vice presidents have ascended to the White House following the death or resignation of a president. Four of the presidents died of natural causes, four were assassinated, and only one resigned.

FACT

When Vice President John Tyler learned of William Henry Harrison's death, he was at his home in Williamsburg, Virginia. The news reached Tyler a day after Harrison died, and it took Tyler another day to travel back to the capital. During this two-day period, there was no president—the longest such vacancy in our nation's history.

Given the ambiguities in the Constitution regarding the specific nature of presidential succession (that is, whether the vice president assumed the presidency itself, or just the powers of the presidency), the first four vice presidents to take office through succession were considered by many to be illegitimate. This sentiment was so strong that all four—John Tyler, Millard Fillmore, Andrew Johnson, and Chester Arthur—failed to win renomination by their own parties for an independent term of their own. None of the four served with any distinction, and Andrew Johnson was actually impeached over a political decision.

Theodore Roosevelt was the first vice president elevated to office to win a full term on his own, when he trounced Democrat Alton Parker in

1904. Ironically, the Republican Party bosses had chosen Roosevelt as William McKinley's running mate because they disliked his progressive platform as governor of New York, and wanted to put him in a position where he would be powerless!

When Harry S. Truman took office following Franklin Roosevelt's death in 1945, the United States was at war with Germany and Japan. Roosevelt had kept Truman in the dark about the development of the atomic bomb, so it came as a great surprise when Truman was informed of the weapon only hours after being sworn in as president.

Richard Nixon was the first president to replace his vice president, when he appointed Gerald Ford to the office following Vice President Spiro Agnew's resignation in 1973. The following year, President Gerald Ford nominated New York governor Nelson Rockefeller to fill the vacancy created by Ford's ascension to the presidency.

Twenty-fifth Amendment

Following President Kennedy's assassination in 1963, political leaders realized that it was time to clarify the succession process. In 1967 the Twenty-fifth Amendment was ratified. It established four points:

1. In the case of the president's death or removal from office, the vice president becomes president.
2. If the office of vice president is vacated, the president must nominate a new vice president, to be confirmed by a majority in both houses of Congress. (Prior to this, the vice presidency remained unoccupied if the office was vacated either through death or succession.)
3. If the president is temporarily unable to discharge the duties of the office, he must inform both the Speaker of the House and the president pro tempore of the Senate in writing, at which time the vice president becomes acting president. Once the president is able to resume his duties, he must again inform both Congressional leaders in writing. In 1985, President Reagan was the first to invoke this

provision while undergoing a procedure to remove a cancerous growth from his colon.

4. If a majority of the cabinet members (as well as the vice president) determine that the president is unable to discharge the powers of the office, they must inform the Speaker of the House and the president pro tempore in the Senate in writing, at which time the vice president would become acting president. This provision has not yet been tested.

Selecting a Vice President

The process of selecting a running mate has undergone a dramatic transformation over the past two centuries. This change has coincided with the evolution of the office of the presidency, and the nature of campaigns.

Who Chooses the Vice President?

For most of the nineteenth century, the vice presidential candidate was selected by party bosses, and was usually the result of "backroom" negotiations and compromises among various factions of the party. The presidential candidates typically had little input into this decision.

Often, this process resulted in candidates and running mates who barely knew each other, or—worse—didn't get along. Vice President George Clinton didn't even attend James Madison's inaugural, while John C. Calhoun went so far as to cast the tie-breaking vote in the Senate against Andrew Jackson's nominee for ambassador to Great Britain, Martin Van Buren.

Backroom deal-making among party bosses gave way to nominating conventions in the early twentieth century as the preferred method of choosing a running mate. During the election of 1900, both William McKinley and William Jennings Bryan threw their vice presidential nominations to the convention floor, and consequently were handed running mates they did not like. In 1920, the delegates to the Republican convention actually rejected Warren G. Harding's choice of Senator Irwin Lenroot in favor of Massachusetts governor Calvin Coolidge, who later succeeded Harding after the president's sudden death. In 1956, the Democratic convention took twelve ballots before it decided on Estes Kefauver as

Adlai Stevenson's running mate. Kefauver edged out five candidates, including a young senator from Massachusetts named John Kennedy.

Taking Control over the Process

Over the past three decades, presidential candidates have taken the lead in the vice presidential selection process. It has become routine that shortly after being assured of his party's nomination, the candidate forms a search committee composed of his closest advisers to produce a "short list" of potential running mates. This committee usually completes its work by early summer, and in most cases the presidential candidate chooses some-one from that short list. The selection is usually unveiled prior to the party convention as a way to generate extra buzz and momentum.

FACT

In 2000, Dick Cheney headed George W. Bush's vice presidential search committee. After rejecting the list of a half-dozen potential running mates, Bush took the unusual step of offering the position to Cheney himself. President Bush said that after working closely with Cheney for several months, it became apparent that he was the best person for the position.

Factors to Consider

Modern presidential candidates take into account a combination of factors when narrowing down the list of potential running mates:

- **Regional balance.** Having separate regions of the country represented on the presidential ticket is a frequent consideration. In 1988, Massachusetts governor Michael Dukakis selected Texas senator Lloyd Bentsen as his running mate. Bentsen was well known and regarded in the South, while Dukakis's base of support was in the Northeast. Two decades earlier, fellow New Englander John F. Kennedy also looked to a Texan, Lyndon Johnson, to balance his ticket.
- **Ideological balance.** Like regional balance, ideological balance also helps a presidential ticket appeal to a wider audience. In 1980, Ronald Reagan selected George H. W. Bush primarily because Bush's moderate

views helped lessen concerns among some voters that Regan was too conservative.

- **Carrying a state.** In some instances, the need to carry an important state is the key factor in choosing a running mate. In 1952, Dwight Eisenhower chose to run with California senator Richard Nixon, whom he did not like, though he liked California's electoral votes more than he disliked Nixon.

- **Buzz factor.** Candidates far behind in the polls will sometimes select a running mate who can possibly change the dynamics of the election—in other words, introduce the "buzz factor." Facing long odds of unseating popular incumbent Ronald Reagan, Walter Mondale made two-term Representative Geraldine Ferraro the first woman to run on a major party's national ticket, in the hope of shaking up the election. It failed to ignite the electorate, however; Reagan carried every state except Mondale's home state of Minnesota.

- **Who would be the best president.** Once in a while, a presidential candidate will select a running mate solely on the basis of his belief that the nominee would make a good president.

QUESTION?

Where does the vice president live?
The vice president makes his residence at the Naval Observatory, which is located several miles from the White House. The first veep to live at the Observatory was Walter Mondale. Prior to 1976, the nation's second highest officeholder lived at his own residence.

The Vice President's Campaign Role

Historically, vice presidential candidates have played a minor campaign role in presidential elections. It is widely believed that Americans cast their vote for the person leading the ticket, and not the running mate. As Richard Nixon famously put it, "The number two man goes along for the ride." In 1988, the Democrats tried to make Senator Dan Quayle's relative youth and inexperience a campaign issue against George H. W. Bush, but it failed to register with the voters.

Over the past several decades, vice presidential candidates have begun to assume a larger role in the election. Increasingly, they have been called upon to serve as the campaign "hatchet man," cutting down the opposition with sharp attacks. As Gerald Ford's running mate in 1976, Senator Bob Dole created a stir when he blamed the Democrats for starting four wars in the twentieth century. Four years later, Vice President Mondale called into question Ronald Reagan's fitness to serve as president.

The high point of the campaign for the two presidential running mates is the vice presidential debate—the one time when the candidates for vice president get to square off. Notwithstanding the hype leading up to it, this debate usually takes a back seat to the presidential debates and rarely has an impact on the campaign. In 2000, Dick Cheney and Joe Lieberman showered each other with pleasantries and compliments during their only faceoff, in sharp contrast to the two presidential debates.

FACT

The most memorable moment of the 1988 campaign came during the vice presidential debate, when Senator Dan Quayle compared his experience to that of John F. Kennedy, to which Lloyd Bentsen responded: "Senator, I served with Jack Kennedy. I knew Jack Kennedy. Jack Kennedy was a friend of mine. Senator, you're no Jack Kennedy." It is one of the most often repeated lines in politics.

The Changes Continue

No other office in American government has undergone a greater transformation than the vice presidency. For its first 150 years, it was mostly inhabited by little-known politicians, and served primarily to provide an understudy for the president. As the federal government expanded during the latter half of the twentieth century, so did the responsibilities of the vice president. In just the past decade, this once forgotten office has emerged as one of the most powerful positions in Washington—a trend that is likely to continue in the future. Ⓔ

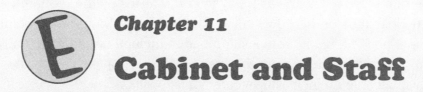

Chapter 11

Cabinet and Staff

Some of the most influential people in American government are those who advise the president. Although they serve in nonelected positions, these advisors have the ability to shape and influence both domestic and foreign policy. Presidential advisors come in three categories: cabinet members, White House staff, and nongovernmental advisors. In this chapter, you'll learn about the cabinet, White House staff, and others who have the president's ear. The next chapter will examine the rest of the federal bureaucracy.

History and Purpose of the Cabinet

The idea behind a nonelected cabinet to advise the chief executive has its roots in the British system of government. In the seventeenth century, the English Parliament devised the "cabinet council"—a small group of men who advised the king on political issues and administered certain government departments—as a way to curb abuses by the monarch and keep close tabs on his governance. The king was allowed to appoint the cabinet council, but its composition had to include members of Parliament. Over time, the cabinet assumed greater responsibilities as the Crown became an increasingly ceremonial position.

Cabinet and the Articles of Confederation

The British idea was borrowed by the Congress under the Articles of Confederation. Because Congress was required by the Articles to both legislate and administer the laws of the land, it had set up several executive departments to manage the administrative functions of government.

Just months after the ratification of the Articles of Confederation, the Congress set up the Department of Foreign Affairs and appointed Robert Livingston as the Secretary of Foreign Affairs—the first cabinet officer in our nation's history. Ten years later, the Department of Foreign Affairs was renamed the State Department; thus, the cabinet actually predates the Constitution by nearly a decade.

FACT

In Federalist No. 70, Alexander Hamilton—one of the few proponents of a strong executive—made the case for omitting the cabinet from the Constitution. He believed that it was undemocratic and unworkable to have a system in which a nonelected cabinet could overrule an elected president. "A feeble Executive implies a feeble execution of government," he concluded.

In the Constitution

The role of the president and his advisors was one of the most hotly contested issues at the Constitutional Convention. A majority of the delegates agreed that a weak president was preferable to one who resembled a monarch, but disagreed over how best to restrict his authority.

Some argued that having three presidents would effectively limit the power of the office, but the idea was dismissed as unworkable and too stifling. Others proposed a single president with a strong cabinet—one who shared the decision-making process with him—as a compromise solution, but the delegates couldn't agree on the exact powers of the cabinet. Unable to reach a consensus, the framers decided on a single executive with limited powers, and purposely omitted any reference to a cabinet in the Constitution so as not to give credence to the notion of a "president by council."

Evolution of the Cabinet's Role

Among the many precedents established during Washington's presidency, the role of the cabinet ranks near the top of the list in importance. Washington believed that cabinet staff should serve as policy advisors and department managers. He frequently convened his cabinet as group meetings to discuss both specific departmental items and general matters of national governance. However, Washington never considered the cabinet an instrument for collective policymaking. Instead, he viewed it as a forum for open discussion and debate on national issues. This was an important distinction.

FACT

Though usually a consensus seeker, President Lincoln wasn't above pulling rank on his cabinet every now and again. After presenting a draft of the Emancipation Proclamation to his cabinet during a lengthy meeting, Lincoln asked them if he should present it to the nation. When his entire cabinet opposed the idea, Lincoln quipped, "Seven nays and one aye, the ayes have it."

Washington also believed that cabinet selection should be based solely on merit—whoever is most qualified to perform the job—and should represent political and geographic diversity whenever possible. However, with the rise of political parties, and the advent of the patronage system, much of Washington's philosophy regarding cabinet appointments was lost on future generations. Cabinet selection, for the most part, simply became another opportunity for the president to reach out to various interest groups and strengthen his political base.

Name That Cabinet Department

As of January 1, 2003, there are fifteen cabinet departments working with the president. Can you tell which is which?

1. The fourth largest department in terms of employees, this agency was elevated to cabinet status in 1889. This department conducts research to improve agricultural activity, provides assistance to farmers and ranchers, and works to protect national forests from fire and disease.

   Department of Agriculture

2. Established in 1789, this department develops foreign policy, negotiates treaties, and handles diplomatic relationships with foreign governments. Its head is the first cabinet official to succeed to the presidency in the case of national disaster. Thomas Jefferson, Dean Acheson, and Henry Kissinger have all headed this department.

   State Department

3. Established in 1849, this was the first cabinet department created after the original three of 1789. One of its responsibilities is to supervise Native American affairs. It also oversees the national parks system and is responsible for wildlife conservation. In 2001, Gail Norton became the first woman to head this agency.

   Interior Department

4. The mission of this department is to create affordable housing and home ownership opportunities for all Americans. Established as one of the Great Society programs of the 1960s, it's the second smallest department in terms of the number of its employees.

   Department of Housing and Urban Development (HUD)

5. This agency is responsible for setting workplace conditions, and monitoring contract negotiations between unions and management. In 2001, department head Elaine Chao became the first Asian-American woman to head a cabinet agency.

Department of Labor

6. By far the largest cabinet department with almost 700,000 employees, this agency provides for the national defense, manages the armed forces, and operates military facilities. Donald Rumsfeld holds the distinction of being both the youngest and oldest person to head this department, having served in the post under President Gerald Ford and George W. Bush.

Department of Defense

7. This department enforces federal criminal laws and provides legal advice to the president. It was formed in 1789, although it did not become a cabinet-level department until 1870. More than a dozen smaller agencies report to this department, including the Federal Bureau of Investigation (FBI).

Justice Department

QUESTION?

Which cabinet department resides outside of Washington, D.C.? The Pentagon, which houses the Department of Defense, is located across the Potomac River in Alexandria, Virginia, only five miles from downtown Washington. With approximately 30,000 employees, the Pentagon is considered the world's largest office building.

8. Created in 1988, this department promotes the welfare of veterans of the U.S. Armed Forces. It is estimated that more than 500,000 veterans and their spouses receive benefits from this agency every year.

Department of Veterans Affairs

9. The purpose of this department is to promote economic growth and job creation, and protect the interest of businesses. It was founded in

1903 and became its own department in 1913. It's also responsible for the national census, patents and trademarks, and promoting U.S. travel and tourism.

Commerce Department

10. Established in 2002, this department's primary responsibility is to protect Americans at home from terrorist attacks. Airport luggage checkers, the Coast Guard, the border patrol, and many others now report to this agency. President George W. Bush appointed former Pennsylvania governor Tom Ridge to be the first head of this department.

Department of Homeland Security

11. This department is responsible for providing safe and easy travel within the United States. Created in 1967, its sub-agencies include the Federal Aviation Administration (FAA), the Federal Highway Administration (FHWA), and the National Transportation Safety Board (NTSB), which investigates plane crashes and other transportation-related accidents.

Department of Transportation

12. Established in 1977, this department is responsible for promoting the conservation of energy and resources, conducting research and development for alternative energy sources, and overseeing radioactive and nuclear materials at home and abroad.

Energy Department

13. Originally created in 1953, this department was renamed and given a slightly different mandate in 1979. It promotes the health and welfare of the American people, and is the largest grant-making agency in the federal government. The Food and Drug Administration and Centers for Disease Control are just two of the many sub-agencies that report to this department.

Department of Health and Human Services (HHS)

14. The smallest cabinet department, with approximately 5,000 employees, this agency coordinates federal programs and policies meant to improve the quality of education nationwide. Since its creation in 1979, there have been several unsuccessful attempts to abolish this department.

Department of Education

15. One of the three original cabinet departments established in 1789, this one oversees the nation's fiscal policy and economy, and is also responsible for protecting the president and his family. Former department heads include Alexander Hamilton, James Baker III, and Robert Rubin.

Treasury Department

ESSENTIAL

For the first 150 years, the cabinet served as the predominant source of presidential counsel and decision-making. Over the past fifty years, however, the White House staff has replaced cabinet personnel as the president's primary advisors and policymakers.

Why Are New Departments Created?

Over the past two centuries, cabinet departments have been created approximately once every couple of decades. The longest period between new additions was the fifty-one-year gap between the Department of Navy (1798) and the Department of the Interior (1849). New departments are created by Congressional legislation, and must be signed into law by the president.

Some cabinet departments are born of a specific necessity. The Department of Homeland Security was formed in response to the terrorist attacks of September 11. At the urging of President George W. Bush, it took the Congress less than a year to conceive, draft, and pass the bill authorizing the department—a remarkable accomplishment given the enormity of the task. The Department of the Interior was established in response to the rapid expansion of the western territories during the mid-nineteenth century. The settlers needed government assistance in dealing with Native Americans, and in resolving such issues as public land usage and the harnessing of natural resources.

Several cabinet departments, such as the Department of Agriculture, Department of Labor, and Department of Commerce, were created to serve narrow—but powerful and highly organized—constituencies (in these cases, farmers, workers, and business groups, respectively). All three of these interest groups lobbied Congress intensely for long periods of time before finally getting their own cabinet departments.

Other cabinet departments are created to serve the interest of the general public, such as the Department of Energy and the Department of Transportation. It's the mission of the Department of Energy to coordinate national policy and find alternative sources of energy. Transportation is charged with coordinating the various modes of transportation, including highways, railroads, air transport, sea carriers, and mass transit, at the national level.

A few cabinet departments have been created or elevated to cabinet status as a symbolic act or a gesture of political favoritism. President Carter created the Department of Education mostly to keep a campaign promise to the teachers unions that supported his campaign. President Reagan elevated the Veterans Administration to the Department of Veterans Affairs, in part to heal the wounds of the Vietnam War and attract voters who were veterans.

No Guarantee to Last

In some cases, cabinet departments may be downgraded in status. For instance, the Department of Navy, formerly a cabinet department, eventually merged with other departments to form the Department of Defense. In theory, cabinet departments can be dissolved as well, although this has never occurred. When the Republicans took control of Congress in 1994, one of their first agenda items was to consolidate and abolish several departments—something Republicans had been campaigning on for years. However, dismantling the Department of Education—first on the Republicans' hit list—proved to be more difficult than anticipated, and the Congress soon gave up on downsizing the cabinet.

FACT

The Department of Agriculture provides information, assistance, and subsidies to America's farmers. At the time of its creation during the Civil War, 90 percent of Americans were farmers. Today, farmers represent about 1 percent of the work force, which means that there is one Department of Agriculture bureaucrat for every three farmers in this country!

Those Who Serve in the Cabinet

Putting together a cabinet is one of the first orders of business for a president-elect. Generally speaking, the composition of a president's cabinet reflects his political philosophy.

The head of the president's transition team usually chairs a search committee that puts together a short list of potential cabinet secretaries for each post. An extensive background check is done for the persons on the short list (with their permission), and the president typically interviews multiple candidates for each position.

Presidents take into account several factors when selecting their cabinet members:

- **Longtime friends.** Every president has included longtime friends—people he had known for decades—in his cabinet. Former Secretary of Labor Robert Reich first met President Clinton while the two studied at Oxford University in their early twenties. President John F. Kennedy raised a few eyebrows when he appointed his brother Robert as attorney general, which he had done mostly at the urging of his father.
- **Campaign loyalists.** It's not unusual for a president to fill a spot or two in his cabinet with campaign loyalists who've helped get him elected. Richard Daley, heir to the famed Daley political machine in Chicago, was rewarded for his campaign service with the top job at the Commerce Department during Bill Clinton's second term. Ed Meese became attorney general after engineering Ronald Reagan's victory over Jimmy Carter in 1980.

- **Member of the opposite party.** It has become a semi-tradition that at least one member of the opposite party be included in the cabinet. President Clinton chose Republican senator William Cohen of Maine to serve as secretary of defense during his second term, while President George W. Bush appointed former Democratic Congressman Norman Mineta as his secretary of transportation. Democratic stalwart Daniel Patrick Moynihan served several positions in the Nixon administration before running for the Senate in New York.

QUESTION?

Who was the first woman to serve in the cabinet?
Appointed secretary of labor in 1933 by President Franklin Roosevelt, Frances Perkins headed the Labor Department for twelve years and three months—the longest tenure of any cabinet secretary in history. In 1980, the Department of Labor headquarters was renamed the Frances Perkins Building.

- **Superstar.** Presidents often search out political "superstars" to serve in their cabinet for the expertise and prestige they bring to the administration. During the election of 2000, candidate George W. Bush let it be known that former Chairman of the Joint Chiefs of Staff Colin Powell would be included in a Bush administration—a move he hoped would appeal to moderate and undecided voters. George H. W. Bush scored a minor coup when he convinced conservative icon Jack Kemp to serve as his secretary of housing and urban development, a post that is not generally regarded as one of the more glamorous cabinet positions.
- **Elected officials.** Most cabinets include former members of Congress. George W. Bush made Spencer Abraham his secretary of energy after the one-term senator was defeated for re-election in Michigan. Abraham had served on the energy committee, and was highly regarded on Capitol Hill.
- **Experts from the private sector.** Most presidents look to the private sector to fill one or two cabinet positions. For example, President Clinton chose longtime educator and University of Wisconsin President

Donna Shalala to head the Department of Health and Human Services, where she served for eight years.

White House Staff

Throughout the nineteenth century and into the twentieth, the cabinet played a critical role in advising and counseling the president. Outside of personal servants, clerical helpers, and aides, the president had almost no White House staff to help with the administration of the executive branch. President Herbert Hoover actually took some heat for doubling the White House staff from two to four—a move that did not sit well with Congress.

This all changed, however, with the dramatic expansion of the federal government during the Roosevelt administration. As the New Deal became law, dozens of agencies were created to administer the new programs. Roosevelt understood that the White House required increased staff to properly administer and oversee these new federal programs.

Executive Office of the President

In 1939, President Roosevelt proposed a major reorganization of the executive branch. Although Congress rejected most of FDR's proposal, it authorized the creation of the Executive Office of the President (EOP) as a way to staff the White House. In its first year, the EOP created six positions to help Roosevelt discharge his duties. Today, the EOP consists of ten staff agencies with more than 600 employees working at the White House.

Of the ten staff agencies created by the EOP, four in particular make up the majority of the White House staff:

1. **White House Office.** Established in 1939, it is the oldest and most influential staff agency within the White House. Personnel in this department include the chief of staff, press secretary, communications director, legal counsel, appointments secretary, senior advisors, and others who look out for the political interests of the president. Campaign veterans and longtime allies usually serve in these positions, and they tend to have the most access to, and influence with, the president.

2. **National Security Council.** Created at the onset of the cold war, the primary function of the National Security Council (NSC) is to advise the president on domestic and foreign policy matters involving national security. The council consists of nineteen members, including the vice president, secretary of defense, secretary of state, and the national security advisor, one of the highest profile positions in the administration. The NSC has more than 200 staff members who monitor global events on a twenty-four-hour basis from the situation room of the West Wing of the White House.

3. **Council of Economic Advisors.** Established in 1946, this three-member group advises the president on issues relating to the economy. Its main responsibility is to devise economic policy and prepare the president's annual economic report to Congress. The president's primary economic advisor during the campaign usually serves as the chairman of the Council of Economic Advisors.

4. **The Office of Management and Budget.** Reorganized during the Nixon administration, the primary responsibilities of the Office of Management and Budget (OMB) are to prepare the annual budget, help set fiscal policy, and supervise the administration of the federal budget. The director of the OMB is considered the "chief accountant" for the federal budget.

The other six staff agencies of the Executive Office of the President include the Office of the United States Trade Representative, Council on Environmental Quality, Office of Science and Technology Policy, Office of Administration, Office of National Drug Control Policy, and the Office of Policy Development.

The Staff's Roles

Since World War II, the White House staff has gradually supplanted the cabinet as the nucleus of the administration and the president's chief policy advisors. As the Executive Office of the President has grown in size, so too have its responsibilities.

Because campaign loyalists, personal friends, and longtime allies of the president staff a vast majority of the EOP positions, modern presidents have grown increasingly comfortable with their staffs setting policy direction, drafting legislation, devising legislative strategy, and communicating the agenda—tasks once handled primarily by the cabinet. The White House staff is also aided by its close proximity and regular access to the president—two crucial ingredients when exercising power in the executive branch.

Policy initiatives that originate from the cabinet are usually reviewed and sometimes revised by the White House staff before meeting the president's approval. At times, this process has been the source of friction between the White House and the cabinet. Richard Nixon believed that his cabinet was captive of the bureaucracy, and regularly encouraged his staff to undermine them. President Lyndon Johnson and his staff spent considerable time figuring out ways to circumvent his department heads. President Clinton's staff simply ignored policy overtures from the cabinet a good deal of the time.

FACT

Relations between President Carter's staff and cabinet grew so strained that a presidential retreat was held at the Catoctin Mountains so that the two camps could work out their differences. Apparently, little was accomplished—not long after, the president fired nearly half of his cabinet and appointed a new chief of staff.

In addition to assuming greater responsibilities, the White House staff has also taken on a higher media profile in recent years. It's not unusual for as many as a half-dozen West Wing staffers to regularly appear as administration spokespersons on television news programs. In the age of the twenty-four-hour news cycle, it has become more practical for White House staffers—not cabinet members—to set the agenda, respond to events, and "spin" policy positions through the media.

Nongovernmental Advisors

Every president has sought the advice of friends and allies outside of government at one time or another. Typically, these advisors serve as unbiased "sounding boards" for the president—ones who don't have a bureaucratic constituency or staff territories to protect. Most presidents turn to them infrequently, and only for counsel on specific matters for which they offer a special expertise.

Andrew Jackson was the first and perhaps only president to rely exclusively on counsel from a small circle of friends. This group was dubbed the "Kitchen Cabinet" by the press because they sneaked through the White House kitchen to meet with him. Jackson distrusted his formal cabinet, and didn't even meet with them until his third year in office. President Franklin Roosevelt had a similar group of informal advisors, whom he referred to as "the brain trust," although he called on such advisors less frequently than did Jackson.

FACT

President Roosevelt's closest informal advisor, Harry Hopkins, actually lived in the White House residence for long stretches of time during World War II. Roosevelt liked having "Harry the Hop" nearby, and believed it was better for the chronically ill Hopkins to be looked after by the White House staff. Hopkins and Roosevelt died within a year of each other.

In recent times, the late Clark Clifford served as an informal counselor to every Democratic president from Harry Truman to Bill Clinton. Clifford was highly regarded in Democratic circles, and considered an invaluable presidential resource. Washington superlawyer Vernon Jordan was a close (and highly public) confidant of Bill Clinton.

Chapter 12

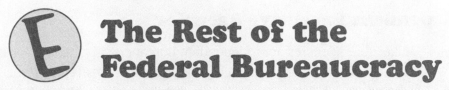

The Rest of the Federal Bureaucracy

Although it's nowhere to be found in the Constitution, the federal bureaucracy is sometimes referred to as the fourth branch of government. Since its inception, the bureaucracy has been a frequent source of presidential frustration. Every chief executive has tried to bring the bureaucracy under his control, but few have succeeded.

Basic Organization

The federal bureaucracy is divided among four types of structures. In addition to cabinet departments, which were examined in Chapter 11, there are also three types of "noncabinet" agencies—independent executive agencies, independent regulatory commissions, and government corporations.

Independent Executive Agencies

Executive agencies are independent bureaucracies that are located outside the cabinet department structure. These agencies report directly to the president, who appoints and removes their chief officials. Presidents prefer an executive agency to remain independent when it has a narrow mission that requires special consideration.

There are approximately seventy independent executive agencies of varying sizes. Some employ tens of thousands of people; others, several hundred. The Central Intelligence Agency (CIA), Small Business Administration (SBA), National Aeronautics and Space Administration (NASA), Environmental Protection Agency (EPA), and the Peace Corps are independent executive agencies.

FACT

When the CIA was created in 1947, the Department of Defense lobbied to have it placed under its jurisdiction. The Congress decided against this because it wanted civilian control over intelligence gathering and spying. The Department of Defense failed to win responsibility for NASA for the same reason when it was created in 1958.

Independent Regulatory Commissions

These commissions are formed with the express purpose of regulating particular sectors of the economy and promulgating rules. They are intended to be totally independent from the president and the executive branch. Congress came up with independent regulatory commissions in order to delegate its oversight responsibilities without giving too much power to the executive branch.

Most regulatory commissions are run by boards of commissioners, who are appointed to fixed terms by the president and confirmed by the Senate. The appointments are bipartisan (no party can have more than a one-person majority), and the president cannot remove a commissioner absent any malfeasance. Most commissioners are either industry experts, academics, or former elected officials.

The first of these commissions appeared in 1887, when Congress established the Interstate Commerce Commission (ICC) to regulate the rapidly industrializing economy. Since then, scores of commissions have been created, including the Federal Reserve Board of Governors (1913), the Federal Trade Commission (1914), the Securities and Exchange Commission (1934), the National Labor Relations Board (1934), the Equal Employment Opportunity Commission (1964), and the Nuclear Regulatory Commission (1974). Most of these commissions have fewer than 2,000 employees.

Government Corporations

Sometimes referred to as quasi-governmental agencies, these entities are created when the government activity is commercial in nature. Government corporations behave like private companies in that they generate revenues through buying and selling property, lending money, or participating in other market activities.

ALERT!

Government corporations should not be confused with government sponsored entities (GSEs), which are shareholder-owned companies that are chartered by the federal government to promote certain social policies, such as home ownership. The Federal National Mortgage Association (Fannie Mae), the Federal Home Loan Mortgage Corporation (Freddie Mac), and the Student Loan Marketing Association (Sallie Mae) are all GSEs.

Like a private corporation, a government corporation is headed by a chief executive officer, who is chosen and supervised by a board of directors or commissioners. The board of directors is selected by the president, much the same way as for an independent regulatory commission. Unlike private corporations, however, a government corporation has no public shareholders, retains all its profits, and does not pay taxes. The United States Postal Service is the most recognizable government corporation. With almost 900,000 employees, it is the largest employer in the United States. The Federal Deposit Insurance Corporation (FDIC), Export-Import Bank, and Amtrak are also government corporations.

The Bureaucracy's Role in Government

The primary purpose of the bureaucracy is to administer the laws and policies passed by Congress and the president by establishing programs, promulgating rules and regulations, and creating infrastructures to deliver benefits in accordance with the language and intent of the enabling legislation. Sometimes, however, bureaucracies make policy as well. This occurs in two ways.

Iron Triangles

The term "iron triangle" is used to describe the alliance formed by Congress, bureaucrats, and interest groups to make public policy in the group's domain. These iron triangles are often referred to as "subgovernments," and typically operate outside the conscious view of Congress, the president, and the public.

A first cousin of the iron triangle is the "captured agency." This occurs when an agency promulgates rules favorable to (not critical of) the interest group it's supposed to be regulating. Interest groups "capture" agencies by applying political pressure to members of Congress, who in turn apply pressure to the regulating agency.

Iron triangles have been making policy for several decades, and they operate on the theory of mutual self-interest. Bureaucrats are dependent on Congress for continued authorization and funding, so it is in their interest to work closely with Congressional committees and subcommittees that have jurisdiction over their departments. Likewise, members of Congress gladly solicit legislative input and direction from the interest groups in return for campaign contributions and electoral support. In the end, all parties benefit from the relationship: Congress receives campaign contributions, interest groups get favorable legislation, and bureaucrats preserve their jobs and enhance their standing.

Issues Networks

As the federal government has grown in size and complexity, policymaking has become more nuanced and subtle. With control of both houses of Congress and the White House changing more frequently than in previous eras, "issues networks" have begun to replace iron triangles as the preferred method of policymaking.

Issue networks are composed of individuals and groups that coalesce around a particular policy initiative and then lobby Congress, the president, the courts, and even the bureaucracy to adopt this public policy. Members of the issue network may include legislators, bureaucrats, scholars, activists, and even members of the media.

In 2002, Senator John McCain and his network of supporters—which included Democratic legislators, academics, good-government activist groups, and members of the broadcast and print media—won passage of campaign finance reform (the McCain-Feingold bill), a bill that President George W. Bush opposed but was pressured into signing. It's not unusual for issue networks to form around opposing sides of the same policy debate.

Who Are the Bureaucrats?

More than 90 percent of the federal work force is composed of career civil servants—nonpolitical appointees who retain their positions regardless of the administration in the White House. Many of these career bureaucrats develop vast expertise and institutional knowledge regarding their particular niche and, in some cases, their own personal agendas. In addition to career civil servants, the bureaucracy is also staffed by political appointees. For the most part, the president makes the appointments for top positions in the federal bureaucracy; rarely does Congress make any appointments.

FACT

The Civil Service Reform Act of 1978 established the Office of Personnel Management (OPM), which acts as a clearing-house to recruit, interview, and evaluate potential civil servants. The OPM makes recommendations to the hiring agency, but the agency itself ultimately decides whom to select.

Through most of the 1800s, all government jobs were political, causing high turnover and corruption. Congress established a merit-based civil service act in 1883 after President Garfield was assassinated by a disappointed office-seeker. While creating a class of career bureaucrats improved continuity and independence, some believe it has contributed to an increasingly inert and unresponsive federal bureaucracy.

Getting Appointed

How does one get a political appointment to a federal position? After every presidential election, the Government Printing Office (GPO) publishes United States Government Policy and Supporting Positions (also known as "the plum book" because of all the plum positions listed). Beginning with the transition period and lasting well into the first year of office, the White House fills the positions listed in the "plum book."

The president takes into consideration a combination of factors—political affiliation, area of expertise, work experience, personal characteristics, and background—when selecting a candidate for a particular job. Thousands of appointments are made every year, most of which require Congressional approval. With the increased partisanship in Washington, it's not unusual for these positions to remain empty for months or even years at a time.

Most political appointees remain in their positions for a brief period of time; the average term is less than two years. This being the case, career civil servants are typically disinclined to aggressively implement their current boss's directives because it's likely that the appointed boss will be gone in a year or two. They are further emboldened to disregard their supervisors' policies because it's nearly impossible to discharge a career civil servant—less than one-tenth of 1 percent are fired every year. This high turnover rate among appointees, combined with the inability to fire career civil servants, has led to a bureaucracy that is difficult to bring under control and slow to implement change.

Controlling the Bureaucracy

Congress established bureaucratic agencies because it did not have the resources or expertise to regulate the growing economy. In the process, Congress delegated some authority to the executive branch to help administer these agencies, although it retained the most important function: oversight. It's the responsibility of Congress to make certain that each agency remains true to its mission and is properly performing its duties. As former senator Phil Gramm put it, "Congress's duty doesn't end with passing a law—we have to make sure that the law works." This is accomplished in several ways.

When career civil servants disagree with a particular policy direction, the preferred method of resistance is inaction, not confrontation. Both the State Department and Defense Department stalled on multiple orders from the Kennedy administration to remove Jupiter missiles from Turkey before finally relenting. During the Nixon administration, the FBI simply ignored the president's many requests to use "dirty tricks" to get back at his political opponents.

Pulling the Purse Strings

Congress's most effective oversight tool is the authorization and appropriations process. When an agency is established, Congress must authorize funds for it. In some cases, such as the Social Security Administration (SSA), this is a permanent authorization, meaning it never has to be renewed. For others, such as NASA, this authorization is periodic—it must be renewed every few years. In light of this, Congress wields much greater control over agencies that require periodic authorizations.

Congress also controls the annual budgets for both permanently and periodically authorized agencies through the appropriations process. This gives Congress the ability to abolish or modify agency programs by eliminating or cutting back funding. Many times, Congress will make agency appropriations contingent upon specific policy changes. In rare cases, Congress will do just the opposite, giving increased funding beyond what was requested for programs it finds particularly effective. Agency heads periodically testify before the Congressional committees and subcommittees with jurisdiction to request increased funding.

Nonappropriations Methods

Congress also has several nonappropriations tools that it uses to oversee the bureaucracy—some more effective than others:

- **Hearings and investigations.** Congress can investigate agencies and call bureaucrats to testify before committees and subcommittees to determine whether the agency is complying with Congressional intent. It can also ask the Government Accounting Office (GAO) and the Congressional Budget Office (CBO) to investigate particular agency actions and conduct oversight studies.
- **Legislative vetoes.** The legislative veto allows Congress to reject (by majority vote) an agency's policy proposal or action. Although the Supreme Court declared legislative vetos unconstitutional in 1983, Congress continues to enact them and agencies continue to abide by them.
- **Mandatory reports.** Congress can require agencies, departments, and even the president to periodically assess programs and report their findings. Through these reports, Congress can determine whether the laws it has passed are having their intended effect. For example, the anti-drug law of 1986 requires that the president submit an annual report to Congress on whether nations that produce and transport

narcotics are cooperating with the U.S. government. Congress can cut off aid to a nation if it is found not in compliance.

- **Inspectors general.** Virtually every agency has inspectors general (IGs) who reside outside the bureaucratic chain of command. These inspectors regularly meet with Congress to report on waste, fraud, and abuse within the agency. On occasion, Congress will direct the IGs to perform specific audits and investigations on its behalf.

Bureaucratic Whistleblowers

The term "whistleblower" is used to describe someone who brings attention to (blows the whistle on) illegal or corrupt behavior, gross inefficiencies, or mismanagement. Whistleblowers show up in both the private and public sectors. Relying on whistleblowers for oversight is a recent phenomenon.

FACT

Perhaps the most famous whistleblower in U.S. history is the character of "Deep Throat" from Bob Woodward and Carl Bernstein's book *All the President's Men*. The duo credited Deep Throat with providing invaluable information regarding the Watergate burglary and coverup. To this day, only Woodward, Bernstein, and their editor Ben Bradlee know the whistleblower's identity.

Bureaucratic whistleblowers play an important role in agency oversight. They have been an invaluable resource for Congress and the public for aiding understanding of bureaucratic waste, abuse, and corruption. Whistleblowers may be clerical workers, managers, experts, and even department leaders. Despite legislation that prohibits acts of retaliation against whistleblowers by their superiors, most government whistleblowers end up leaving their jobs within three years of coming forward with their information.

Attempts at Reform

As long as there has been a federal bureaucracy, there have been complaints about its inefficiency, ineffectiveness, arrogance, and lack of responsiveness to the public's needs. Poll after poll has revealed that government bureaucracies consistently rank among the most unpopular institutions in America.

Over the past several decades, Congress has made several attempts to reform the federal bureaucracy and rehabilitate its image. The Government in the Sunshine Act of 1976 requires that federal agencies run by a panel of executives hold their meetings in public sessions. The only exceptions to this rule are personnel matters and court proceedings. Every other type of agency gathering—whether formal or informal—is required to be open to the public, or "in the sunshine." This transparency has helped make some bureaucracies more responsive to Congress and the public.

Given the enormous size and complexity of the federal bureaucracy, the president's most useful tool in shaping bureaucratic policy is his power of appointment and removal. Presidents usually remove top officials hostile to their agendas and appoint ones sympathetic to their goals.

Recently, many states have begun to adopt "sunset laws" as a way to gain greater control over their bureaucracies. Sunset laws create a finite lifespan for a bureaucracy and automatically terminate it at the end of that designated period, unless the bureaucracy is specifically reauthorized by the state legislature. In order to be reauthorized, these bureaucracies must prove their effectiveness and merit. It's only a matter of time before Congress makes greater use of sunset laws.

There has also been a growing trend at the state and federal levels to privatize certain government functions. Supporters of this approach contend that the private sector can provide some services more cost-effectively and with better results. Some prisons, schools, waste management facilities, and homeland security functions have been privatized in recent years. There is a limit, however, to the public services that private companies can perform.

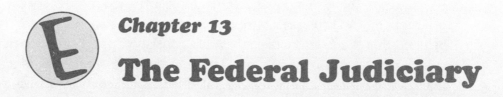

Chapter 13

The Federal Judiciary

Of the three branches of government, the federal judiciary is the least well known and understood. For one thing, its proceedings aren't covered by the press with the same regularity or intensity afforded the executive and legislative branches. Also, few Americans have reason to participate in the federal court system, because most disputes are handled at the state court level. And finally, its role and procedures can seem complex and confusing. We'll try to simplify and demystify the federal courts in this chapter.

History of the Federal Judiciary

One of the many shortcomings of the Articles of Confederation was that it lacked a national judiciary. The delegates who gathered in Philadelphia for the Constitutional Convention realized this, and set out to correct the problem.

However, there were great differences over the exact shape of the judicial branch. The Federalists, proponents of a strong national government, believed that the federal judiciary should consist of trial courts, appellate courts, and one supreme tribunal. The antifederalists, supporters of states' rights, were concerned that an integrated federal judiciary would usurp the states' authority and embolden the federal government. Instead of a three-tier federal judiciary, they proposed that state courts serve as the trial and appellate courts. A national supreme court would hear final appeals.

FACT

One of the antifederalists' biggest concerns was that trials in federal court would be biased against the defendants and would not offer the same protection as did the state courts. They won two key concessions in this regard: The Judiciary Act guaranteed defendants in federal court the right to trial in their district of residence, and also provided that jury selection in federal court would be consistent with the jury selection method of the state in which the district is located.

Like many of the debates that took place in Philadelphia, the dispute over the federal judiciary ultimately ended in compromise, found in Article III of the Constitution: "The judicial Power of the United States shall be vested in one supreme Court, and in such inferior Courts as the Congress may from time to time ordain and establish." Essentially, it was left to Congress to resolve the issue.

Congress wasted little time in doing just that, passing the Judiciary Act of 1789 in its very first session. The bill picked up where the Constitutional Convention left off, forging further compromise between the Federalist and antifederalist factions. The act constructed a three-tier federal judiciary by adding a trial and appellate level, just as the Federalists wanted. At the same time, it limited the jurisdiction of the federal courts, set a high monetary threshold for diversity cases (cases where the litigants are from different states), and gave the state courts concurrent jurisdiction over many federal issues—three provisions the antifederalists insisted upon. In the end, both sides were satisfied with the outcome. The fact that federal judiciary has changed so little over the past two centuries is a testament to its genius.

Sources of American Law

American law comes from a variety of sources: the Constitution, state constitutions, federal and state statutes, and case law. Understanding this is important because litigants must identify the source of law in their complaint to bring suit in federal court.

Federal and State Constitutions

The Constitution of the United States is the supreme law of the land—no law, regardless of its source, can contravene it. In essence, the Constitution establishes a guideline by which all federal and state laws and regulations must adhere; any law found in violation of the Constitution is declared unconstitutional by the Supreme Court. Over the course of 200 years, the Supreme Court has compiled a vast body of constitutional law based on its interpretation of various phrases and clauses found in the Constitution. These interpretations, of course, have sometimes varied from court to court, which is how the law evolves over time.

Likewise, state constitutions are the supreme law within their respective borders, unless they contradict the U.S. Constitution, an act of Congress, or the provisions of a foreign treaty. Just as the Supreme Court interprets the Constitution, so does the highest court in each of the states interpret its own state's constitution.

Legislative Acts

Legislative acts constitute a rapidly growing area of American law. Every year, tens of thousands of legislative bodies promulgate new laws and regulations that govern our lives, covering everything from zoning rules to highway speeds, the disposal of hazardous waste, and criminal conduct. Congress and the state legislatures are the best known of these bodies, but county, municipal, and district governments also contribute to statutory law. It has been estimated that there are nearly 50,000 governmental bodies in the United States that act in a legislative capacity.

Stare decisis, Latin for "let the decision stand," is a doctrine by which the lower courts (as well as the Supreme Court itself) follow precedents established in earlier rulings when deciding a case. While the courts are not absolutely bound by stare decisis, it's highly unusual for them to disregard established case law. Perhaps the biggest violator of stare decisis is the Supreme Court itself.

Case Law

Through the years, decisions rendered by the various courts have formed a body of law referred to as "case law." Unlike statutory law or administrative regulations, which are codified and highly organized, case law is found in court opinions, and is generally tied to the particular facts of a case. Sometimes case law is referred to as "unwritten law," although this is a misnomer.

Case law is a product of our common-law tradition, which was inherited from Great Britain. "Common law" is another way of saying judge-made law. Its origins date back to the Norman conquest of England, when William the Conqueror established a unified legal system based on the rulings of the king's court. The more important decisions from the king's court were collected in something called the *Year Books*, which served as the basis for settling similar disputes.

Case law differs from statutory law in that it is flexible, and can evolve over time to reflect society's changed values. To some extent, it is the ability of case law to adapt to the times that has helped make the Constitution a "living document," as many scholars refer to it. Today, a dozen countries have common-law systems, including former British colonies Canada, Australia, India, and New Zealand.

The Power of Judicial Review

In theory, it's the role of Congress and the president (the two elected branches of government) to make public policy, and it's the job of the courts (the appointed branch) to interpret and apply the law. In reality, however, judges make policy all the time when carrying out this task. This is made possible by a doctrine known as judicial review, the single greatest power of the courts.

In the strictest terms, judicial review is the authority of the courts to determine whether acts of Congress, the executive branch, and the states are constitutional. However, the concept is nowhere to be found in the Constitution; it was established by the Supreme Court in a landmark case called *Marbury v. Madison*, to this day considered the most important decision in Supreme Court history.

FACT

Although the Supreme Court established the power of judicial review in 1803, it used it infrequently through the first part of the nineteenth century. In fact, prior to the Civil War only two federal laws were declared unconstitutional. On the other hand, during the 1930s the Court aggressively used judicial review to strike down dozens of New Deal laws and regulations.

The Case of *Marbury v. Madison*

Judicial review was born out of political expediency more than anything else. Shortly before leaving office in 1801, President John Adams appointed William Marbury the federal justice of the peace. The new president, Thomas Jefferson, then ordered his secretary of state, James Madison, to refuse to recognize Marbury's appointment. In response, Marbury filed a lawsuit against Madison, claiming that Madison's failure violated section 13 of the Judiciary Act of 1789.

Supreme Court Chief Justice John Marshall despised Thomas Jefferson and believed that Marbury should be given his commission. Marshall knew, however, that if he ruled in favor of Marbury, Jefferson would certainly ignore his decision, and the authority of the Supreme Court would be weakened. He also knew that if he ruled in favor of Jefferson, it would appear that he was bowing to political pressure, no doubt undermining the Court's independence.

Faced with this dilemma, Marshall conjured a brilliant solution. He ruled against Marbury, stating that the Supreme Court could not hear the case because section 13 of the Judiciary Act of 1789, which Marbury claimed granted the Supreme Court authority to hear such cases, was itself unconstitutional. In doing this, Marshall established that the Supreme Court had the inherent power to declare acts of Congress unconstitutional, while at the same time not inviting retaliation from Thomas Jefferson, who was delighted that Marbury was denied his commission.

Marshall reasoned that "if the courts are to regard the Constitution; and the Constitution is superior to any ordinary act of the legislature; the Constitution, and not such ordinary act, must govern the case to which they both apply." In the end, he concluded, "It is emphatically the province and duty of the judicial department to say what the law is."

Today, all courts—both at the national and state level—have the power to determine the constitutionality of legislative acts. This aspect of American jurisprudence stands apart from most other Western democracies, in which only the highest courts (if any) exercise the power of judicial review.

Judicial Activism and Restraint

There are two primary schools of thought when it comes to exercising judicial review. "Activist" judges and justices generally believe that the courts should aggressively use judicial review to thwart acts of Congress, executive agencies, and the state legislatures when they find those acts to be excessive in authority or contrary to public policy. "Restraintist" judges and justices, on the other hand, believe that the courts should defer to the judgment of the elected branches of government on legislative matters, and they tend to withhold using judicial review except in cases where a law or rule is clearly unconstitutional.

Today, judicial activism is generally associated with political liberalism, while judicial restraint is linked to conservatism. Democratic presidents typically appoint activist judges and justices who view the courts as vehicles for social change and betterment; Republican presidents typically appoint restraintist judges and justices who believe the courts should have a limited role in making public policy.

FACT

The landmark abortion case *Roe v. Wade* highlights the differing judicial philosophies. Proponents of the decision believe that the Supreme Court properly found that the U.S. Constitution guarantees the right to an abortion as part of its right to privacy, while opponents contend that the court circumvented the will of elected officials by reading new rights into the Constitution. It's unlikely the debate will be resolved in the near future.

The Federal Court System

Think of the federal judicial system as a pyramid: The Supreme Court is on top, followed by an appellate level just below, and the district (or trial) courts at the base. The power flows downward, so the inferior courts are bound by Supreme Court decisions. However, all courts may exercise the same power of judicial review.

District Courts

The U.S district courts represent the starting point into the federal judicial system. Created by section 2 of the Judiciary Act of 1789, the 94 district courts—staffed by more than 600 judges—are the trial courts for the federal judiciary. Every state (plus the District of Columbia, Guam, Puerto Rico, the Virgin Islands, and the Northern Mariana Islands) has at least one district court, and the larger states have several (New York, California, and Texas are the only states with four district courts). Each district court has more than one judge presiding, which allows for multiple trials to take place simultaneously (the Southern District of New York, which consists of Manhattan and the Bronx, has the most with twenty-eight judges).

The district courts hear three types of cases. The most common are criminal matters, which are initiated by the U.S. attorney for that district. Federal income tax evasion, counterfeiting U.S. currency, and trafficking narcotics across state lines are examples of criminal cases that would be tried at the district court. It also tries civil cases when the dispute is based on matters of civil law, such as contractual obligations, copyright infringement, unlawful trademark infringement, and the like. The least common are public law cases, in which citizens or private organizations sue governmental agencies for failing to act in accordance with their statutory obligations.

Court of Appeals

Losers at the district court can appeal to the U.S. court of appeals. The appellate courts are divided among thirteen geographic circuits, and they hear appeals from the district courts located within their respective circuits. The circuits are divided as follows:

1. Maine, New Hampshire, Rhode Island, Massachusetts, and Puerto Rico
2. New York, Connecticut, Vermont
3. Pennsylvania, New Jersey, Delaware
4. West Virginia, Maryland, Virginia, North Carolina, South Carolina
5. Texas, Mississippi, Louisiana
6. Michigan, Ohio, Kentucky, Tennessee
7. Wisconsin, Illinois, Indiana
8. North Dakota, South Dakota, Minnesota, Nebraska, Iowa, Missouri, Arkansas
9. California, Nevada, Arizona, Oregon, Washington, Idaho, Montana, Hawaii, Alaska, Guam, Northern Mariana Islands
10. Utah, Wyoming, Colorado, Kansas, Oklahoma, New Mexico
11. Alabama, Georgia, Florida
12. District of Columbia
13. The Federal Circuit (no geographic jurisdiction)

The appellate courts have no discretion to refuse cases—they must accept all appeals brought before them. Because they are not trial courts, the appellate courts only review questions of law (whether the law was properly applied to the facts), not questions of fact (such as whether an event really took place). Because the Supreme Court takes very few cases, court of appeals rulings are rarely overturned.

FACT

The court of appeals for the Thirteenth (Federal) Circuit has no geographic jurisdiction. Instead, it has nationwide jurisdiction over certain specialized cases involving federal policy, such as patent infringement, or actions in which the United States government is the defendant. Congress created the Federal Circuit in 1982 by consolidating the Court of Claims and the Court of Customs and Patent Appeals.

Getting into Federal Court

There is no automatic right to appear in federal court. In fact, the overwhelming majority of legal actions that occur in the United States take place in state courts, not the federal court. Two requirements must be met before an action can be judged in the federal system: jurisdiction and standing.

The Question of Jurisdiction

The federal judiciary is composed of courts of limited jurisdiction, meaning it can only hear cases where there is express authority to do so. Article III, section 2 of the U.S. Constitution dictates two such situations. The first is when the disputed matter involves a question of federal law. The "federal question" can derive from the Constitution, an act of Congress, an executive branch ruling, or a dispute arising under a treaty.

The second type of federal jurisdiction occurs when the litigating parties are citizens of different states. This is "diversity of citizenship" jurisdiction. The amount in controversy must exceed $75,000, however, in order for diversity jurisdiction to be established. Disputes between U.S. citizens and foreign governments or citizens also satisfies diversity requirements.

The Question of Standing

In order to bring suit in federal court, the moving party (the party bringing the lawsuit) must have legal "standing." Standing is simply another way of saying that the litigant is entitled to appear before the court. Four conditions must be present to show standing:

1. There must be a conflict. Federal courts do not rule on hypothetical situations or give advisory opinions. In 1997, the Supreme Court overruled a lower court's judgment that the presidential line-item veto was unconstitutional. The Court found that the six congressmen who had brought the suit weren't actually harmed by the line-item veto, because it hadn't been used yet.
2. The plaintiff—or person bringing the action—must have been harmed in some way by the defendant, and there must be a remedy under the law for that harm. Generally speaking, litigants cannot bring suit on behalf of other injured parties (except in the case of minors).
3. The conflict at issue cannot be "moot," or have been resolved prior to adjudication. In one anti–affirmative action case that made its way before the Supreme Court, the high Court determined that the controversy had become moot when it learned that the plaintiff (a student) was admitted to the law school (defendant) subsequent to the legal action. It refused to rule on the merits of the case.
4. There must be a specific plea alleged in the complaint. In order for a court to hear an action, the dispute must be based on a specific violation of law, whether it's a constitutional, statutory, or common law.

State Courts

State courts serve the same function as the federal courts, except they function at the state level. They interpret the meaning of the state constitution, rule on matters of state statutory law, and create a body of state case law. As mentioned earlier, the vast majority of the legal proceedings that occur in the United States take place in state courts. Cases tried in state courts may deal with any of the following matters:

- Felony and misdemeanor crimes
- Business and real-estate disputes
- Divorce and child custody cases
- Will, estate, and trust probates
- Personal injury and other private tort actions
- Private economic (contract) disputes
- Matters involving state regulation of business and professional services

States have varying methods for selecting jurists to their court of last resort. Eight states, including Pennsylvania and Texas, hold partisan elections for these positions. Thirteen states hold nonpartisan elections. The governors of New York, New Jersey, New Hampshire, and Maine appoint their high court jurists, while Rhode Island, South Carolina, and Virginia vest that power with their state legislatures.

While no two state court systems are organized exactly alike, most states divide their court system among four general categories: trial courts of limited jurisdiction, trial courts of general jurisdiction, appellate courts, and the "court of last resort."

Trial Courts of Limited Jurisdiction

Upward of 80 percent of all the courts in the United States are state courts of limited jurisdiction. These include juvenile courts, city courts, county courts, family courts, municipal courts, and magistrate courts, to name a few. Typically, these courts hear minor cases, such as criminal misdemeanors (cases for which jail sentences would be less than one year), and civil disputes involving less than $1,000. These cases rarely go to trial—most are quickly resolved out of court.

Trial Courts of General Jurisdiction

Most states refer to their general jurisdiction courts as either district or superior courts. For some unknown reason, New York refers to it as the supreme court. These courts handle major cases, such as felony crimes (cases for which jail sentences would be longer than one year) and civil disputes greater than $1,000. Most states divide their general trial courts into judicial circuits or regions according to existing boundaries, such as counties or parishes.

Intermediate Appellate Courts

As their name implies, appellate courts hear cases on appeal from the trial courts of limited and general jurisdiction. Only three-quarters of the states have intermediate appellate courts; the others designate their court of last resort as the sole court of appeal. In most situations, these appellate courts have mandatory jurisdiction, meaning that they must accept all cases brought before them. Some states have one court of appeals with statewide jurisdiction, while other states have regional appellate courts that service a specific group of trial courts.

Court of Last Resort

Every state has a highest court, or court of last resort. Most states refer to it as the supreme court, with New York being the notable exception (it calls it the court of appeals). For the most part, state courts of last resort behave similarly to the United States Supreme Court in that they have discretionary jurisdiction (they choose their cases), only rule on matters of law (they don't hear evidence), and are the final arbiters on matters of state law. Only a narrow band of cases can be appealed from a state court of last resort to the United States Supreme Court (more on this in the next chapter). Ⓔ

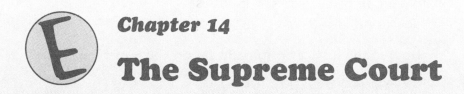

Chapter 14

The Supreme Court

On the first Monday of each October, the U.S. Supreme Court begins a new session. Between October and July, it rules on 80 to 100 cases, and, in the process, creates and refines a body of case law. Some decisions will go unnoticed; others will please, anger, or activate Congress and the president, interest groups, the media, and the public. The Supreme Court's mission has remained the same: to interpret the meaning of the Constitution and determine the constitutionality of the laws that govern our land.

Through the Centuries

In the eighteenth century, the Supreme Court produced few important rulings. The justices spent a good deal of time on administrative functions as they tried to figure out the role of the Court. It wasn't until the landmark decision of *Marbury v. Madison* in 1803 (discussed in Chapter 13) that the Court began to assert itself.

QUESTION?

How many justices originally sat on the Supreme Court?
In its first year of existence, the Court had five justices. This number changed six times before Congress finally settled on the current total of nine justices in 1869. In 1937, President Franklin Roosevelt tried to increase the bench to fifteen members, but Congress rejected his "court-packing" plan.

Nineteenth-Century Court

From 1801 through 1835, Chief Justice John Marshall—the longest-serving chief justice in history—guided the Court through a period of rapid expansion in its power. Marshall was a strong believer in the pre-eminence of the federal government, and his views pervaded the Court's decisions. Despite early political resistance to Marshall's activist Court, his rulings came to be accepted by the other branches of government.

John Marshall's successor, Chief Justice Roger Taney, presided over a markedly different Court. The Taney Court took a narrow interpretation of the Constitution, finding fewer federal powers and more states' rights than did the Marshall Court. Its philosophy led to the *Dred Scott* decision of 1857, considered by many to be the low point in Supreme Court jurisprudence. *Scott* ruled that slaves were not citizens of the United States, and that federal laws limiting slavery violated the Constitution. *Scott* was later overturned by the Fourteenth Amendment.

Over the next seventy years, the Supreme Court continued to look suspiciously at the growth of the federal government. It overturned a series of laws and regulations aimed at the economy, and crafted extremely narrow interpretations of the Civil Rights Amendments.

One such decision was the *Slaughterhouse* case of 1873, which held that the Fourteenth Amendment did not protect the right to private property. A quarter century later in *Plessy v. Ferguson*, the court concluded that the Fourteenth Amendment did not prohibit public segregation by law, so long as it was "separate but equal." The doctrine survived until 1954, when the Supreme Court reversed itself in *Brown v. Board of Education*.

Twentieth-Century Court

During Franklin Roosevelt's presidency, the Supreme Court underwent another dramatic transformation. As justices hostile to the New Deal began retiring, Roosevelt replaced them with liberal jurists who believed that the federal government had broad power to regulate commerce and the economy.

With the exception of Jimmy Carter, every twentieth-century president named at least one justice to the Supreme Court. Franklin Roosevelt appointed eight during his thirteen years in office, far and away the most of any president. During his one year in office, President Warren G. Harding had the good fortune of making two appointments.

Over the next forty years, the Supreme Court aggressively pursued an agenda of expanded civil rights, civil liberties, and business regulation. *Brown v. Board of Education* ended school segregation; *Gideon v. Wainwright* created the right to counsel in criminal proceedings; *Miranda v. Arizona* established that police must inform suspected criminals of their rights (known as the Miranda Rights); and *Roe v. Wade* expanded the right to privacy to include the right to an abortion.

Under the stewardship of current Chief Justice William Rehnquist, the Court has shed its activist past and moved back toward a more narrow interpretation of the Constitution. The Rehnquist Court has eroded some of the criminal rights established by previous Courts, and has chipped away at the right to privacy, including abortion. Still, the current Court seems to be as equally divided as the electorate on many of great political issues of the day.

Appointing Justices

Filling a Supreme Court vacancy ranks among the most important decisions a president can make. It's one of the few opportunities he has to influence the policy debate beyond his time in office. Over the past two decades, the composition of the Supreme Court has become an increasingly prominent issue in the presidential election. During the 2000 campaign, George W. Bush promised supporters that he would appoint "strict constructionists" to the high Court, while Al Gore made it known that he favored more activist jurists.

FACT

Clarence Thomas received the narrowest confirmation margin in history, 52–48. Thomas's nomination was nearly derailed when a former colleague named Anita Hill alleged that he had sexually harassed her while the two worked together at the Equal Employment Opportunity Commission. Thomas riveted the country with his testimony, at one point referring to the proceedings as a "high-tech lynching."

When choosing a nominee to the Supreme Court, presidents take into consideration several factors, including the following:

- **Ideology.** Over the past two decades, ideology has become the predominant consideration. President Clinton's appointments of Ruth Bader Ginsburg and Steven Breyer, jurists generally considered moderate, reflected his centrist approach to governing. Not surprisingly, Ronald Reagan appointed Justice Antonin Scalia, considered by many to be the most conservative member of the current court. President George H. W. Bush nominated Clarence Thomas, in part to make amends with his conservative base after appointing David Souter a year earlier.
- **Confirmability.** Given the increased politicization of the confirmation process, confirmability—the likelihood of the nominee being confirmed by the Senate—is a factor that has grown in importance. George H. W. Bush's primary motive for choosing David Souter, a

little-known judge on the New Hampshire Supreme Court, was that he lacked a "paper trail" of views. The Senate had little choice but to confirm him.

- **Age.** Because it's a lifetime appointment, age can be the deciding factor if two candidates are otherwise equally matched. In addition to being a reliably conservative vote, Clarence Thomas's relative youth—he was forty-three at the time of his nomination—made him an attractive appointment. Should he remain in good health, it's conceivable that Thomas could spend the greater part of his life on the bench.

- **Race and gender.** It's undeniable that both race and gender play a role in today's nominating process. President Clinton's appointment of Ruth Bader Ginsburg was in keeping with a campaign promise to make his administration look more like America. It was no coincidence that an African-American, Clarence Thomas, replaced Thurgood Marshall, the court's first black justice. Many court-watchers expect President George W. Bush to make White House counsel Alberto Gonzales the first Hispanic nominee to the court.

Making It to the Supreme Court

One of the most confusing and misunderstood aspects of the Supreme Court is how a case reaches the high court. Not every legal action can be appealed to the highest court in the land—the Supreme Court must have jurisdiction in order to hear a case. This can be achieved one of two ways.

Original Jurisdiction

Article III, section 2 of the Constitution gives the Supreme Court jurisdiction as the trial court over certain types of cases. These cases of original jurisdiction may be brought directly to the Supreme Court and are adjudicated (judged) only once without the possibility of appeal. Cases of original jurisdiction are extremely rare; fewer than 200 have been decided in the Court's history.

The Constitution lists seven types of disputes that are entitled to original jurisdiction:

1. Cases arising under treaties
2. Cases affecting ambassadors
3. Cases of maritime jurisdiction
4. Cases between two states
5. Cases in which the U.S. government is a party
6. Cases between a state and a citizen of another state
7. Cases between states and foreign countries or citizens

In 1998, the Supreme Court heard a case of original jurisdiction between the state of New Jersey and the state of New York regarding ownership rights to Ellis Island, a well-known landmark and tourist attraction. The Court decided in favor of New Jersey, giving that state ownership rights to most of the island.

Appellate Jurisdiction

Most disputes reach the Supreme Court through its appellate jurisdiction, meaning that the case has already been decided by either the lower federal courts or a state supreme court.

Cases arising through the federal court system begin in the U.S district courts, and involve disputes between citizens of two different states or criminal violations of federal law, such as the interstate trafficking of drugs, murdering a federal law enforcement official, espionage, and so on. The losing side can appeal the decision to one of thirteen U.S. courts of appeals, which are divided among geographic circuits. Whichever party loses in the court of appeals can make a final appeal to the Supreme Court. Most cases of appellate jurisdiction arise through the federal courts system.

Cases arising through the state courts system follow a similar route, only at the state level: A trial court makes a ruling, the losing party can appeal to the state court of appeals, and that loser can appeal to the state supreme court. It can get confusing at times because some states refer to their highest court as the court of appeals, while other states refer to it as the supreme court. Whatever the case may be, all state remedies must be exhausted before the U.S. Supreme Court can consider hearing the case on appellate jurisdiction.

With disputes arising through the state court system, an extra requirement is necessary to establish the Supreme Court's appellate jurisdiction: The appellant must show that an issue of federal law is in dispute. This may seem odd, since cases involving federal law are always settled in federal court, not state court. However, in some cases arising under state law, issues of federal law—such as the violation of a constitutional right (the right to free speech, right to due process, etc.)—are raised and must be resolved at the Supreme Court. In those situations, the Supreme Court can only rule on the federal issue in question. It cannot re-examine matters of state law involved in the case.

FACT

During the 2000 presidential election recount, George W. Bush's legal team appealed to the Supreme Court on three grounds regarding the Florida Supreme Court decision to let the recounts go forward: It violated Article 2, section 1 of the Constitution, failed to comply with an obscure federal statute, and violated the equal protection clause of the Constitution.

How the Court Selects Its Docket

Only after a case has worked its way through the federal or state courts and jurisdiction has been established may the losing party appeal to the Supreme Court. The vast majority of these requests come in the form of a petition for a writ of certiorari, which is a fancy way of saying "petition for a hearing." Appellants may also seek requests for certification (taking a look at the validity of laws used in the lower courts), per curiam decisions (decisions given without an opinion), or petitions for an "extraordinary writ" to get before the high court (that is, to get the high court's hearing before the case has been tried at a lower court). However, these measures are rarely used.

Reasons to Accept a Case

At least four justices must agree to hear a case before it makes it onto the docket. This is called the "rule of four." The justices never publish a reason for accepting or declining a case, so the selection process remains a bit of a mystery. When the Court refuses a case, it's essentially affirming the lower court's decision.

ALERT!

Contrary to popular belief, there is no absolute right of appeal to the Supreme Court. While every year the court is flooded with thousands of petitions from aggrieved parties, only about 1 percent will get a hearing.

The Supreme Court looks for one of several situations when deciding to accept a case. If the lower courts are in disagreement over the same legal issue, the Court will usually intervene to resolve it. The same holds true when a lower court's ruling conflicts with a Supreme Court decision. Sometimes the Court will hear a case that involves an issue that it has not yet ruled on. And once in a while, it will choose a case if the Court believes that the legal principle at stake could have an impact beyond the litigants involved.

Rendering a Decision

Once a case makes it onto the docket, the litigants are required to submit briefs summarizing the legal issue to be resolved. Because the Supreme Court is not a trial court, it does not hear evidence; instead, it relies on the litigants' briefs, the official record, and the case abstract (past rulings from similar cases) to make its judgment on the matter at hand. In most cases, the Court also holds oral arguments to further explore the legal question at issue.

Oral Arguments

For most lawyers, making an oral argument before the U.S. Supreme Court is the defining moment of his or her legal career—the Super Bowl of trial law. In reality, very few lawyers ever get the opportunity. Although these sessions have never been televised (there is a small viewing gallery open to the public), most Americans are somewhat familiar with the proceeding and its purpose.

Oral argument serves two purposes: It allows litigants to emphasize certain arguments and supplement their briefs, and gives the justices the opportunity to delve further into the legal issues by probing the lawyers.

Given the extraordinary interest in *Bush v. Gore*, the Supreme Court broke with tradition and released an audio version of the oral argument to the media for rebroadcast. Normally, transcripts of the oral argument are sent to the National Archives and Records Administration, where the public can access them.

Each side is given thirty minutes to make oral arguments. Typically, the lawyers have only a couple of minutes of uninterrupted time before the justices interject with their questions. They do this, in part, to control the direction of the argument and rattle the lawyers. Although some court-watchers believe that a particular justice's vote can be discerned by his or her line of questioning during oral argument, this has never been proved a reliable predictor.

Some justices are more active than others during oral argument. Recently, Antonin Scalia and William Rehnquist have been known for their frequent and sometimes abrasive questioning, while Clarence Thomas almost never queries the lawyers. Justices David Souter and John Paul Stevens have been generally considered the most cordial and temperate in their questioning.

Taking a Vote

Once oral arguments have been completed, the justices convene a conference that same week to discuss the merits and take a vote. Only the nine justices attend the conference. Clerks, staff, and even stenographers are barred.

The chief justice begins by summarizing the case and then stating his point of view. The other justices then share their thoughts and vote, in descending order of seniority (measured by service on the Court, not age). The justices rarely engage in debate or change their minds during the conference. As Justice Scalia once put it, "To call our discussion of a case a conference is really something of a misnomer, it's much more a statement of the views of each of the nine Justices, after which the totals are added and the case is assigned."

After the votes have been tallied, the chief justice—if he's in the majority—assigns an associate justice to draft the opinion (or the chief justice can do it himself). If the chief justice is not in the majority, then the most senior justice in the majority makes the assignment. During the drafting process, the justices receive considerable assistance with the research and writing from their clerks.

Decisions and Opinions

Once the opinion has been drafted and circulated, the justices are given the opportunity to either sign on or dissent; they are not bound to their original conference vote. Some use this time to "negotiate" concessions from the authoring justice in exchange for their vote. The other justices are allowed to circulate their own opinions as well at this point. The real debate of ideas occurs during this process of exchanging and negotiating opinions.

Checks on the Supreme Court

Just like the legislative and executive branches, the Supreme Court is subject to certain checks on its authority. These checks are intended to limit the Court's ability to "legislate" or make policy from the bench. With the lifetime appointment of its members, however, the Supreme Court is the most independent of the three branches of government, as was intended by the framers of the Constitution.

The Powers of Congress

If Congress disagrees with a statutory interpretation made by the Supreme Court, it can amend the statute or pass a new one to invalidate it. Congress enacted the Civil Rights Act of 1991, in part, to overturn a series of discrimination-related rulings that it found too conservative. In 1998, Congress passed the Curt Flood Act in order to partially overturn major-league baseball's anti-trust exemption, which was established a quarter-century earlier in the landmark case *Flood v. Kuhn.*

Like other federal officials, Supreme Court justices can be impeached and removed for "treason, bribery, and other high crimes and misdemeanors." In 1803, Samuel Chase became the first and only Supreme Court justice to be impeached. The Senate acquitted him two years later. In 1969, Justice Abe Fortas resigned from the bench in scandal before he could be formally impeached.

Nevertheless, there are times when the Supreme Court has the last word in its battles with Congress. In 1993, Congress passed the Religious Freedom Restoration Act (RFRA) to overturn a 1990 Supreme Court ruling that it found too restrictive on religious freedoms. A few years later, however, the Supreme Court declared the RFRA unconstitutional.

Once in a great while, Congress will take the extraordinary measure of amending the Constitution to invalidate a Supreme Court decision. This has occurred four times, most recently in 1971 when the Twenty-sixth Amendment was ratified. By establishing the voting age at eighteen years of age for both federal and state elections, it overturned *Oregon v. Mitchell,* a 1970 Supreme Court decision that declared it unconstitutional for Congress to set the voting age in state elections.

The Powers of the President

Aside from making judicial appointments, the president's only other influence over the Supreme Court resides in his power to enforce—or choose not to enforce—judicial decisions. This power is known as judicial implementation. As President Andrew Jackson once remarked about a ruling he disagreed with, "[Chief Justice] John Marshall has made his decision; now let him enforce it."

What Jackson was referring to is the Supreme Court's inability to carry out its rulings. The Supreme Court can only interpret the law—it must rely upon the president and Congress to enforce its judgments and decrees. Most of the time this is not a point of contention, but if the president vehemently disagrees with a court ruling, it's within his discretion to refuse or delay enforcing it.

Following the landmark *Brown v. Board of Education* decision in 1954, which resulted in the order to desegregate public schools, a reluctant President Eisenhower was forced to send federal troops to Arkansas after the governor used the state's National Guard to block African-Americans from entering Central High School in Little Rock. Eisenhower only ordered the troops in after Governor Orville Faubus created a riot at Central High.

FACT

In 1997, the Supreme Court accepted the Paula Jones sexual harassment case to resolve the issue of whether President Clinton could be sued while in office. The Court ruled that a sitting president could face civil proceedings, as long as the proceedings didn't interfere with his ability to perform the job. The lawsuit was eventually settled out of court.

Disobeying a Supreme Court decision is a drastic political move fraught with danger for the president. Even Richard Nixon complied with the Court's ruling that he turn over his secret White House tapes to the special prosecutor. He knew that noncompliance would further erode his legitimacy and probably result in immediate impeachment. Only in the rarest circumstances will a president ignore or act contrary to a Supreme Court decision. Ⓔ

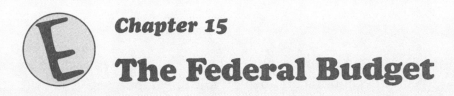

Chapter 15

The Federal Budget

In 2003, the federal government spent more than $2 trillion on thousands of programs, from the space program and national defense to the national endowments for the arts and humanities, Social Security, Medicare, interstate highway construction, and even midnight basketball. The federal budget determines how the government allocates its funds to all these programs. The budgeting process is enormously confusing and complex, and is frequently the source of bitter partisan debate.

Control over the Federal Budget

As an institution, the federal budget has undergone a dramatic transformation over the past two centuries. Historically, the transformation may be broken down into three distinct periods: legislative dominance (1789–1921), presidential dominance (1921–1974), and legislative-executive conflict (1974–present).

Passing the budget is one of the few mandatory functions of Congress and the president. It must be done every year, or the government will cease to operate. Perhaps more than any single document, the budget is a reflection of the president's priorities, agenda, and direction for the country.

Legislative Dominance (1789–1921)

The Constitution gives Congress the power to raise funds (tax) and appropriate (spend money). The framers believed that the enormous power of taxing and spending was best left to the Congress, because it was feared that the president could abuse the power to serve his own ends, and perhaps even overthrow the government. The theory was that Congress could check the power of the presidency by controlling the resources at his disposal.

The Constitution is vague about how the budget process should work. Chapter 2 explained that Article 1, section 8 of the Constitution provides only four general guidelines for federal spending:

1. All money drawn from the treasury must result from an appropriations bill.
2. Congress must account for all expenditures from "time to time."
3. Appropriations that support the military expire after two years.
4. All expenditures must be made for the "general welfare" of the United States.

FACT

The Constitution is purposefully vague about the budgetary process because at the time of the Constitutional Convention, the practice of budgeting had not been established yet. The budget process was conceived in Europe during the nineteenth century, and wasn't duplicated in the United States until the early twentieth century.

As required by the Constitution, all spending bills originated in the House of Representatives and were sent to the Senate once the House had completed its work. (Today they may be introduced simultaneously in both chambers.) All appropriations were made in one single bill, and the goal was to achieve a balanced budget—even though the Constitution doesn't require it. In fact, between 1789 and 1921, a balanced budget or surplus was achieved two-thirds of the time. The only time federal spending surged was during times of war—quadrupling during the War of 1812, doubling during the Mexican War, and increasing twentyfold during the Civil War. Public debt was paid off quickly, however, as lawmakers and the public viewed deficit spending as a moral shortcoming.

Following the Civil War, Congress took a first step toward creating a budget system when it established appropriations committees in both the House and Senate to handle all spending matters. Prior to that, there was no committee in charge of spending; the entire chamber worked on appropriations, which was a cumbersome and messy process. At this point in time, the president played virtually no role in determining federal spending, except to sign or veto appropriations legislation. Congress dominated the process.

Presidential Dominance (1921–1974)

Following World War I, Congress conceded that it was no longer capable of controlling spending, as federal expenditures skyrocketed from $725 million in 1915 to $19 billion in 1920 (and the public debt soared from $1 billion to $26 billion). In response to heightened public scrutiny, Congress passed the Budget and Accounting Act of

1921, which created a presidential budgeting process that still exists today. The act gave the president a formal role in the process, requiring him to submit an annual budget to Congress. It also barred federal agencies from making appropriations requests directly to Congress, which they had done in the past, and established the Bureau of Budget (renamed the Office of Management and Budget in 1970) to help the president set his budget.

QUESTION?

When was the last year that annual federal spending decreased? In 1954, the federal government spent $70 billion, which was $6 billion less than the previous year. President Eisenhower was a firm believer in fiscal austerity and responsibility. During his eight years in office, federal spending grew at its slowest rate during the twentieth century.

Beginning with Franklin Roosevelt, presidents began to use their newfound budgeting powers to shape public policy and dominate the national agenda. Rather than control federal spending, the Budget Act of 1921 spurred an explosion in the growth of government, as presidents linked ambitious legislative programs like the New Deal and the Great Society to their annual budgets. During this time, Congress played a secondary role in the budgeting process; while it still appropriated federal spending, it increasingly deferred to the president's proposals and estimates.

Legislative-Executive Conflict (1974–Present)

Throughout the 1960s, budget tension between the president and Congress mounted, as lawmakers grew increasingly disenchanted with the direction and cost of the Vietnam War. Hostility between the two branches reached a boiling point in the early 1970s, when President Nixon refused to spend billions of dollars appropriated by Congress.

In response to this, Congress passed the Congressional Budget and Impoundment Control Act of 1974, which President Nixon signed into law just a month before resigning from office. The act called for Congress to adopt its own budget resolution, as well as set revenue and spending goals. It also established the Congressional Budget Office (CBO), which provided Congress with its own economic assumptions, program analysis, and budget recommendations. With the CBO, Congress no longer had to rely on the president's estimates and recommendations. This was an important development in the legislative-executive budget relationship.

Thanks to the passage of the 1974 act, Congress and the president have an equal role in the budget process. However, because of that equality, the process has become acrimonious, partisan, and excruciatingly deliberate. Over the last two decades, some of the most contentious political fights have been over budgetary matters, including President George H. W. Bush's reneging on his "no new taxes" pledge, and the 1995 government shutdown.

FACT

In January of 1995, following their takeover of Congress for the first time in four decades, the Republicans tried to cut taxes and control spending. President Clinton responded by twice vetoing the Republican budget, and in the process temporarily shut down the government. With public pressure mounting, it was the Republicans who capitulated as President Clinton's approval ratings soared during the shutdown.

Office of Management and Budget

The Office of Management and Budget (OMB) has one of the most difficult—and important—tasks in the federal government. Created in 1921 as the Bureau of Budget, it is responsible for putting together the president's budget, which is then submitted to Congress.

The 500-person agency is housed in the Executive Office of the President, and is considered a part of the executive branch. The OMB is composed both of political appointees (top managers who come with one president and depart with the next) and career civil servants (staff members who continue their work no matter who's in office).

The OMB performs several functions:

- Estimates total revenues, spending, and the size of deficits (surpluses).
- Determines where spending should be increased or reduced in order to meet the president's budget plan.
- Reviews budget requests submitted by executive branch agencies and makes recommendations to the president.
- Compiles the budget.
- Monitors Congressional appropriations and analyzes proposals put forward by the Congressional Budget Office (CBO).
- Reviews the costs and benefits of proposed federal regulations.
- Assesses the effectiveness of federal programs.

Moreover, the OMB director serves as an important economic and budgetary advisor to the president.

The Budget Process Today

The current budget process is an amalgamation of precedents, procedures, and reforms adopted over the past two centuries. It has a strict timeline that Congress and the president are supposed to meet (although that's not usually the case). The following are descriptions of the most important dates.

The Process Begins in the Spring

It takes upward of eight months for the White House to prepare its budget. Because the president is required to submit his budget to Congress prior to the first Monday in February, the budget-writing process must begin the previous spring. At that time, the president sends budget guidelines to each executive agency and department. The agencies formulate a budget according to the president's directive, and submit it to the Office of Management and Budget for review. This process is usually completed by the end of the year.

First Monday in February

Once the budget is ready, the president has about a month to formally submit it to Congress on the first Monday in February. Once there, the Congressional Budget Office reviews the budget and provides an economic report to the House and Senate budget committees.

March 15

The House and Senate budget committees have until March 15 to develop their own budget estimates. The committees are not bound to follow the president's recommendations. To create concurrent budget resolutions, the committees hold hearings at which representatives from the federal agencies and the OMB testify before the committees to defend their budgets.

April 15

Congress is required to adopt a budget resolution by April 15. This resolution does not have the effect of law, nor does it provide specific details on how federal funds are to be spent. The budget resolution simply establishes a framework for Congress to formulate spending and revenue targets. It's not unusual for Congress to fail to pass a budget resolution.

May 15

Even if the budget resolution has not been passed, the House and Senate appropriations committees begin working on the thirteen regular appropriations bills that make up the budget. The bills are assigned to thirteen permanent subcommittees, which conduct hearings at which agency officials can defend their budget requests. The thirteen regular appropriations bills that must be passed each year are:

- Agriculture and Food & Drug Administration
- Departments of Commerce, Justice, and State
- Department of Defense
- District of Columbia
- Energy and Water Development
- Foreign Operations
- Department of Interior

- Departments of Labor, Health and Human Services, and Education
- Legislative Branch
- Military Construction
- Department of Transportation
- Treasury and Postal Department
- Departments of Housing and Urban Development and the Veterans Administration

June or August

Once the subcommittees have completed their work, the entire Appropriations Committee votes on the measure. If it passes the Appropriations Committee, the bill goes to the House and Senate floors for a final vote. A conference committee irons out any differences between the House and Senate version. Both chambers must pass the conference committee bill before it can be sent to the president for his signature. This is usually one of the most contentious moments of the budget process.

October 1

The federal government's fiscal year begins on October 1. If the budget is not enacted by this time (which is almost every year), continuing appropriations must be passed in order to keep the federal government running. These have become a very common practice in Washington. In 1995, Congress and the president twice failed to agree on continuing appropriations, which led to the temporary shutdown of the federal government.

Where Does the Money Go?

The $2.4 trillion spent by the federal government in 2003 represents about 20 percent of our nation's gross domestic product, or the total monetary value of all goods and services produced in the United States during one year. To put it in perspective, federal spending in the United States exceeds the value of the gross domestic product of virtually every country on the planet save a handful, which is testament to the awesome size of the U.S. economy.

What does the federal government spend $2.4 trillion on? Every year in Washington, the biggest political fights are reserved for that very question: Who gets the money? For starters, federal spending is divided into two categories—mandatory spending and discretionary spending.

Mandatory Spending

As its name implies, mandatory spending includes those government expenditures that must be paid and do not require annual approval. Social Security, Medicare/Medicaid, and interest on the national debt are the three largest mandatory government payments. Social Security and Medicare/Medicaid are sometimes referred to as "entitlement" programs, because qualified recipients are entitled to receive benefits every year.

To put the dizzying growth of Social Security and Medicare/Medicaid spending in perspective, consider a few numbers. In 1970, $61 billion was spent on the three programs combined. In 1980, that number increased fourfold to $260 billion. It doubled to $560 billion in 1990, and doubled again to nearly a trillion dollars in 2000. It is estimated that the number will exceed $3 trillion in 2010 (more than the current federal budget), and will surpass $25 trillion in 2050.

As a percentage of the federal budget, mandatory payments have ballooned over the past four decades. In 1960, they accounted for approximately 30 percent of government expenditures. In 2003, they represented nearly 70 percent of the federal budget.

The Government Accounting Office (GAO) estimates that mandatory payment programs, if left unchanged, will constitute 90 percent of the entire federal budget by the year 2025. Today, there is mounting political pressure on lawmakers to find alternative ways of funding future entitlement programs without bankrupting the government.

Discretionary Spending

Discretionary spending is everything that is not mandatory spending. Or, put another way, it is funding that Congress and the president have control over on an annual basis. During the budget process, funding levels for discretionary spending can be raised, lowered, or even eliminated completely. Unlike mandatory spending, discretionary spending must be appropriated every year. If it isn't, the money isn't allocated.

The largest discretionary spending item is national defense, which accounted for half of all nonmandatory spending in 2003. Following the end of the cold war in the early 1990s, defense spending actually decreased substantially (in both real dollars and as a percentage of discretionary spending) for nearly a decade. That trend changed, however, following the September 11 terrorist attacks. Defense spending is now at an all-time high, and is likely to continue to grow for the foreseeable future.

The newly created Department of Homeland Security is another rapidly growing discretionary spending item. The tab for homeland security topped $250 billion in 2003, making it second only to defense spending ($400 billion) for that year. At this point, it's uncertain how rapidly homeland security spending will grow in the future. No other discretionary spending item exceeded $70 billion in 2003.

FACT

After the departments of Defense and Homeland Security, spending for the Department of Agriculture comes in third ($65 billion in 2003), followed by Transportation, Veterans Affairs, Labor, Education, Housing and Urban Development, Energy, Justice, NASA, Interior, the State Department, and Commerce.

Pork-Barrel Spending

Pork-barrel spending is an unflattering term used to describe spending projects earmarked for a particular member's district that are buried deep inside appropriations bills. These projects are hidden in mandatory appropriations bills so as to ensure passage while keeping them hidden from the public and even other members of Congress. The biggest culprits in pork-barrel spending typically are powerful committee and subcommittee chairmen, as well as other senior members. Some lobbying firms in

Washington, D.C., specialize in securing pork-barrel projects for both public and private interests. In response to the sharp decline in federal revenues following the September 11 terrorist attacks, OMB Director Mitch Daniels publicly admonished Congress to "moderate its appetite for these programs"—a warning that went unheeded.

Members use pork-barrel projects to maintain their popularity back home and reward campaign contributors. Former New York senator Al D'Amato built a career around bringing federal projects back to his state. Senator Robert Byrd of West Virginia, arguably the most capable parliamentarian in Senate history, is recognized as the undisputed "king of pork" for his ability to secure federal projects for West Virginia. According to the last count, seven buildings in the state were named after Byrd!

The watchdog group Citizens Against Government Waste estimated that pork-barrel spending projects totaled $20.1 billion in 2002. Some of the more egregious projects in recent years have included $800,000 for Satsuma orange research in Alabama; $400,000 for the Montana Sheep Institute; $250,000 for seaweed control in Hawaii; $50,000 for a tattoo removal program in San Luis Obispo, California; and $2 million for the Center on Obesity at West Virginia University (no doubt the handiwork of Senator Byrd).

In 1975, Senator William Proxmire of Wisconsin started the Golden Fleece Awards as a way to draw attention to wasteful pork-barrel spending. Every month for fourteen years, Proxmire issued humorously worded rebukes of outrageous spending projects. Proxmire once lampooned an $84,000 National Science Foundation study into "Why People Fall in Love."

Deficits and Debt

Since the early twentieth century, the budget process has been characterized by annual deficits and mounting public debt. Deficits occur when government spending exceeds revenues (that is, the amount that it takes in). Since revenues and spending goals are estimated a year in advance of their enactment, these figures are frequently incorrect. This occurred most recently following the terrorist attacks of September 11, when tax revenues declined sharply and federal spending increased unexpectedly to fight the war on terrorism. Several years of surpluses (having more money than the amount needed for spending) were wiped out in a matter of months.

Sometimes the government will purposefully "deficit spend" in order to prevent the economy from going into a recession, or to bring it out of one. In both 2001 and 2003, a combination of tax cuts, increased discretionary spending, and one-time tax rebates were enacted to stimulate the economy. In 1993, a similar stimulus package was helpful in ending a two-year recession.

Public (or national) debt is the accumulation of years of deficits. As of 2003, the national debt exceeded $7 trillion, which is three times the size of the federal budget. Every year, one of the largest government expenditures—more than $200 billion—goes toward paying interest on the national debt. Were there no national debt, that expenditure could be used for other purposes. Some economists contend that large deficit spending stunts economic growth because it drives up long-term interest rates; others maintain that accumulated debt has no real impact on the economy.

Raising Revenues

Revenue is the money that the government collects from taxes, fees, borrowing, and other sources. Before 1913, when the Sixteenth Amendment was passed, Congress didn't have the power to enact an income tax. Before then, the federal government's chief revenue sources had been tariffs and excise taxes. Things have changed quite dramatically since then. In 2003, approximately 40 percent of all revenues came from individual income taxes, while 35 percent came from Social Security (payroll) taxes, 12 percent from corporate taxes, 7 percent from borrowing, and 5 percent from excise taxes.

Lawmakers have several ways to increase government revenues: raise marginal tax rates on income (as they did in 1993), increase the payroll tax, close tax loopholes, eliminate corporate subsidies, or increase government borrowing.

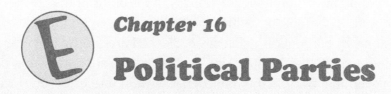

Chapter 16

Political Parties

Political parties rate among the least popular institutions of American government. Poll after poll has revealed that a sizable percentage of Americans hold the two major parties—the Republicans and Democrats—in low esteem. In many respects, however, political parties are the lubricant that allows democracy to function smoothly. Parties inform citizens of the issues, teach democratic values, and reach out to voters. They bring citizens and officeholders together in policy coalitions, and facilitate the wheels of government, turning public preferences into policy.

Evolution of the Two-Party System

Contrary to popular belief, the two-party system is not institutionalized in the Constitution. In fact, most of the delegates at the Constitutional Convention were hostile to the idea of political parties. George Washington worried about the "baneful effects of the spirit of party" would have on the young Republic. Thomas Jefferson was more blunt in his criticism: "If I could not go to heaven but with a party, I would not go there at all."

Nonetheless, convention delegates coalesced around two general principles while writing the Constitution. The Federalists supported a strong national government, while the antifederalists were interested in preserving the states' autonomy. As we have learned, many provisions of the Constitution resulted from compromise between the two factions.

Federalists and the Democratic-Republicans

Following the 1787 convention, the two factions battled over the ratification of the Constitution, with the Federalists—led by Alexander Hamilton and John Adams—winning out. Hamilton, who was appointed treasury secretary by George Washington, had a bold vision for the country. He believed that it should be the role of the federal government to promote a robust national economy that produced a thriving manufacturing and commercial class. In order to win passage of his programs through Congress, Hamilton cultivated and organized a group of like-minded allies to form the first political party, known as the Federalists. They recruited candidates in subsequent elections to increase their majority in Congress.

Naturally, opponents of Hamilton's policies formed their own political party. Led by James Madison and Thomas Jefferson, who was serving as Washington's secretary of state, the Democratic-Republicans believed that the federal government lacked the constitutional authority to implement Hamilton's agenda. The Democrats, as they would eventually become known, supported an agrarian-based economy that promoted the well-being of farmers and tradesmen.

The Democratic-Republicans scored their first victory in the election of 1800, when Jefferson defeated John Adams for president. Buoyed by their success, the Democratic-Republicans began organizing at the state and local level as well, and within several years became the dominant political party. The Federalists failed to innovate or make inroads with the electorate, and in 1816 fielded their last presidential candidate, who lost in a landslide to James Monroe.

ALERT!

The election of 1800 represents one of the first peaceful transfers of power between opposing political parties, and certainly the first in a democracy. The victorious Democratic-Republican Party, predecessor of the modern Democratic Party, is considered to be the oldest continuous political party in the world.

Democrats and the Whigs

With the demise of the Federalists, the Democratic-Republicans came to dominate the political landscape, so much so that James Monroe's presidency would come to be known as the "era of good feeling." During this time, eligible voter turnout dropped dramatically—from more than 40 percent in 1812 to less than 10 percent in 1820—as voters had little reason to go to the polls.

Intra-party squabbles, however, soon led to factions within the Democratic-Republican Party, and in the presidential election of 1824 the party fielded five candidates to succeed James Monroe. Although war hero Andrew Jackson won the popular vote, he failed to receive a majority of electors. Thus, the election was thrown into the House of Representatives, where runner-up John Quincy Adams emerged victorious after striking a deal with third-place finisher Henry Clay.

Jackson's supporters were outraged by the backroom deal-making, and splintered off to form the Democratic Party. Reviving the old Jeffersonian coalition of farmers and tradesmen, the Democrats effectively organized at the national, state, and local level, forming clubs and committees, holding rallies, establishing a chain of newspapers, and raising money for their candidates. Their rallying cry was the elimination of corruption in Washington.

Supporters of President Adams responded by cobbling together the remaining factions of the Democratic-Republican Party with remnants of the old Federalist Party. The Whigs, as they became known, lacked the Democrats' organization, and were soundly defeated in 1828, 1832, and 1836. They scored their only presidential victories in 1840 and 1848 with war heroes William Henry Harrison and Zachary Taylor, respectively.

Looking to galvanize party members for the coming election, the Democrats held the first-ever national convention in 1832. Convening in Baltimore, Maryland, the convention was little more than a well-organized pep rally, but it did help smooth over differences between several factions, and rally the party behind a single candidate for president.

While the parties were consistent in their economic policy (the Whigs supported a national bank and tariffs that protected manufacturers; the Democrats opposed the bank and advocated low tariffs that helped farmers), both were badly split over the slavery issue. Although both tried to suppress slavery from becoming a national issue, this proved impossible as feelings and emotions intensified.

Democrats and Republicans

In 1854, a coalition of anti-slavery forces organized to form a third party, called the Republicans. The Republicans attracted anti-slavery members from the two major parties, and absorbed the pro-business elements of the dying Whig coalition. Their first presidential candidate, John Fremont, was defeated in 1856, but their second, Abraham Lincoln, was victorious in the following election. With that, the Republicans became the first and only third party in American history to ascend to major party status.

Since the Civil War, Republicans and Democrats have been the two major political parties. The Republicans dominated national politics from 1860 to 1932, controlling Congress for most of that time and winning all but four presidential elections. During this period, the Republicans stood for national expansion, laissez-faire (free market) capitalism, and colonialism, while the Democrats were the party of immigrants, farmers, and tradesmen.

FACT

During the 1840s and 1850s, the Know-Nothing Party competed with the Republicans to replace the Whig Party as the Democrats' major opposition. The Know-Nothings got their name because their members were sworn to secrecy, and could only reply with "I know nothing about it" when asked of their party affiliation. At one point, the Know-Nothings included six governors, five senators, and forty-three House members in their ranks.

Franklin Roosevelt's election in 1932 brought about a "realignment" of the political parties. With the Great Depression in full bloom, the Republicans' policies of industrialization, high tariffs, and unregulated commerce were replaced by Roosevelt's New Deal—a patchwork of federal spending programs and government regulations designed to create a social safety net for low-income Americans, particularly union workers, immigrants, minorities, and small-business owners. Between 1932 and 1980, the Democrats won seven of eleven presidential contests, and held both chambers of Congress for all but a few years.

Republicans and Democrats Today

Ronald Reagan's victory in 1980 marked the beginning of a second realignment of the political parties. With his defeat of Jimmy Carter in 1980 and landslide victory over Walter Mondale in 1984, Reagan forged the foundation for a new Republican coalition. His message of cutting taxes, defeating communism, and resurrecting moral values appealed to traditional Democratic constituencies including socially conservative immigrants, blue-collar workers, and small-business owners—crossover voters who were dubbed "Reagan Democrats" by the media. Reagan's coalition, however, did not translate to significant Congressional gains.

In 1994, Newt Gingrich broadened this coalition with the Republican takeover of Congress. Gingrich's "Contract with America" repeated many of the themes that Reagan had popularized a decade earlier—cutting taxes, modernizing the military, and reducing the size of government—and helped bring about one of the most dramatic swings in Congressional history. Not since the Eisenhower administration had the Republicans controlled both houses of Congress.

FACT

Most of the gains for the Republicans have come in the South, which over the past two decades has switched from solidly Democrat to solidly Republican. During the 2000 election, President Bush swept the states that composed the old Confederacy, including Al Gore's native Tennessee.

President George W. Bush seemed to have cemented this realignment of the parties after leading the Republicans to an unprecedented victory during the 2002 midterm elections. For the first time in half a century, the Republicans took control of both branches of government, as well as a majority of the governorships and state legislatures.

The Party Issues

According to the most recent polls, roughly one-third of the American electorate identifies with the Republicans, one-third with the Democrats, and the remainder consider themselves independents. What makes someone a Republican or Democrat? Where do the parties stand on various issues? Although individual members of both parties sometimes differ with their leadership, the Republicans and Democrats generally disagree on the following issues:

- **Taxes.** Republicans favor broad-based tax cuts; Democrats favor targeted tax cuts directed at lower income Americans. In 2001 and 2003, President George W. Bush won passage of two of the largest tax cuts in American history.
- **Government spending.** Democrats support larger federal spending programs administered from Washington; Republicans favor reduced spending in the form of "block grants" to the states. Democratic

spending proposals usually outpace the rate of inflation, while Republican proposals usually remain at or below the rate of inflation.

- **Foreign policy.** Democrats favor working through international organizations such as the United Nations and the North Atlantic Treaty Organization (NATO) to combat terrorism; Republicans believe that the United States has the right as a sovereign nation to act alone against terrorist threats, and subscribe to the "Bush Doctrine" of pre-emptive strikes when necessary.
- **Abortion.** Democrats believe abortion should remain legal; Republicans believe there is no constitutional right to an abortion. No Republican president or vice president has ever been pro-choice.

Although abortion law has not changed since the 1973 landmark decision *Roe v. Wade*, it remains one of the most divisive issues in American politics. While virtually every Democrat in Congress is "pro-choice," only two-thirds of Republicans are "pro-life." Pro-choice Republicans are considered moderate Republicans, while pro-life Republicans are regarded as conservative.

- **Affirmative action.** Democrats support the use of preferential treatment to achieve racial diversity; Republicans oppose race-based quotas and set-asides, but support economic-based affirmative action. In 2003, President Bush spoke out against a University of Michigan affirmative action policy that used race as a numerical factor in the admissions process.
- **Social Security reform.** Republicans favor partially privatizing Social Security and the creation of individual retirement accounts; Democrats oppose privatization and individual retirement accounts.
- **Health care.** Democrats support universal health-care coverage guaranteed by the federal government; Republicans favor health maintenance organization (HMO) reform and incremental coverage. Both parties support improving prescription drug benefits.
- **Education.** Republicans favor less federal spending and greater local control; Democrats favor increased federal spending and control.

In 1995, the Republican Congress tried to abolish the Department of Education, but was rebuffed by President Clinton.

- **Minimum wage.** Democrats support regular increases in the minimum wage; Republicans oppose it. During the Clinton administration, the minimum wage increased from $4.25 to $5.15, the largest increase during an eight-year period.
- **Same-sex unions.** Democrats generally favor same-sex unions and gay rights; Republicans oppose them.

Why a Two-Party System?

The two-party system distinguishes American government from most other democracies. Most Western democracies, particularly those in Europe, have multiparty elections and parliaments, but the American government traditionally has had a two-party system,and since the Civil War the two parties have been the Republicans and Democrats. Although the issues, coalitions, and constituencies have evolved over time, the two-party system has remained intact. From time to time, third parties have gained traction with the electorate, most recently the Reform Party, led by Ross Perot, and the Green Party. However, few third-party candidates hold elected office at the state and national level.

Winner Takes All

Our electoral system is commonly referred to as "winner-takes-all," meaning that the candidate who receives the most votes is the one who takes office. If there are five candidates running for a Congressional seat, and candidate Jane Smith receives the highest vote total with 30 percent, she wins the election. The other finishers receive nothing.

In a winner-takes-all system, there is a strong tendency toward two parties because voters act strategically, preferring to vote for legitimate contenders than cast a "spoiler" vote for a third-party candidate. As a consequence, most voters eventually gravitate toward either the Republican or Democratic candidate.

Parliamentary systems, which are common in Europe, do not employ winner-takes-all elections. Instead, they use "proportional representation," meaning that a political party receives legislative representation (seats in parliament) proportionate to the percentage of the vote it receives during the election. If a third party garners 5 percent of the vote, it receives 5 percent of the seats in parliament. As a result, many European countries have upward of a dozen parties represented in parliament!

QUESTION?

What does the term GOP mean?
GOP is an abbreviation for Grand Old Party, and is another name for the Republican Party. The nickname is a bit of a misnomer in that the Democratic Party actually predates the Republican Party by three decades.

Duality of Political Issues

Another reason the two-party system thrives in American government is the duality of political issues. For the most part, there are only two sides to a given conflict. From the time of our founding (Federalism versus antifederalism), to the present (pro-choice versus pro-life), most of our political debates have been two-sided affairs. It's difficult for a third point of view—and consequently a third party—to gain political traction in a two-sided debate.

That's not to say it has never occurred. At times, third parties have articulated positions and issues that have resonated with the public. What has often been the case, however, is that one of the two parties has then "co-opted" or adopted that issue as their own in an attempt to poach the third party's constituency. In the 1968 presidential election, Alabama governor George Wallace won five southern states by appealing to "white resentment" of minorities. Four years later, President Richard Nixon incorporated much of Wallace's message as part of his "southern strategy," and won all five states. In the midterm elections of 1994, Republican challengers successfully exploited popular Reform Party issues like term limits, a balanced budget, and government accountability to end the Democrats' forty-year dominance in Congress.

FACT

In 1992, Reform Party candidate Ross Perot received 19 percent of the presidential vote, one of the highest third-party tallies in history. In the following election he received 8 percent, another solid third-party showing. Both times, however, he received no electoral votes, even though in several states he defeated one of the major party candidates.

Third Parties Today

Even though third-party members hold very few elected offices, they still play an important role in the electoral process. Voters disenchanted with the Republicans and Democrats can opt for one of several alternative parties.

Green Party

The central tenet of the Green Party is that corporations and other moneyed interests exploit average Americans for their own narrow interests, and that citizen-activists need to participate in the political process. "Greens" believe in radical social and economic reform, and are considered splinters of the far left wing of the Democratic Party. In the 2000 presidential election, Green Party candidate Ralph Nader garnered 2.7 percent of the national vote—the most of any third-party candidate that election—and is widely believed to have tipped the election for George W. Bush in Florida, where Nader pulled crucial votes from Al Gore.

Reform Party

Founded by billionaire H. Ross Perot, the Reform Party was established in the mid-1990s to facilitate Perot's presidential ambition. At one point, the party made a serious bid to become a viable alternative to the two major parties. Since Perot's second presidential campaign, however, the Reform Party has lacked a coherent vision. In 2000, it nominated right-wing political pundit Pat Buchanan as its presidential candidate. Buchanan's poor showing (he finished behind Ralph Nader in most states) combined with intra-party squabbles have greatly diminished the party's stature.

The only Reform Party candidate to hold statewide office was former professional wrestler Jesse "The Body" Ventura, who served one term as Minnesota's governor. Ventura pulled off one of the biggest upsets in political history, defeating two well-known major-party candidates. Midway through his term, Ventura quit the Reform Party and declared himself an independent.

Libertarian Party

The smallest of the three "major" third parties, Libertarians believe in radically limited government. Their organizing principle is that government should perform only two functions: protect our borders and keep civil order. Libertarian candidates tend to draw votes from disenchanted Republican voters, much the same way that Green candidates appeal to Democratic constituencies. Although it has been around the longest, the Libertarian Party is not as well organized or funded as the other third parties. At this point, it represents a philosophical movement more than a political party.

QUESTION?

Which two animals represent the Democrats and the Republicans? The elephant represents Republicans, and a donkey represents the Democrats. The animal mascots first appeared in an 1874 *Harper's Weekly* cartoon.

The Role of Political Parties

Although the two parties are not as organized or powerful as in years past, they still play an important role in modern American politics. In particular, they perform five critical functions:

1. **Recruitment of candidates.** Parties need officeholders at the local, state, and national level to shape policy. National and state committees spend considerable time recruiting and training candidates to challenge incumbents and seek open seats. Both parties look for candidates with strong knowledge of the issues, deep ties to the community, and the ability to raise money. However, with the proliferation of primaries and

caucuses, both parties now have a diminished role in the candidate selection process.

2. **Raising money.** As former senator Phil Gramm of Texas was fond of saying, "Money is the mother's milk of politics." With the cost of campaigns increasing exponentially each election, the two parties spend nearly every waking minute raising money—and lots of it. In a given election cycle, both parties will raise hundreds of millions of dollars at the national and state level, and distribute the proceeds to candidates deemed to have a legitimate chance of winning office. Since taking control of Congress in 1994, the Republican National Committee has consistently outpaced the Democratic National Committee in fundraising by a 2 to 1 margin.

FACT

In 2002, the McCain-Feingold campaign finance reform legislation banned the two parties from raising "soft money" (unlimited corporate and individual donations). Now the parties must rely on "hard money," or capped contributions from individuals. In the short time McCain-Feingold has been law, Republicans have widened their fundraising advantage by a margin of 3 to 1.

3. **Campaign support.** At one time, political parties completely ran political campaigns; the candidate simply served as a proxy for the party. Today, the parties provide numerous "support services" for candidates, including polling, opposition research, voter lists, position papers, legal and strategic counsel, phone banking, and media buying. Both parties focus their attention and resources on vulnerable incumbents and challengers running for open seats.

4. **Government organization.** Both parties are responsible for organizing the three branches of government. Party members in the legislative branch select the leadership, introduce legislation, and confirm executive branch appointments. In the executive branch, the party in power is responsible for thousands of appointments, including judgeships. It would be hard to imagine the effective operation of government without political parties.

5. **Advocacy of political issues.** The political parties are expected to define the issues and advocate a position consistent with their core values. This is especially important when new issues arise, such as human cloning, domestic terrorism, and the taxation of Internet commerce. Voters look to political parties to offer direction and solutions for issues both new and old.

How the Parties Are Organized

Both political parties resemble "pyramid-shaped" organizations, meaning there is a single leader at the top (national chairman), a broad base of grassroots workers at the bottom (precinct captains), and several layers of local, state, and national committees in between. Decision-making, however, is not simply a "top down" process; the different committees are actually in loose confederation with each other and maintain a certain level of autonomy.

National Organization

Each party has a national organization—the Republican National Committee (RNC) and the Democratic National Committee (DNC). The purpose of the national committee is to organize party functions, coordinate activity with state and local committees, raise money for officeholders and state parties, advocate policy positions in the media, and provide strategic and tactical support for candidates. The Democrats and Republicans have different methods for selecting national committee members, though both draw heavily from state organizations and elected officials.

Each national committee is led by a national chairman, who acts as the principal spokesperson for the party. In theory, the national committees are supposed to choose the national chairman; in practice, the two presidential candidates usually make this selection. In 2002, President George W. Bush replaced Republican National Chairman Jim Gilmore with close friend and ally Marc Racicot, the former governor of Montana. Both national chairmen are elected every two years, and rarely serve more than two terms.

FACT

Following Al Gore's defeat in the 2000 presidential election, prolific fundraiser Terry McAuliffe was voted Democratic national chairman, edging out former Atlanta mayor Maynard Jackson in a bitterly divisive contest. The selection of McAuliffe was somewhat unusual in that he was widely viewed as Bill Clinton's candidate because of his close ties to the former president and first lady.

Every four years, both national committees host a national convention, where their candidates for president and vice president are formally nominated. This time is also used to vote on national committee membership, adopt a national platform, and discuss rule changes for the primary system. The national conventions mark the beginning of the general election.

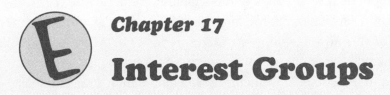

Chapter 17

Interest Groups

In 1834, the famous French chronicler Alexis de Tocqueville remarked that America was a nation of joiners. That observation still holds true today. Americans love to form and join groups. There are more than 200,000 associations in the United States, and it is estimated that two-thirds of all Americans belong to at least one. While not every one of these organizations is politically active, the fact remains that through the years interest groups have come to play an important role in American government.

What Are Interest Groups?

Interest groups are associations or organizations of individuals who share a common interest and assert their collective strength in the political process to protect—and in some cases, expand—that interest. These groups may form for many reasons: to celebrate a common heritage, pursue a political or social agenda, shape a policy debate, or strengthen a profession or avocation. Some interest groups, such as the National Association for the Advancement of Colored People (NAACP), are well known; others, like the National Anti-Vivisection Society, are obscure.

Often, mass social movements such as the fight for racial equality or the effort to outlaw alcohol consumption spawn the formation of interest groups. It's not unusual for countergroups to appear in response. For instance, Putting People First (PPF), a 35,000-person organization, mobilized to counteract the efforts of People for the Ethical Treatment of Animals (PETA).

FACT

By making charitable donations to nonprofit organizations tax deductible, and by exempting nonprofit organizations from paying federal taxes, the federal government actually encourages the formation of interest groups. The government also gives nonprofit organizations special discounted mailing rates. Many critics of the tax code contend that it should not be used for this type of "social engineering."

Every year, thousands of interest groups are formed, each with its own distinct purpose and agenda. With the proliferation of communication technologies such as the Internet and mobile phones, it's easier than ever for individuals to form groups, communicate with each other, and act in unison. Who knows how civil rights or women's suffrage organizations would have benefited from the information superhighway!

Historically Speaking

Organized lobbying by individuals, interest groups, and associations actually predates the Republic. During the colonial era, merchants, manufacturers, religious and ethnic minorities, and other groups hired agents to lobby (try to influence) members of the British Parliament for favorable legislative treatment. These eighteenth-century lobbyists used many of the strategies and tactics still employed today: Cultivating relationships with key members of Parliament, organizing letter-writing campaigns, drafting legislation, making financial contributions, and forming coalitions with like-minded lobbyists and associations. Some went as far as lobbying members of Parliament at their own homes, a practice that would be frowned upon today.

The Revolutionary Period

As the relationship between the colonies and the British government deteriorated, more public interest organizations began to appear. The Bill of Rights Society was a radical English group dedicated to bringing suffrage to the colonies; their primary tactic was to attack government officials. In response to the passage of the Stamp Act of 1765, patriot Sam Adams founded the Sons of Liberty, a secretive group of laborers, tradesmen, and merchants committed to repealing unjust British laws. The Sons gained notoriety throughout the colonies for orchestrating the Boston Tea Party and other acts of protest.

The delegates to the Constitutional Convention weren't exempt from outside pressure and lobbying. A decision was made early on to hold the convention in secret and behind locked doors so as to prevent lobbyists and other special interest groups from influencing the proceedings. The delegates didn't even keep an official record of the proceedings because they feared that their intentions would leak out and attract lobbyists.

It wasn't long after the Constitution was ratified that interest groups, associations, and organizations began to flourish. Most of these groups, like the National Trades Union, had narrow self-interests. A few, however, such as the Anti-Slavery Society and the American Temperance Union, aimed to transform society. As the country underwent rapid expansion and industrialization following the Civil War, new business and commercial entities emerged. These large-scale corporations and trusts hired armies of lobbyists—paid agents whose sole purpose was to influence the legislative process—to block Congress from passing laws and regulations hostile to their industries. These lobbyists weren't above showering lawmakers with cash and gifts in exchange for favorable treatment.

A Questionable Reputation

Not surprisingly, it was around this time that lobbyists began to develop an unflattering reputation with the public and in the press. Poet Walt Whitman referred to them as "crawling serpentine men, born freedom sellers of the earth." *The Nation Magazine*, one of the country's most influential and respected journals, described a lobbyist as "a man whom everybody suspects; who is generally during one half of the year without honest means of livelihood; and whose employment by those who have bills before a legislature is only resorted to as a disagreeable necessity."

Some good did come from special interest lobbying during this time, however. Pressure from various activist organizations and associations brought about much-needed electoral reforms, child labor and wages-and-hours laws, anti-trust and business regulations, a federal income tax, and women's suffrage, among other things.

The nineteenth-century *Dictionary of American Politics* contained the following unflattering definition for lobbying: "Lobby, The, is a term applied collectively to men that make a business of corruptly influencing legislators. The individuals are called lobbyists. Their object is usually accomplished by means of money paid to the members, but any means that is considered feasible is employed."

Perhaps the most successful interest group from that era was the Anti-Saloon League, the driving force behind the adoption of the Eighteenth Amendment, which from 1919 until its repeal in 1933 banned the sale of alcohol in the United States. The group left nothing to chance during its twenty-year quest to outlaw alcohol consumption, publishing monthly newsletters, staging rallies at the Capitol, forming local temperance groups, organizing letter-writing campaigns, making political contributions to friendly lawmakers, and targeting hostile members of Congress who lived in districts where the citizens favored prohibition. Many historians consider the Anti-Saloon League the most successful single-issue group in U.S. history.

Types of Interest Groups

Interest groups vary greatly in their missions and memberships. Some are dedicated to a single issue; others represent professional organizations and associations; still others are advocates for the "public interest." Their size can range from millions of members to several dozen. Some wield enormous clout while others have limited influence. Most interest groups can be classified into three categories: economic, public-interest, and single-issue.

Economic Interest Groups

The primary purpose of a vast majority of interest groups is to provide economic benefits to their respective memberships. Business groups, labor organizations, and professional associations are examples of interest groups that seek to gain economic advantages.

One of the most influential business groups is the U.S. Chamber of Commerce. Representing more than 200,000 companies nationwide, the Chamber's annual dues exceed $30 million. The Chamber lobbies on behalf of its members for laws and regulations that promote economic growth and commercial activity. With a budget of $25 million, the National Association of Manufacturers is another powerful business lobby. Its sole focus is to support legislation that creates manufacturing jobs and oppose bills that eliminate them. In 1993, it lobbied frantically against the passage of the North American Free Trade Agreement (NAFTA) because it feared that the agreeement would result in the exportation of manufacturing jobs to Mexico and Canada. Although NAFTA eventually became law, the association did win several concessions that helped mitigate the impact of the agreement on its membership.

Labor unions are another type of business interest group. The American Federation of Labor and Congress of Industrial Organizations (AFL-CIO) ranks among the most powerful interest groups, with more than 13 million members. Every year it contributes millions of dollars to political candidates and provides grassroots campaign support at the local, state, and national level. The overwhelming majority of its campaign contributions and assistance is given to Democratic incumbents and challengers. The Teamsters and the United Auto Workers (UAW) are also powerful labor lobbies, with 1.5 million and 800,000 members, respectively.

Professional associations compose another type of economic interest group. The American Medical Association (AMA), Screen Actors Guild (SAG), and American Bar Association (ABA) are three of the most influential professional associations in America. During the 2000 election, the AMA contributed several million dollars to candidates, making it one of the largest political contributors in America. The Screen Actors Guild often uses the star power of its membership to lobby Congress and the White House for favorable treatment.

Although not often thought of as a business interest group, the American Farm Bureau Federation, with its 5 million members, is one of the oldest and most influential business lobbies in Washington. Founded in 1919, the federation has been instrumental in winning generous subsidies, price supports, and tax advantages for the nation's food growers.

Public-Interest Groups

A fairly recent category of interest groups is the so-called public-interest group. The mission of public-interest groups is to protect the rights, resources, and liberties common to all Americans—in other words, to act "in the public interest."

The American Civil Liberties Union (ACLU) is the granddaddy of public-interest groups, dating back to the First World War. Known primarily for its involvement in legal battles related to the abuse of civil liberties, the ACLU is also a forceful lobby on Capitol Hill against legislation that impedes the Bill of Rights, particularly the First Amendment.

The modern public-interest movement traces its origins to the 1960s, when citizen-activist Ralph Nader created a consumer watchdog group called Public Citizen. Over the past four decades, Nader has formed or sponsored more than fifty public-interest groups, including Citizen Works, the Health Research Group, and the Public Interest Research Groups (PIRG), an activist organization funded and controlled by college students.

Common Cause, another grassroots public interest group, played an important role in winning passage of the Twenty-Sixth amendment (which extended the right to vote to eighteen-year-olds), the "Government in the Sunshine" laws of the mid-1970s, and campaign finance reform. It works on nonlegislative issues as well, such as achieving greater voter registration.

FACT

Ralph Nader shot to national prominence in 1965 with the publication of his book *Unsafe at Any Speed*, which chronicled General Motors's attempt to conceal from the public dangerous defects in its rear-engine Corvair car. GM tried to discredit Nader by investigating his past, for which Nader retaliated with a lawsuit. It was ultimately settled in his favor for $400,000.

Environmental organizations such as Greenpeace, the Environmental Defense Fund, the Sierra Club, and the National Wildlife Federation (NWF) are considered public-interest groups. Greenpeace takes a more radical approach to fulfilling its vision, while the Sierra Club, NWF, and others work within the political system to achieve policies that protect the environment. The Nature Conservancy uses contributions from its members to purchase and preserve undeveloped open spaces.

Single-Issue Groups

Some of the most prominent and powerful interest groups in America are "single-issue" groups. These organizations have one thing in common: an extremely narrow and intense focus on a particular issue. The abortion debate, for example, has created single-issue groups on both sides of the argument. The sole focus of the National Abortion Rights Action League (NARAL) is to keep abortion legal; the Right to Life Committee would like to see abortion outlawed. Both camps aggressively advocate their positions on Capitol Hill, in state capitols, and through the media.

A Model Interest Group

Many observers consider the American Association of Retired People (AARP) to be the most powerful interest group in the United States. With a membership of nearly 35 million, it's far and away the largest dues-paying association in America. It's also the leader in grassroots lobbying, as it regularly mobilizes its membership to contact their elected officials on various issues.

Over the years, AARP has been influential in shaping scores of federal and state programs and laws geared toward older Americans, including the formation of Medicare and Medicaid, increases in the cost-of-living increases (COLAs) for Social Security benefits, and stricter guidelines for lending to the elderly. Many lawmakers on both sides of the aisle blame AARP for standing in the way of Social Security reform.

FACT

In the spring of 2003, actor Charlton Heston stepped down as the president of the National Rifle Association (NRA), one of the most powerful single-interest groups in Washington. Every election cycle, the NRA contributes hundreds of thousands of dollars to elected officials and challengers who believe that the Second Amendment provides an absolute right to bear arms. Most of the NRA's contributions go to Republican candidates.

Strategies and Tactics

Since the very first Congress, interest groups have played an important role in shaping legislation. They have used an assortment of methods to influence legislators and impact public policy. These tactics can be divided into two categories: direct and indirect techniques.

Direct Techniques

Lobbying policymakers directly is the preferred method of influencing the process. Many interest groups hire specialized lobbying firms or retain lobbyists on their staff to help gain access to key decision-makers. With their vast network of contacts and intricate knowledge of the political process, former legislators and staff members typically make the best lobbyists.

Lobbyists perform a variety of functions to shape government policy:

- Setting up private meetings with lawmakers, staff, and executive agency bureaucrats to inform them of their clients' interest
- Providing both policy and political information to decision-makers
- Assisting lawmakers and their staffs in drafting legislation
- Testifying before Congressional committees, subcommittees, and executive rule-making agencies on proposed legislation and rules related to their industry
- Interpreting the impact of proposed legislation and rules
- Organizing protest demonstrations
- Hosting campaign fundraisers for candidates
- Talking to the media
- Running advertisements in the media
- Filing lawsuits or engaging in other litigation

ALERT!

Former members of Congress take full advantage of certain privileges when lobbying their former colleagues, such as continued access to their respective chambers' gym, dining room, and floor. The only catch is that former lawmakers are prohibited from directly lobbying members of Congress for one year after they leave government.

Most interest groups aren't shy about offering campaign assistance to lawmakers in order to gain access and shape policy. The larger interest groups have special fundraising committees called political action committees (PACs), which distribute campaign contributions to various federal and state lawmakers. Interest groups give PAC donations to incumbents and challengers that they believe are sympathetic to their cause. Since the late 1970s, the number of PACs has quadrupled to nearly 5,000, with the size of their contributions increasing tenfold to $500 million. Labor PACs give most of their dollars to Democratic candidates, while corporate donations tend to favor the Republicans.

A few prominent interest groups, such as the Americans for Democratic Action (ADA), the American Conservative Union (ACU), and the League of Conservation Voters, publish an annual "scorecard" whereby they rate the performance of every member of Congress. For example, if a lawmaker has an ACU rating of 80, it means that he voted in favor of the ACU's position 80 percent of the time on legislation that the group deemed important.

In their effort to defeat the passage of NAFTA, dozens of consumer, environmental, labor, and manufacturing groups formed an "umbrella" organization called the Citizens Trade Campaign. By pooling their resources, the groups were able to reduce expenses, avoid duplicating each others' efforts, and give the appearance of broad-based support.

Indirect Techniques

Sometimes, interest groups will work through third parties to influence legislators and shape public policy. One of the most commonly used indirect techniques is constituent lobbying, whereby members of an organization write, phone, and e-mail legislators to communicate their concerns. When done correctly, this type of grassroots lobbying can be extremely effective because it demonstrates the size, intensity, and political savvy of an interest group—something elected officials monitor closely.

In some cases, well-funded and high-profile interest groups try to generate a groundswell of public pressure through mass mailings, public demonstrations, media advertising, and public relations campaigns. In 1993, the Health Insurance Association of America, a group opposed to Hillary Clinton's nationalized health-care proposal, spent $17 million on a series of television commercials for the purpose of discrediting the first lady's plan. The memorable ads generated national buzz and were highly effective in turning public opinion against "Hillary-Care."

Regulating Lobbyists

Although it tried on several occasions, it wasn't until 1946 that Congress finally passed the first law regulating lobbying activity—the Federal Regulation of Lobbying Act.

The primary purpose of the act was to provide public disclosure of lobbying activities. It required lobbyists (defined as any person or organization that was paid to influence Congress) to register with the clerk of the House of Representatives or the secretary of the Senate, state their purpose for lobbying, and provide quarterly updates on their clients and fees.

The law quickly proved to be ineffective, however, as lobbyists exploited several loopholes to avoid compliance. It was further weakened by a 1954 Supreme Court decision that held that the act only applied to paid lobbyists, groups, or organizations whose principal purpose was influencing Congress, and lobbyists who contacted members of Congress directly. Individuals who lobbied Congressional staff, were unpaid, or who performed other services in addition to lobbying did not have to register with Congress. As a consequence, fewer than 7,000 individuals and organizations registered as lobbyists.

On June 11, 1995, at a public event in Manchester, New Hampshire, President Clinton and House Speaker Newt Gingrich shook hands on a promise to pass campaign finance and lobbying reform. While the former pledge was forgotten, the latter was acted upon, as the two parties came together to pass the Lobbying Disclosure Act of 1995. The law overhauled the 1946 act with six new provisions:

1. It defined a lobbyist as anyone who spent more than 20 percent of his or her time lobbying members of Congress, their staff, or executive branch officials.
2. It banned for life former U.S. trade representatives and their staffs from lobbying for foreign interests.

3. It banned nonprofit groups that lobby Congress from receiving federal grants.
4. It required lobbyists to file semiannual reports disclosing the specific issues and bills worked on, the amount of money spent, and the branches of government contacted.
5. It required lawyers who represent foreign entities or U.S–owned divisions of foreign-owned companies to register with Congress.
6. It exempted grassroots lobbying efforts and lobbyists who are paid less than $5,000 semiannually.

The law had an immediate impact, as the number of registered lobbyists doubled almost immediately. It also revealed the size and scope of the lobbying activities of foreign governments in Washington, and helped bring about two separate Congressional investigations of the Chinese government's attempts to influence the Clinton administration.

Influence over Foreign Policy

While foreign governments are prohibited from lobbying the institutions of government, scores of ethnic-American organizations regularly lobby Congress and the president on behalf of their countries of concern. The American Israel Public Affairs Committee (AIPAC) was rated by *Fortune* magazine as the fourth most powerful lobbying group in Washington. The Cuban American National Foundation (CANF) is considered the second most influential ethnic lobby in Washington. Persistent lobbying by CANF helped win passage of Helms-Burton, a 1996 law that tightened the U.S. embargo against Cuba. CANF and other Cuban-American lobbying organizations demonstrated their influence during the Elian Gonzalez controversy. Although polls showed that upward of 70 percent of the American public favored the return of young Elian to his father in Cuba, Cuban-Americans were able to help stall the boy's deportation for more than half a year.

Chapter 18

The Media

Outside of government institutions, no other entity has more influence in shaping policy decisions and elections than does the mass media. Although the framers of the Constitution could never have envisioned the proliferation of mass media that we enjoy today, they were acutely aware that the press would play a critical role in the burgeoning democracy. It's no coincidence that freedom of the press constitutes the First Amendment in the Bill of Rights.

An Emerging Influence

The media's role in government dates back to the colonial era, when daily newspapers were the sole source of political as well as other news for the colonists. Newspaper publishing was an expensive and time-consuming process at that time. The fastest printing presses could only produce 250 newspapers an hour. The reporting of "breaking" news was a matter of weeks, not days. Sometimes it took months for information to travel through the colonies.

Around the time of the American Revolution, twenty-five weekly newspapers served the colonies. Some were vocal supporters of the cause of independence, while others adamantly opposed it. Just about all of them lost money, because publishing costs far exceeded the demand for daily papers.

FACT

The mass media has undergone an incremental transformation over the past 200 years. Much of that change has occurred since the mid-1990s, with the advent of the Internet and all-news cable television channels. As those and other communication technologies continue to evolve at lightning speed, the role of the media in government will also continue to change.

It wasn't long after the creation of political parties that the Federalists and antifederalists began publishing their own newspapers. These papers were little more than crude party organs that advocated the party platform, promoted their candidates, and relentlessly attacked the opposition. These party-affiliated papers had small audiences, and relied heavily on their respective parties for financial support. In light of this, each newspaper aggressively championed the views of its political party, even if the publisher had reservations about doing so. The primary audience was the party faithful, not the general public.

The Golden Era of Newspapers

With the advent of the steam-powered printing press in the 1830s, the situation began to change. Able to produce a greater number of newspapers at a cheaper cost, newspaper publishers began to forgo support from the political parties—and stopped advancing their partisan causes—in order to attract larger audiences. In the mid-1830s, the *New York Herald* ushered in the era of the penny press when it dropped its price to a penny and expanded its news coverage to include human-interest stories, crime, business news, and social events. Its readership soared, and imitators followed suit almost immediately.

The intense competition for mass readership led to a rapid expansion in the number of daily newspapers and in their circulation. Between 1870 and 1900, newspaper circulation grew from 3 million to 15 million—a 600 percent increase. It was around this time that successful publishers began creating chains of newspapers across America. The Scripps brothers were among the first to build a chain of newspapers, owning twenty-two by 1910. Not one to be outdone, William Randolph Hearst operated close to forty newspapers by 1935, and could boast that one in four Americans read one of his newspapers.

The period of 1880 to 1925 is considered the golden era of newspapers, as daily papers wielded enormous influence with politicians, business leaders, and the public. Publishers and editors used this power to influence public opinion, shape policy decisions, and highlight social injustices.

Newspapers were so influential during the late nineteenth century that the Hearst and Pulitzer chains virtually forced Congress to declare war on Spain over the Cuban government's policy of forcing rural people to move to towns where groups of soldiers were stationed. One critic of the war effort dubbed it "Mr. Hearst's" war, while the Spanish prime minister lamented that American newspapers had more power than did the American government.

Radio and Television

In 1920 the Westinghouse Corporation's KDKA in Pittsburgh became the nation's first commercial radio station, but it took a decade for the new medium to catch on with the public. By 1930, however, almost 40 percent of the households in America owned radios, and that number would double again before the end of the decade. President Roosevelt helped to popularize the new medium during the Great Depression with his weekly "fireside chats." With its ability to deliver breaking news instantly, radio replaced newspapers as the primary source of news for most Americans.

FACT

As advertising dollars began to move from newspapers to radio, one newspaper association organized a boycott of the radio industry. During the boycott, radio stations were prohibited from using newspapers and wire services as a source of information for their news stories. The boycott quickly failed, however, and the newspaper industry resigned itself to competing with the new medium.

Television enjoyed an even faster rise to prominence. In 1939, fewer than 5 percent of the households in America owned a television. In 1950, that number had grown to 90 percent. One survey revealed that by the mid-1960s, a majority of Americans received their news information from television. As the Vietnam War dragged on, Americans increasingly turned to television for a "firsthand" account of the war. Coverage of other big events, including President Kennedy's assassination, Watergate, and the Apollo 13 crisis, also helped cement television's primacy as the predominant source of news and information in America. A 1994 poll revealed that 74 percent of Americans received their news from television—the high-water mark of the medium's dominance. Since that time, the Internet has begun to erode television's news monopoly.

The Impact of the Internet

In some sense, the Internet has become a check on the mass media—primarily the major networks and newspapers—because it communicates directly without the filter of editors, publishers, and corporate parents like Viacom, Disney, Time-Warner, and General Electric. Web sites such as Drudgereport.com, Andrewsullivan.com, thesmokinggun.com, and many others receive millions of hits a months from visitors seeking news, information, and opinions that aren't found in the mainstream media.

In 1998, it was controversial cyber journalist (some would call him cyber gossip columnist) Matt Drudge who broke the Monica Lewinsky scandal. Drudge didn't do the firsthand reporting on the story; he simply revealed that the magazine *Newsweek* had the story but was undecided about publishing it. Drudge's revelation forced *Newsweek* to print the story, setting off a chain of events that ultimately led to President Clinton's impeachment. Since then, dozens of political stories have originated in cyberspace, only to cross over to the "mainstream" media.

The Internet has been an invaluable tool for journalists to perform research, gather information, and report from distant parts of the globe. It has allowed the media to be more comprehensive and timely in its reporting, and has effectively reduced the news cycle from twelve hours to a matter of minutes.

ALERT!

Former *New Republic* editor Andrew Sullivan is the leading "blogger" (Web logger), or self-published opinion journalist, in cyberspace. Andrewsullivan.com attracts hundreds of thousands of unique visitors per month. Sullivan's two-year crusade against former *New York Times* editor-in-chief Howell Raines's political and professional biases helped contribute to the editor's dismissal following a highly publicized plagiarism scandal.

The Role of Media in Government

In a democracy, the free flow of information, ideas, and opinions is critical. To this end, the media has three primary responsibilities: setting the agenda, investigating the institutions of government, and facilitating the exchange of ideas and opinions.

Setting the Agenda

Who determines the news? The answer, to some extent, is that the media determines the news. Every day, hundreds of decisions, activities, and events take place in Congress, the executive branch, and the courts that could potentially have an impact upon millions of Americans. It's the job of the media—print, television, radio, and the Internet—to determine which actions merit coverage and which do not. This is part of the news-gathering process. After all, print and broadcast media have a finite amount of time and space to dedicate to news coverage. Therefore, news editors and producers use their discretion in determining what receives coverage.

The process of determining the news—setting the agenda—is not a perfect science. What one editor considers "hard news" might not be viewed as newsworthy at all by another. It's a highly subjective process that leaves many news-gathering organizations open to criticism from groups dissatisfied with their coverage. For years, political conservatives have complained that "elite" media institutions such as the *New York Times, Washington Post*, and the three broadcast networks (ABC, NBC, and CBS) were biased toward liberal causes. Many on the right contend that the issue of homelessness was prominently covered by the media during the Reagan and Bush administrations and then suddenly dropped from the radar while President Clinton was in office, only to reappear after George W. Bush was sworn in. Liberal advocates hold the opposite view, contending that because large corporate conglomerates own the major news organizations, they have a vested interest in preserving the status quo.

FACT

Liberal lawmakers and activists have singled out Fox News Channel as being biased toward conservative causes, even though the channel purports to have "fair and balanced" news coverage. Since the terrorist attacks of September 11, Fox News has enjoyed a ratings bonanza, surpassing CNN as the most watched cable news network. In 2003, former vice president Al Gore announced that he was forming a "progressive" news channel as an alternative voice to Fox News.

Editors and producers typically take several factors into consideration when determining the news value of an event, ruling, decision, or trend, such as the number of people affected by it, the impact, the long-term consequences, and the effect on future actions or decisions. Prior to

September 11, 2001, the threat of domestic terrorism received virtually no news coverage, because news decision-makers—and many others—believed that there was little likelihood of such an attack. Since then, however, it has overshadowed every other issue, and will likely continue to do so for some time.

Serving the Public Trust

As we have learned, the framers of the Constitution established multiple checks and balances to guard against tyranny. Their biggest fear was that one branch of government would monopolize power and rule against the will of the people. One of the checks they established is the First Amendment, which guarantees a free press.

Investigative journalism dates back to the 1800s, when a new breed of reporters dubbed "muckrakers" sought to expose public corruption and social injustices. Author Upton Sinclair is considered the "grand-father" of muckraking because of his book *The Jungle*, which was a groundbreaking depiction of the unsanitary conditions of the meat-packing industry. The Meat Inspection Act and Pure Food and Drugs Act were passed a year after the book's publication.

In this regard, the media serves as a kind of "super-check" on all three branches of government. For more than two centuries, the press has called attention to corruption, deception, incompetence, fraud, abuse, and the misuse of power at every level and branch of government. It was a vigilant press that exposed massive corruption in the Grant administration, brought attention to unsanitary working conditions in factories and the misuse of child labor around the turn of the twentieth century, and uncovered government deception and lying during the Vietnam War, among other things. Perhaps most famously, it was Bob Woodward and Carl Bernstein, two novice *Washington Post* reporters, who conducted an investigation of the Watergate burglary that led to the resignation of

Richard Nixon—the only time in history that a president has resigned from office.

With the proliferation of cable television, talk radio, and the Internet, the media is more active than ever in serving as a public watchdog. Entire publications, news programs, and Web sites are dedicated to exposing government malfeasance, corruption, and waste. In the past decade, enterprising journalists have exposed scores of crooked politicians, government officials, and corporations.

Opinion Journalism

It's almost impossible to turn on the television or radio and not be bombarded with the sights and sounds of political pundits—sometimes referred to as "talking heads"—screaming at one another. Although this may not seem like a service to democracy, opinion journalism plays an important role in our system of government, because it gives lawmakers, activists, interest groups, academics, and concerned citizens a forum in which to discuss and debate the pressing issues of the day.

Every day, tens of millions of Americans listen to talk-radio personalities such as Rush Limbaugh, Sean Hannity, Michael Savage, Don Imus, and others to get their perspective on the day's news and events. Audiences do not listen to these programs to receive objective information or dispassionate analysis; quite the opposite, they usually share the host's political point of view. In recent years, liberal lawmakers and interest groups have complained that a majority of radio talk-show personalities are political conservatives. To some extent, this observation is accurate, because right-wing commentators have dominated radio for more than a decade. In the marketplace of ideas, however, all points of view have equal access to the airwaves.

The cable news landscape is equally saturated with opinion journalism. Stations such as MSNBC, Fox News, CNN, and CNBC provide lawmakers and opinion leaders with nearly endless opportunities to debate pressing issues and ideas. It's not unusual to see a talking head appear on multiple programs (on different stations, no less) during the same evening. Lawmakers use programs such as *Crossfire*, *Hardball with Chris Matthews*, and *The O'Reilly Factor* as a way to increase their visibility and develop a national profile. Prior to embarking on his bid for the Democratic nomination for president, little-known freshman senator John Edwards made frequent appearances on the "big four" cable networks—Fox, MSNBC, CNBC, and CNN—in an effort to develop a national following.

FACT

During the Congressional election of 1994, right-wing radio talk show host Rush Limbaugh railed against the Congressional Democrats and was a forceful advocate for the Republicans' "Contract with America." Limbaugh was made an honorary member of the "Class of '94" after the Republicans swept both houses of Congress, and was the keynote speaker at the Congressional Republicans freshman orientation session.

Serious lawmakers and opinion leaders use the Sunday morning shows—*Face the Nation, Meet the Press, Fox News Sunday, This Week*, and *Late Edition*—to influence the debate, shape policy, and make headlines. A strong appearance on one of these programs can sometimes change the discourse surrounding a political issue, and catapult a personality to national prominence. During the height of the Monica Lewinsky scandal, Lewinsky's lawyer William Ginsburg set a "talking head" record when he appeared on all five Sunday shows in one morning. It was the first time this rhetorical feat had been accomplished.

Influencing the Media

Elected officials, nonelected government workers, and political candidates spend a considerable amount of time figuring out ways to shape media coverage. The following five techniques are most commonly used:

1. **Staged events.** The most common (and reliable) way to attract media coverage is by staging an event. In 1994, the House Republicans had a "signing ceremony" on the Capitol steps to launch their "Contract with America" campaign theme. The event received enormous press coverage.

2. **Off-the-record conversations.** Politicians, bureaucrats, and candidates have off-the-record conversations with reporters when they want to disseminate certain information, but don't want that information associated with them. Reporters usually attribute off-the-record comments to anonymous or unnamed sources.

3. **Sound bytes.** Most elected officials are adept at giving "sound bites" (concise and colorful quotes) to reporters. Officials who consistently deliver the best sound bites usually receive the most coverage. New York senator Chuck Schumer is regarded as a terrific source of sound bites.

4. **Trial balloons.** From time to time government officials will float "trial balloons"—anonymous program or policy ideas—to the press in order to gauge the public's reaction. Trial balloons allow officials to test ideas or potential appointments without taking responsibility for them. During the recent stem-cell research debate, the White House floated a trial balloon about keeping the controversial research on embryonic stem cells legal, but decided against it after the administration's conservative base reacted negatively.

5. **Leaks.** Almost every day in Washington, confidential information is passed from government officials to the media. Leakers do this for one of two reasons: to cast a negative light on their opponents, or to strengthen their point of view on a particular matter among their colleagues. Investigations in particular tend to be rife with leaks. There were so many leaks during the Monica Lewinsky investigation that the leaks themselves became a separate legal inquiry.

The Function of Media in Political Campaigns

The media exercises its greatest influence during elections. Every aspect of a political campaign, from fundraising and press announcements to staged events and major speeches, is planned with an eye toward garnering media coverage. Political candidates need television, newspapers, radio, magazines, and the Internet to reach voters with their message. Candidates who lack an effective media strategy are likely to be destined for failure.

Political Advertising

The vast majority of media coverage during political campaigns comes in the form of paid political advertising. With the cost of television advertising skyrocketing, candidates are forced to spend an inordinate amount of time fundraising. One senatorial candidate estimated that time to be five hours per day.

Candidates routinely spend 80 percent of their "war chests" on television and radio advertising. In larger states such as California, Texas, and New York, television advertising is the only way for candidates to reach the tens of millions of voters. In 2000, political novice John Corzine spent a mind-numbing $60–80 million of his own money—most of it on television commercials—to win a Senate seat in New Jersey.

One of the most effective negative ads in political history was the "Daisy ad," which Lyndon Johnson ran against Senator Barry Goldwater during the 1964 presidential election. The ad depicted a little girl picking the petals off a daisy as she counted to herself. It ended with a mushroom cloud filling up the screen. The clear implication was that Goldwater would lead Americans to nuclear war.

Most television advertising comes in the form of thirty-second commercials. Increasingly, the trend has been toward negative advertising (or "contrast" ads, as political pros refer to them), mostly because they have proved to be highly effective—even though voters claim to be turned off by them. Political professionals have learned that it is easier to be critical of an opponent during a thirty-second commercial than it is to lay out a positive agenda.

Spinning the News

All candidates supplement their paid media with free (or earned) media. Free media is another way of saying news coverage, and it's invaluable in establishing the reputation and credibility of a candidate. Lawmakers and candidates can shape the news coverage in several ways.

The most obvious is by planning campaign events at photogenic or inter-esting backdrops (known as photo-ops)—something that President Reagan's handlers mastered very well.

Astute politicians also develop close relationships with particular reporters by granting them exclusive interviews, sharing campaign informa-tion, and coming up with fresh campaign stories on a daily basis. All of these are things that make reporters' jobs easier. And of course, all candi-dates and their staffs are adept at "spinning" the news, a process by which they try to convince reporters that their interpretation of the news is the correct one. "Spin doctor" is a derisive term used to describe cam-paign staffers whose sole responsibility is to spin the media.

FACT

On May 1, 2003, President George W. Bush pulled off one of the most memorable photo-ops in recent years when he co-piloted an S-3B Viking jet onto the USS *Abraham Lincoln*, an aircraft carrier anchored off the shore of California. The president spent hours greeting hundreds of seamen on the runway, and later delivered the Operation Iraqi Freedom victory speech to a national audience from the flight deck.

The Media and the Presidency

Perhaps no other institution has helped shape the presidency more than the media. In the age of twenty-four-hour news coverage, virtually every moment of the president's public life is chronicled. Prior to the advent of television, the president rarely interacted with the press, except to occa-sionally grant interviews to newspapermen. Today, the press reports on the president's every movement, which at times has resulted in an adver-sarial relationship between the two.

Beat Reporters

Covering the president has become an industry unto itself. Hundreds of "beat reporters"—journalists who cover the White House on a daily basis—work from the basement of the White House. Twice a day, these reporters meet with the president's press secretary to get a briefing on the day's activities. Television cameras covering these briefings have been a frequent source of friction between the press secretary and the press, as some journalists use these press briefings as an opportunity to grandstand for the cameras. Typically, the press is on call twenty-four hours a day, unless the press secretary puts a "lid" on the news, which means that no big announcements are planned.

Most presidents have "feuded" with particular journalists and publications at one time or another. Richard Nixon detested the *Washington Post* and *New York Times*, and had his vice president publicly attack them. The Clinton White House singled out Sue Schmidt of the *Washington Post* as a reporter with a vendetta against the president. President George W. Bush publicly used an expletive to describe *New York Times* reporter Adam Clymer, a sentiment that Vice President Cheney agreed with. President Kennedy, on the other hand, enjoyed a cordial relationship with the press corps, partly because he singled out favorites for special treatment in return for favorable coverage.

The role of presidential press secretary is one of the most demanding and visible positions in Washington. The press secretary serves as a conduit for information between the White House and the press corps. Very few press secretaries serve a full presidential term; the average tenure is about two years. Many in the media consider Mike McCurry, President Clinton's third press secretary, among the finest ever to serve in that position.

In spite of the tension between the president and the press corps, the two have a symbiotic relationship. The president needs the press to deliver his message, and the press needs access to the president in order to do its job.

It's not uncommon for White House staffers to leak information to select journalists in order to shape the coverage. Sometimes the president will grant exclusive interviews to certain reporters as a way to dominate the headlines. During the early months of his presidency, President George W. Bush adopted nicknames for his favorite reporters, a tactic that was described as the "charm offensive."

FACT

Once or twice a year, the president holds a press conference with the White House reporters. This is the only opportunity for the press to ask any question directly of the president of the United States. The question order is usually predetermined. It's not unheard of for the opening questions to be "plants" from the White House staff—a deal they strike with reporters eager to be in the spotlight.

Pool Reporting

The reporters who cover the White House beat form a tight-knit fraternity. When the president travels abroad or makes domestic appearances, only a limited number of reporters can travel with him. When this occurs, the reporters adopt something called "pool coverage," which means that the reporters attending the event share their notes with the "pool"—the reporters not in attendance. Some beat reporters collaborate with their colleagues from other news outlets to make certain that they haven't missed any details or facts from a presidential event. Ⓔ

Chapter 19

Presidential Primaries and Elections

Presidential elections are held every four years, and in most cases it's a long, contentious, and sometimes even entertaining process. Candidates spend years organizing their campaigns, and as soon as one election concludes, another one begins. Seeking the highest office in the land requires persistence, stamina, single-mindedness, and the willingness to live in a media "fishbowl." As an observer once noted, running for president is not for the faint of heart.

The Process

Before someone can become a major party presidential candidate, he must first receive the nomination. During the winter months of each presidential year, the Democrats and Republicans hold primaries to select their respective nominees. Incumbent presidents seeking a second term rarely face a primary challenger—George H. W. Bush was a notable exception—as most are renominated automatically.

The primary process officially begins with the Iowa caucus, and concludes when one candidate has accumulated enough delegates to receive his party's nomination (which usually occurs in the early spring). Once the two major parties have determined their nominee through the primary process, the general election process begins.

Getting Organized

Running for the presidency is a massive undertaking. To be successful, the candidate needs an enormous political network of supporters—contributors, volunteers, organizers, and many others. The first challenge any candidate faces when considering a run for the Oval Office is putting together a campaign organization. Serious White House aspirants begin this process within months after the conclusion of the prior election. They focus on several key tasks, including raising money, organizing the campaign network, and establishing contacts with the media.

Raising Money

Raising money—and lots of it—may be the most critical function for a presidential candidate. Seeking the White House is a wildly expensive proposition. Most experts agree that a minimum of $20 million to $30 million is required just to build an organization and be viewed as a legitimate candidate. Professional fundraisers are extremely sought-after commodities. Candidates spend much of their time in the early months trying to line up proven fundraisers. It's almost a "contest within a contest" among the candidates (and with the press) to see who can sign up the biggest fundraisers.

FACT

For the 2004 election, freshman North Carolina senator John Edwards was accorded "first tier" status after a surprisingly strong showing in the spring 2003 campaign funds report. The following quarter, it was little-known Vermont governor Howard Dean who vaulted to top-tier status after raising $5.7 million—most of it from the Internet.

Serious presidential candidates spend the majority of their time in the months leading up to the primary season crisscrossing the country in search of campaign cash—most spend upward of eight hours a day "dialing for dollars" and attending fundraising events. Every quarter, the candidates must file a campaign contributions report with the Federal Election Commission, detailing how much money they've raised and spent. The report is available to the press, which separates the serious candidates from the "also-rans" according to how much money they raised.

Lining Up Campaign Consultants

Just as candidates compete for prominent fundraisers, they also jockey for the services of campaign consultants. Candidates look to consultants to help devise strategy, organize statewide campaigns, produce commercials, conduct polling, provide issues and opposition research, and give counsel and direction to the campaign. Political consultants with proven track records at the presidential level are difficult to come by, and highly sought. The press looks to consultant signings as another way to separate the first-tier candidates from the long shots.

Creating State Campaigns

Because the nominating process and thus the general election are determined by state elections, candidates must have well-run state campaigns. One of the first things prospective candidates do is put together a campaign organization in the key primary states. In states like Iowa, New Hampshire, South Carolina, and Arizona (the first four caucuses and primaries), there is an intense competition to win the support and backing of the governor, members of the state legislature, members of Congress, state party leaders, county chairmen, and even precinct leaders. It's not unusual for candidates to call and visit county chairmen, town leaders, and precinct captains directly to sign them up. In states like Iowa and New Hampshire, where "retail" politics (door-to-door campaigning) is considered an art form, organization is particularly important. Candidates rely on their state organizations to get out the vote on Election Day.

In the 2000 Republican primary race, Senator John McCain pulled off a resounding upset over George W. Bush in New Hampshire, mostly on the strength of his well-oiled state campaign. Less than a week later, Bush returned the favor with a lopsided victory in South Carolina, where his forces were much better organized than were McCain's.

Courting the Media

During the early part of the nominating process, media attention is difficult to come by. Like everything else, candidates compete for press coverage, usually by issuing position papers, staking out bold positions, and making themselves available. National media coverage can make fundraising and organizing much easier, and elevate candidates to first-tier status.

Debates and Straw Polls

The candidates don't actually begin the process of competing for votes until the primary season begins, but they spend years organizing, fundraising, and piecing together their campaigns.

Debates and voter forums typically begin a full year prior to the first primary. These events give voters a chance to compare the candidates, and allow the media the opportunity to assess the relative strengths and weaknesses of each candidate. More than anything, debates give the candidates a chance to gain "traction" and build momentum for their campaigns. In 1996, political commentator Pat Buchanan used the debates and other candidate forums to hammer away at Republican front-runner Bob Dole and build enthusiasm for his campaign. His upset victory in

New Hampshire is credited, in part, to his masterful performances in the debates leading up to it. John McCain employed a similar strategy in 2000 against George W. Bush, who struggled during the early debates.

FACT

Ronald Reagan delivered one of the most memorable moments in New Hampshire primary history when he scolded the organizers of the New Hampshire primary for turning off his microphone prior to the start of the debate. "I paid for that microphone!" he retorted to the stunned moderator, setting a new tone for the campaign.

In addition to debates, the candidates also compete for momentum and perceived strength at "straw poll" conventions. These contests are usually held a month or two in advance of the primary season, and are little more than mini-conventions where citizens show up (they usually pay an entrance fee) and cast a vote for one of the candidates. The Florida straw poll contest is considered the most important. Candidates spend hundreds of thousands of dollars organizing their support at this event in order to give the appearance of strength. Hordes of media outlets cover the Florida straw poll, handicapping the strengths and weaknesses of each candidate's performance. A good candidate showing at the Florida straw poll can generate momentum heading into the Iowa caucus, while a poor show can potentially cripple a campaign. Often, the front-runners heading into the Florida straw poll opt not to participate in it out of fear of being upset and losing momentum.

Winning the Nomination

States are free to choose how they select their political candidates. Most states use primaries to elect their political candidates; a few use caucuses. Caucuses are similar to primaries, with the big difference being that voters don't select a candidate directly. Rather, they select delegates to attend the nominating convention. Caucuses tend to have lower turnouts than do primaries, but the participants are generally more knowledgeable about the issues and committed to their candidates.

The Iowa Caucus

The most important presidential caucus is the Iowa caucus, which is usually held during the first week in February of the election year and kicks off the formal nominating process. Presidential aspirants spend years organizing their Iowa campaign with hopes of making a strong showing.

Typically, candidates finishing among the top three in Iowa gain momentum heading into the New Hampshire primary, which takes place the following week. Candidates who fail to finish among the top three, or perform below expectations, usually begin to see their fundraising dry up and momentum stall.

In 1976, Jimmy Carter went from relative obscurity to presidential front-runner after winning the Iowa caucus. Carter, who held no elected office at the time, spent months prior to the caucus living in Iowa and meeting with voters. In 1996, Texas senator Phil Gramm, one of the early Republican favorites, was forced to drop his candidacy after finishing fifth behind Bob Dole, Pat Buchanan, Lamar Alexander, and Steve Forbes in the Iowa caucus. In 1988, televangelist Pat Robertson vaulted to top-tier candidate after finishing in second place to Senator Bob Dole, and ahead of George H. W. Bush. In 2000, Senator John McCain made the wise choice of deciding not to participate at all in Iowa, knowing full well that he probably wouldn't defeat George W. Bush. He spent the extra time campaigning in New Hampshire.

The New Hampshire Primary

The primary in New Hampshire is the first in the nation, and takes place a week after the Iowa caucus. The candidates spend the week leading up to the primary traveling all over the state meeting as many voters as possible. New Hampshire voters are known for being astute and informed, and they appreciate retail politicking.

If the Iowa caucus begins the process of winnowing the field, then the New Hampshire primary concludes it. In most situations, the top two or three finishers in New Hampshire maintain enough momentum and support to continue running for president. The other finishers usually see their fundraising and organization dissipate and dissolve as their supporters begin migrating to the more viable candidates. It is said that the top three finishers have a ticket out of New Hampshire, while the rest have a ticket home.

ALERT!

The winner of the New Hampshire primary almost always goes on to capture the nomination. Two notable exceptions, however, are the two most recent. In 2000, Senator John McCain won New Hampshire, while in 1996 Pat Buchanan was the winner.

Because New Hampshire is such a critical contest, candidates devote hundreds of days to meeting with voters at small gatherings and events during the two-year period leading up to the primary. In no other state does this "intimate" form of campaigning take place.

Regional Primaries

After New Hampshire, the candidates who remain begin traversing the country, competing in the primaries in Arizona, Michigan, and South Carolina. Following those contests, the candidates face off in what has been dubbed "Super Tuesday"—a day when multiple primaries (mostly in the South and West) take place. The participating states devised Super Tuesday as a way to maximize their importance in the process.

Over the past decade, more and more states have begun holding their primaries earlier in the season in order to achieve greater impact on the selection process. This is known as "frontloading" the process, and has been criticized by some because it favors the candidate with the most money and best organization—not necessarily the best candidate.

It used to be that the primaries lasted well into the early summer, and the eventual nominee wasn't selected until the party convention. In the past few election cycles, however, the process has become increasingly frontloaded so that most primaries take place in early March. This means that the nominating process is over sooner, and it also means that the candidate who raised the most money prior to New Hampshire usually stands the best chance of winning. In 2002, George W. Bush was clearly the beneficiary of frontloading as John McCain couldn't overcome

Bush's vast resources. In 1996, the same was true for Bob Dole, as he took advantage of the frontloaded schedule to stamp out the insurgent Pat Buchanan campaign. Frontloading doesn't allow "dark horse" or long-shot candidates enough time to build momentum.

FACT

There are three types of presidential primaries: open, closed, and blanket. Most states have closed primaries, meaning that only registered party members can vote for their nominee. Several states, including Michigan and Arizona, have open primary contests, meaning that voters can choose which primary to vote in regardless of party affiliation. Only Alaska, Washington, and Louisiana have blanket primaries, where voters can vote in all the parties' primaries.

Nominating Conventions

By the end of March, the presidential nominees for both parties have been all but established. Although primary contests continue through early June, the outcome is not in doubt. Between the last contested primary and the nominating conventions, there are several weeks of "downtime" during which the candidates focus on selecting a running mate, devising a general election strategy, and creating television commercials.

During these summer months, the incumbent president enjoys a big advantage. While his opponent is typically cash-strapped from the bruising primary campaigns, the president is usually flush with cash and can flood the airwaves with television commercials touting his record and attacking his opponent's. He also enjoys the advantage of incumbency, which means bill-signing ceremonies, unlimited media coverage, and the ability to set the agenda. In 1996, President Clinton dominated the airwaves between March and September with ads attacking Bob Dole, while the Republican could do little but watch. Many experts credit Clinton's aggressive use of paid advertising during the slow summer months for his wide margin of victory.

The political conventions take place in August, and represent the formal nominating process for the two major party candidates. In past years, the conventions offered some suspense about who would be chosen as running mates (and in some cases who would be the nominee), but today they're nothing more than staged events with little real drama. In fact, the conventions have become so stale and devoid of news that the media networks have drastically reduced their coverage over the past decade. Whereas the conventions used to be covered gavel to gavel by the networks, today only the acceptance speeches are still televised. It wouldn't be surprising if, in the future, networks skipped the conventions entirely, leaving it to cable news networks such as CNN, Fox News, and MSNBC for coverage.

General Election

The general election campaign formally kicks off after the conventions have ended. Voters traditionally begin paying attention to the presidential contest after the Labor Day weekend, as they return from summer vacation.

Taking a Stand on the Issues

The candidates and their staffs devise a strategy for the general election that they believe will win the necessary 270 Electoral College votes required for victory (more on the Electoral College later in the chapter). The strategies usually revolve around two central ideas: which issues should be emphasized (or de-emphasized), and how those issues should be framed. Months of polling and focus-group testing go into determining the issues and the language used to discuss them. Beginning in the late summer, both candidates use daily tracking polls in key states to detect any change in momentum.

Once they've settled on a strategy, the candidates travel to the states that they believe are necessary for victory, where they attend rallies, meet with voters, and talk to the local press to get their message out. The candidates' goal is to garner media coverage while at the same time "staying on message." Given the hordes of media that follow the candidates' every move, staying on message can be difficult. A botched phrase, misspoken word, or incorrect statement can dominate the news cycle for days.

Pollsters use focus groups to gain insights into how the public views the candidates and the issues. The information gathered allows campaign strategists to understand the emotions and anxieties behind certain issues. Most focus groups are highly segmented, meaning that they target particular demographics—senior citizens, blue-collar workers, ethnic groups, younger Americans, and so on.

The candidates typically "contrast" their records and philosophy with their opponent's, pointing out the strengths in their candidacy and the weaknesses in their opponent's. As Election Day draws near, this type of negative campaigning usually intensifies—especially if the contest is close. During the waning days of the campaign, it is not unusual for a candidate to drop an "October surprise"—a particularly nasty revelation—about his opponent with the hopes of gaining a slight advantage. Just days before Election Day in 2000, it was leaked to the press that George W. Bush had a DWI arrest in the 1970s. Some believe it was just enough to slow his momentum and throw the race into a dead heat.

Media Coverage

Media coverage intensifies as the general election begins in earnest following the nominating conventions. Dozens of reporters travel with both candidates, reporting on their every move, utterance, gesture, and campaign squabble. With information closely guarded by the campaigns, reporters are often left to report on the machinations of the campaigns rather than the candidates themselves. News coverage tends to focus on the "horse-race" aspect of the contest, as daily polls track who's up, who's down, and why.

The general election debates are the only unguarded—some would say unscripted—moments of the campaign, leaving the candidates to their own devices. The presidential candidates participate in two debates, which are televised on all the major networks. For the candidate who is trailing, the debates represent the best opportunity to change the dynamics of the race. In 1988, Vice President George H. W. Bush used the debates to pull away from Massachusetts governor Michael Dukakis, who was tripped up by a question from CNN newsman Bernard Shaw. Dukakis's emotionless answer to Shaw's difficult question about rape turned off many voters. In 1992, President Clinton turned in a commanding performance in a town hall–style debate with President George H. W. Bush and Ross Perot, leaving little doubt that he was up to the task of leading the nation.

FACT

Heading into the presidential debates, both campaigns play the "expectations game" as they try to convince the media that the other candidate is expected to perform much better. In 2000, the Bush campaign masterfully lowered expectations for their candidate, so much so that when Al Gore failed to deliver a knockout blow during the first debate, it was considered a Bush victory.

Not all of the media coverage is serious. Comedy programs such as the *Tonight Show, Late Night with David Letterman*, Comedy Central's *The Daily Show*, and *Saturday Night Live* spend months lampooning, satirizing, and simply poking fun at the candidates and campaigns, sometimes with alarming effectiveness. During the 2000 campaign, the *Saturday Night Live* parody of the presidential debates was very effective in portraying the public's perception that the Gore campaign team made the vice president watch a videotape of his performance in order to convince him not to roll his eyes while George Bush was speaking. Some Americans learned more about the campaign through *Saturday Night Live*'s Will Ferrell (Bush) and Darrell Hammond (Gore), than from the candidates themselves. Although late-night comedy ripostes directed at the candidates rarely change the dynamics of the race, they sometimes reinforce feelings or attitudes already held by the public.

Election Day

Election Day takes place on the Tuesday after the first Monday in November. In the days leading up to Election Day, the candidates zigzag across the country, visiting key states to make a last appeal to voters. In 1996, Bob Dole campaigned ninety-six hours straight with almost no sleep over the final four days—his "96 in '96" finale.

With little left to be done on Election Day, candidates typically relax with staff and wait for returns. In 2000, Al Gore, running mate Joseph Lieberman, and their families gave hundreds of radio interviews throughout Election Day in an effort to pick up a few extra votes. Gore's bold Election Day strategy likely contributed to his victory in the popular vote.

The media—most notably the television networks—typically try to forecast (or call) the results as soon as the polls have closed. Even though it takes hours for the actual results to come in, they make these predictions based on "tracking polls" that are performed throughout the day. Tracking polls are simply polls that are conducted of voters as they leave the polling place. These polls aren't always accurate, because people often misrepresent their actual vote when speaking to the media. The media combines tracking-poll information with historical voting data to predict results, sometimes with alarming inaccuracy. In 2000, it was the breakdown of this statistical modeling that twice led to incorrect calls in the Florida race.

The Electoral College

As you learned in Chapter 2, the president and vice president are actually elected by the Electoral College. When casting a ballot for a particular candidate, voters are actually voting for a slate of electors. These electors in turn will vote for that candidate in the Electoral College.

The Electoral College system was devised for two reasons: The framers of the Constitution had feared direct democracy (they believed that a college of dispassionate citizens were better suited than the masses to select a president), and they wanted to protect the interests of smaller states and rural areas.

The Electoral College is composed of 538 members—equivalent to 100 senators, 435 House members, and 3 representatives from the District of

Columbia. Each state's number of electors equals their number of representatives and senators. Thus, California has the most electors with 54, followed by New York (33), Texas (32), Florida (25), and Pennsylvania (23). Except for Maine and Nebraska, the Electoral College is a winner-take-all system, meaning whoever carries the state—regardless of the margin—receives all of the state's Electoral College votes.

Calls to Reform

As we learned in 2000, regardless of the popular vote tally (President George W. Bush lost the popular vote by a half million votes), the magic number is 270 electoral votes. The 25 electoral votes accorded President George W. Bush from his several-hundred-vote victory in Florida gave him a total of 271 to Al Gore's 267. Following the 2000 election, there was some discussion about eliminating the Electoral College and replacing it with direct voting. Were that to happen, however, chances are the candidates would focus on large population centers such as New York, California, Florida, and Texas, and ignore the interests of rural and sparsely populated areas.

QUESTION?

How many times has a president been elected without winning the popular vote?
This has occurred four times. The first was John Adams in 1824, followed by Rutherford B. Hayes in 1876, Benjamin Harrison in 1888, and George W. Bush in 2000. Adams, Hayes, and Harrison all were unable to win a second term.

In 1977, President Jimmy Carter proposed a constitutional amendment that would do just that, but the amendment failed to win a two-thirds majority in the Senate. Small-state senators had also rebuffed a measure to eliminate the Electoral College in 1969. The major parties oppose eliminating the Electoral College because it would give more influence to third-party candidates, who under the current system stand almost no chance of winning any electoral votes.

Who Are the Electors?

It's important to keep in mind that the candidates choose their own slate of electors—the Republican candidate has his set of electors, and the Democrat candidate has a different set of electors. State rules determine how these electors are chosen. The Constitution does not require that the electors cast their ballots for their pledged candidate in the Electoral College. However, since the candidates themselves choose their slate of electors, it's extremely unlikely that any elector would vote for someone other than his pledged candidate. During the 2000 presidential recount, the media speculated one or two Bush electors might switch their votes for Al Gore during the Electoral College, an absurd notion.

Chapter 20

State Government

In our system of government (federalism), the federal and state governments share power. Under federalism, the functions of government are divided. The federal government has exclusive domain over international affairs and national defense. Other matters, such as education, crime control, housing, and taxes, fall within the province of both the federal and state governments. There is a healthy tension between the federal and state governments over the roles and responsibilities of each.

Federal Versus State

State government is structured similarly to the federal government, except on a much smaller scale. Every state has a constitution and three branches of government—executive, legislative, and judicial. The states also have a power-sharing relationship with their local and municipal governments that's much the same as the federal system.

The states are often referred to as the "laboratories of democracy" because no two state governments are exactly alike. Often policies, laws, and procedures that are successful in one state are copied in another, and then in the federal government. This tendency to adopt the "best practices" of states has kept state government vibrant and innovative.

State Constitutions

Every state has a constitution that establishes the legal and political framework for government within that state. Some state constitutions are well written, while others are not. None captures the flexibility, durability, and sheer brilliance of the Constitution of the United States. Most are wordy, bulky, disjointed documents that have been amended, revised, and rewritten many times. Alabama has the lengthiest constitution at a mind-numbing 172,000 words—about twenty-five times longer than the U.S. Constitution! Vermont has the shortest at fewer than 7,000 words.

It's important to remember that state constitutions are "subordinate" to the supreme law of the land, meaning that provisions of state constitutions that come into conflict with federal law are considered unconstitutional. However, state constitutions are the supreme law of the state for matters that fall outside of federal law or that aren't expressly prohibited by the Constitution of the United States.

Like the U.S. Constitution, state constitutions enumerate the powers of the three branches of government, create state agencies, establish a bill of rights, and provide for a method to amend the constitution. Beyond that, state constitutions tend to be very detailed (some would say maddeningly so) about certain matters. For instance, the California constitution mandates the size of fruit boxes, while the Louisiana constitution dedicates nearly 5,000 words (almost the entire length of the U.S Constitution) to the creation of the board of commissioners of the port of New Orleans. That same Louisiana constitution also proclaims former governor Huey P. Long's birthday a "legal holiday forever."

In many states, extremely narrow provisions, like Alabama's cap on local tax rates, have forced lawmakers to repeatedly amend the constitution as government has grown in size and complexity. Some constitutions have provisions idiosyncratic to their state, such as Oklahoma's requirement that all public schools teach horticulture, stock-feeding, and agriculture. It's unlikely that a similar provision exists in the New York constitution.

With Governor at the Helm

The governor is the highest elected state official and the most powerful officeholder in the state. Gubernatorial authority is confined to state matters only; a governor does not have any federal powers. Historically, the statehouse has been a wonderful launching pad for national office—twenty-three governors have gone on to serve as president or vice president. In some states, such as New York, California, and Texas, the office of governor is considered more prestigious than that of U.S. senator. In smaller states, however, the position is not as highly coveted.

A Brief History

During the colonial era, governors were appointed by the king of England. The position was considered largely symbolic, because governors were vested with little real power. The elected state legislatures distrusted the governors's ties to the king, and as a result the legislatures and the governors rarely cooperated on anything. Following the Declaration of Independence, the initial state constitutions called for appointed (not elected) governors to serve one-year terms, which left the governors virtually powerless.

After the U.S. Constitution was ratified in 1789, states began rewriting their constitutions to reflect a stronger executive branch. Governorship became an elected position (most states adopted two- and four-year terms) with enumerated powers. Just about every state modeled the new position after the presidency, and as the nation grew more comfortable with executive power at the national level, so too did it begin to accept the governors.

In 1925, Nellie Tayloe Ross of Wyoming edged out Miriam Ferguson of Texas by a mere fifteen days to become the first female governor. In 1989, Douglas Wilder of Virginia became the first and only African-American to date to serve as governor. By 2002, there were six women and one Asian-American but no African-Americans serving as governor.

Throughout the nineteenth century, state governors began to assume more and greater powers. By the end of the nineteenth century, governors were some of the most influential officeholders in the country. They lorded over their political parties, controlled statewide patronage positions, administered state funds, wrote state budgets, and convened special sessions of the legislature. To this day, the governors remain at the epicenter of the political process across the states.

Governors Today

Most governors come to the statehouse with prior political experience in the state legislature or at the county level. Over the past two decades, an increasing number have come from the ranks of wealthy businessmen. Gubernatorial salaries vary greatly, with California the most generous at $131,000 and Arkansas the lowest at $60,000. In just about half the states, the governor is limited to two terms. Virginia is the only state with a one-term limit.

In the larger states such as New York, California, and Florida, the cost of running for governor can easily exceed $20 million per candidate. In 2002, California governor Gray Davis spent a staggering $60 million on his re-election effort, narrowly defeating his underfunded opponent. Less than eighteen months later, a recall petition against Davis forced a special election—the first successful recall petition in the state's history—and Davis was replaced by Arnold Schwarzenegger.

FACT

Only twelve states have the option to recall—a procedure by which voters can remove the governor by way of a special election. In 1921, Lynn Frazier of North Dakota became the first governor to be ousted from office through a recall petition. The voters of North Dakota didn't remain upset for too long, however; shortly after his removal, he was elected to the U.S. Senate.

The statehouse is by far the most popular route to the presidency. Four of the last five presidents—George W. Bush, Bill Clinton, Ronald Reagan, and Jimmy Carter—were governors. Governors tend to make better presidential candidates because they have a wealth of executive experience, understand how to delegate authority and responsibility, and can point to a specific record of accomplishments and successes. Moreover, they usually remain untainted by the partisanship and "inside the Beltway" bickering that saddle senators and congressmen who seek national office.

Gubernatorial Powers

As the chief executive of his or her state, the governor has many responsibilities and duties. Like the president, he has enumerated, constitutional, and symbolic powers. Some states are said to have strong governors, meaning that the office holds many enumerated powers. The strongest governor of the nation is the governor of New Jersey, who has the ability to appoint cabinet positions (including the state attorney general) as well as state supreme court justices. Conversely, the Texas governor has almost no constitutional powers, and is considered the weakest of the fifty governors. The governor's powers can be divided into three primary categories: executive, legislative, and leadership.

Executive Powers

In most states, the greater part of the governor's authority stems from the executive powers outlined in the state constitution. This includes everything from declaring a state of emergency (due to natural disaster, civil unrest, or other unforeseen situations) to calling up the National Guard. Just as the president is the commander in chief of the U.S. military, the governor is the commander in chief of his state's National Guard. Following the terrorist attacks of September 11, 2001, many governors called up the National Guard to help protect their airports, ports, and other public areas.

After leaving office, some governors return to their previous professions, while others seek other elected office. Many take teaching positions at their state universities. Arkansas governor Orville Faubus—a virulent segregationist—had something of a nervous breakdown after leaving office, and wound up taking a job as a bank teller to make ends meet. One former West Virginia governor turned up as a taxi driver in Chicago.

The governor's most important role as chief executive is drafting an annual state budget. At the beginning of each year, the governor submits a budget to the state legislature outlining spending and policy priorities for the year, as well as any tax hikes or cuts. The governor and the state legislature then negotiate back and forth on spending levels and programs until the two branches reach a compromise.

Many states, including New York, California, and New Jersey, have mandatory deadlines for when a budget must be passed. If the governor and the leadership of the state legislature are from the same party, meeting this deadline is rarely a problem. During times of divided government, however, the process can become acrimonious and protracted. In New York, the budget deadline is rarely met.

Legislative Role

Like the president, the governor also has the ability to influence and shape the legislative process. As the highest elected statewide office-holder, the governor can be viewed as a representative of the entire state. As such, most governors—particularly during their first term in office—propose ambitious legislative agendas. Governors will typically travel around the state and meet with community groups, business leaders, and local officials in order to drum up support for their agendas. Upon narrowly defeating incumbent Jim Florio in 1993, New Jersey governor Christine Todd Whitman stumped vigorously for her tax cut plan—the centerpiece of her campaign—and narrowly won passage in the state legislature.

Once a year, the governor lays out his or her agenda in the State of the State address, a speech given before a joint session of the legislature. Like the president's State of the Union address, the State of the State is the one opportunity for the governor to provide a vision and a cohesive plan for the future. In every state except North Carolina, the governor has the ability to veto legislation passed by the state legislature. Just like the presidential veto, the threat of a gubernatorial veto is sometimes more powerful than the veto itself.

Leadership

Part of the governor's power is derived from his or her ability to lead. No other state officeholder can attract media attention, influence national lawmakers, galvanize the public, and shape the national party like the governor.

FACT

Governor Pete Wilson of California dispatched 4,000 National Guard troops in the streets of Los Angeles after rioting broke out following the acquittal of four police officers charged with beating Rodney King. More than fifty people were killed and $1 billion in property damage was incurred before the guardsmen restored civil order.

During the 2000 presidential campaign, moderate northeastern Republican governors including George Pataki, Christine Todd Whitman, and Tom Ridge were credited with keeping presidential candidate George W. Bush focused on moderate and independent voters.

Some governors use the "bully pulpit" of the statehouse to build support for unpopular or controversial policies. In 2000, Illinois Republican governor George Ryan put a moratorium on all death-row executions after it was learned that a few convictions were tainted by questionable evidence. The move initially angered many voters, but after intense public lobbying he was applauded for the decision.

State Legislatures

Every state has a state legislature, which works with its respective governor in creating laws and setting public policy. Many similarities exist between Congress and the state legislatures: They both represent and serve their constituents, work with executive leaders to pass laws, stand for election at regular intervals, and receive their power from a state constitution.

The state legislature is actually the oldest democratic institution in American government, dating back to the early colonial period. Today, there are approximately 7,500 state legislators in the United States.

The power, prestige, and influence of state legislatures vary from state to state. In weak-governor states, legislatures have a greater impact on policy formation and decision-making than they do in strong-governor states. One thing that is consistent throughout the fifty states is the location of the state legislature; each meets at the statehouse, which is located in the state capital.

Who Serves in State Legislatures

Most state legislative positions are part-time jobs with low-paying salaries. Not surprisingly, New York and California pay the best, topping out at more than $90,000 for their upper chamber positions. Alabama occupies the bottom, paying out a mere $10 stipend per legislator for every day in session.

Most state legislatures are in session for only several months a year. The legislators spend the rest of the time providing constituent casework services in their districts. This irregular schedule, combined with the low pay, typically leads to a high turnover rate in most state legislatures. It also leads to "overrepresentation" by lawyers because an irregular legislative schedule fits nicely with a part-time law practice. It's not uncommon for lawyers to constitute a quarter of the state legislatures. Most states have an age restriction on serving in the state legislature, with the average minimum age being twenty-one.

Generally speaking, there are two broad categories of citizens who serve as state legislators. The first are career politicians with upwardly mobile career ambitions. Many congressmen, senators and governors learn their trade in the state legislature, and use it as a launching pad. The second group is composed of civic-minded citizens with long-standing and deep ties to the community. These members share a passion about issues that might seem mundane to others—helmet laws for skateboarders, the size of parking spaces for the handicapped, hunting season dates, and so on.

Size and Organization

State legislatures vary greatly in size. New Hampshire has more than 400 legislators representing only 1 million residents, while New Jersey has 120 legislators representing more than 6 million citizens. Nevada has only 60 state representatives for its population of 1.5 million.

Every state except Nebraska has a bicameral (two-chamber) legislature—Nebraska has a unicameral (one-chamber) legislature. Most states refer to their upper chamber as the State Senate, and their lower chamber as House of Representatives, House of Delegates, State Assembly, or General Assembly.

The leadership in the state legislatures is similar to that of Congress, with a speaker and majority and minority leaders in the lower chamber, and a senate president and major and minority leaders in the upper chamber. Chamber leaders tend to be even more powerful than Congressional leaders because party discipline is stricter and more important at the state level.

Powers and Authority

The process of passing legislation in the state legislatures is similar to that of Congress, although the subject matter can differ greatly. State legislatures take up everything from new state holidays to the medical use of marijuana, gay marriage, assisted suicide, highway speed limits, ban on cell phone usage in cars, and much more. There are five areas in particular where state legislatures focus most of their attention: education, roads and highways, health and welfare benefits, law enforcement, and conservation.

Education

Anywhere from a quarter to a third of most state budgets are allocated to the education system. A majority of the money goes to the state colleges and universities. Tuition for schools such as Rutgers University, the University of Michigan, the University of California at Berkeley, and the University of Texas is much lower than that of comparable private schools because of state subsidies. (At state universities, out-of-state students typically pay more tuition than do in-state students.) In recent years, state universities have been forced to raise tuition for in-state students because of state budget cuts.

While local municipalities are responsible for administering primary and secondary school (more on this in Chapter 21), the state legislature sets the education guidelines, such as the number of days in a school year, graduation requirements, statewide tests, and so on.

Roads and Highways

Most states allocate approximately 10 percent of their annual budgets for the construction and maintenance of roads and highways. This includes constructing highways, filling potholes, removing snow, establishing speed limits and mandatory seat belt usage, and licensing new drivers. For many state legislators, the Department of Motor Vehicles is a source of unending complaints from their constituents.

Health and Welfare Benefits

It's not uncommon for state legislatures to allocate a quarter of the state budget to health and welfare benefits for the sick and unemployed. State agencies administer state hospitals, immunization programs, welfare benefits, unemployment insurance, and scores of other programs aimed at helping needy citizens. They also regulate medical professionals, as well as private hospitals, nursing homes, and other care centers.

Law Enforcement

While local government is primarily responsible for maintaining law and order, every state has its own police system. State police departments are typically responsible for enforcing civility outside of major cities and towns and maintaining highway safety.

FACT

The first statewide police department was the Texas Rangers, which was established in 1835 while Texas was still a republic. It wasn't until the advent of the automobile around the turn of the century, however, that most states began establishing state police departments.

Conservation Efforts

State legislatures play an important role in conserving public lands, establishing state parks, and regulating hunting and fishing. State legislatures can conserve lands by allocating funds to purchase them, or by simply "protecting" them (this is usually done to protect endangered animals or ecosystems).

Other Statewide Positions

In addition to governor and state legislature roles, most states have several other positions. Four in particular are most common: lieutenant governor, attorney general, secretary of state, and state treasurer.

Lieutenant Governor

In most states, the role of lieutenant governor is similar to that of vice president. The primary responsibility of the lieutenant governor is to be the second in command and to succeed the governor if he or she can no longer serve in office. In some states, such as New York and Massachusetts, the governor and lieutenant governor run together as a ticket; in others, such as Rhode Island and Texas, the two run separately. Only eight states do not have a lieutenant governor. In those states, the state senate president succeeds the governor.

Much like the office of vice president, most lieutenant governors have little institutional power. In many states, the lieutenant governor serves as acting governor when the governor is outside of the state. In states where the lieutenant governor is elected separately from the governor (and therefore could be from the opposite party), the governor usually avoids long absences from the state for this very reason.

The state of Texas has the most powerful lieutenant governor office in the nation (many believe it is actually more powerful than the governor of Texas). The lieutenant governor makes committee assignments in the lower chamber and sets the agenda for the upper chamber. As governor of Texas, George W. Bush had a very close working relationship with Democratic lieutenant governor Bob Bullock. Many attribute Bush's successful legislative agenda to this relationship.

Attorney General

Every state has an attorney general, who is the highest legal officer of the state. In most states, this is an elected position (a few, such as New Jersey, appoint their attorney general). Essentially, the attorney general represents the state in legal matters before the state courts. He or she also can interpret and enforce state laws.

In recent years, this office has become one the most powerful in the nation, as attorneys general have been successful in negotiating tobacco, asbestos, and other mass tort settlements. In New York, Attorney General Eliot Spitzer has spearheaded an effort to make Wall Street more accountable to public shareholders. The attorney general's office is a popular steppingstone to the statehouse, but seldom to the White House.

Bill Clinton was the only twentieth-century president to serve as state attorney general.

Secretary of State

The secretary of state position is nothing like the one of federal secretary of state. The primary responsibility of the state position is certifying election results and maintaining official documents and records. In most states, this is an elected position. Only Alaska and Hawaii—the two youngest states—do not have a secretary of state. Perhaps the most famous secretary of state in recent times was Katherine Harris of Florida, who became a prominent national figure during the 2000 presidential recount. Harris later used her notoriety to win a seat in Congress.

State Treasurer

Sometimes referred to as comptroller, this officer is responsible for collecting and investing state money. The treasurer is also responsible for overseeing state agency spending and paying state bills.

Reapportionment and Redistricting

One of the most important functions of state government is the redistricting of Congressional (as well as state assembly and senate) districts. Some of the nastiest fights in recent memory have come over this issue.

You learned in Chapter 2 that Article I, section 2 of the Constitution mandates that the federal government conduct a census of the population every ten years. One of the purposes of taking the census is to reapportion Congressional seats based on population growth and movement. Because the number of seats in the House of Representatives is constitutionally fixed at 435, states that lose population also lose House seats, and states that gain population gain House seats. During the last census in 2000, New York was one of the losers, while California, Texas, and Florida were all winners.

Once the Bureau of the Census determines which states gain and lose House seats, it's up to the state legislatures to redraw the Congressional districts. Under the "one man, one vote" principle established by the

Supreme Court, Congressional districts all must be approximately the same size (within a 5 percent margin of error). Today, Congressional districts have approximately 600,000 citizens. Because the number of representatives (435) will not change in the future, average district size will increase as the population grows.

Since redistricting is an opportunity for the party that controls the state legislature to redraw the political map to its liking, the process is almost always contentious and ugly. The biggest battles are reserved for states that lose Congressional seats. In those situations, unlucky incumbents (depending on the number of lost seats) are forced to run against another incumbent in order to remain in Congress. Legislators will often gerrymander districts—create odd political boundaries in order to capture favorable demographics—in an effort to pick up a few more Congressional seats for their party. In recent years, the Supreme Court has taken a more activist approach in disqualifying absurdly shaped districts.

QUESTION?

What is gerrymandering?

"Gerrymandering" is a term used to describe redrawing Congressional districts for the sole purpose of delivering a partisan advantage to one party. The Supreme Court has held that it is constitutional for state legislatures to manipulate the Congressional map so as to substantially benefit the majority party at the expense of the minority party.

While gerrymandering is patently unfair to residents belonging to the minority party, it has been a seemingly intractable problem. In recent years, voters have become increasingly vocal in voicing displeasure to their state representatives on this issue.

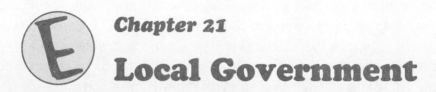

Chapter 21

Local Government

Though we tend to focus on national and state government and politics, most citizens are affected more by their local government. Nevertheless, local government remains something of a mystery to most Americans. It doesn't receive the same press attention as the federal or state government and politics, and many citizens are unaware of how it is organized and executed. This chapter examines county, city, and town government, as well as special districts and regional government.

County Government

The most common jurisdiction of local government throughout the country is county government. Every state but three—Alaska, Rhode Island, and Connecticut—is composed of county governments of varying sizes and population. Although Rhode Island and Connecticut are geographically divided into counties, they do not have county governments. (Connecticut abolished them in 1960.) Alaska refers to counties as "boroughs" because they do not want to stigmatize them as tools of state government; in Louisiana they are called parishes. Loving County, Texas, is the least populous county with only 140 residents, while Los Angeles County is most populous—it's home to 9.2 million people. In total, there are 3,066 counties in the United States, each with its own local government.

ALERT!

Local government is responsible for a myriad of functions: removing and recycling garbage, granting marriage and divorce licenses, providing recreational facilities and programs, building and maintaining local transportation systems, educating children, providing police and fire protection, prosecuting criminals—the list goes on and on.

Counties trace their origins to England, and are modeled after the English shire of the Middle Ages. Back then, each shire was an administrative arm of the national government, as well as the province of local government. Early American colonists adopted the shire as they settled the Eastern seaboard.

Until World War II, county government was little more than a resource for states to administer the services of government. However, with the dramatic growth of suburbs beginning in the 1950s, the role of county government began to change. Over the past several decades, counties have assumed more responsibility and power from the states, and have begun to provide greater services to their residents. Today, county governments are important providers and administrators of critical government services.

Basic Functions

County governments are unique in that, unlike cities, they are not incorporated, and unlike states, they have no reserved or constitutional powers. By and large, the primary task of county government is to administer the functions delegated to them by the state. This includes maintaining rural roads and highways, reassessing property values, keeping official records, providing food and welfare assistance, constructing and maintaining county buildings, awarding county contracts, and collecting taxes. In effect, a county government serves as a middleman between local and state government. For many residents of rural areas, county government provides a crucial link to the larger world.

Over the past two decades, the demands and expectations of county government have grown more substantial. Functions that were historically completed at the state and federal level are now the responsibility of county government. Following the terrorist attacks of September 11, for example, county and local law enforcement and fire departments have played a large role in maintaining homeland security.

Types of County Government

A vast majority of county governments take one of three forms: commission, commission-administrator, and council-executive. In all three forms of government, county commission members receive little or no pay (these are part-time positions) and serve a term of four years. It's not uncommon for county commissioners to seek higher office at both the state and national level. In most states, the county executive position serves as a steppingstone for statewide office, particularly the statehouse. In 1986, Westchester County (New York) executive Andrew O'Rourke was defeated in his bid to unseat Governor Mario Cuomo. O'Rourke was later appointed to the state Supreme Court by Governor George Pataki.

Commission Government

Sometimes referred to as "board of commissioners" or "board of supervisors," the commission is by far the most common form of county government. Two-thirds of the counties in the United States have a commission that contains three to five commission members. In a commission government, the elected board acts as both the legislative and executive branches. It has the power to adopt budgets, enact regulations, set policy direction, and appoint county officials. Most county commissions are composed of elected officials; some are composed of judges, town supervisors, and city officials.

Commission-Administrator Government

In a commission-administrator system, the commission board appoints an administrator, who serves at the board's discretion. In some counties, the administrator is nothing more than a symbolic figure with little power. In other counties, the administrator has a wide range of responsibilities and duties, such as appointing department heads, drafting a budget, overseeing construction projects, and promulgating regulations.

Council-Executive Government

Under this system, a county executive is elected by the county at large, and serves as the chief administrator. The county executive typically has the power to hire and fire department heads, formulate a budget, set policy direction, and veto legislation passed by the county council or commission. The primary difference between the commission-administrator and council-executive forms of government is the separation of powers principle—the elected county executive is totally independent from the council or commission.

Other County Officials

In addition to a county executive and county commissioners, most counties have four other important elected positions:

1. **County clerk.** The county clerk is responsible for keeping the official records of the county, such as birth and death certificates, mortgages,

deeds, and adoption papers, as well as issuing marriage, automobile, and business licenses. The county clerk also oversees elections, and is usually elected to a four-year term.

2. **Sheriff.** The county sheriff is responsible for providing law enforcement to areas of the county that are not incorporated towns. Most county sheriffs oversee the county prison, and are responsible for enforcing court dates. The county sheriff's authority varies from county to county. Some are elected; others are appointed.

3. **County attorney.** Sometimes called the district attorney, prosecutor, or the state's attorney, the county attorney is the legal advocate for the county in all civil lawsuits brought against it. The county attorney also conducts criminal investigations and prosecutes lawbreakers.

4. **County assessor.** The county assessor has one of the most important jobs of local government: He or she is responsible for determining the value of residences within the county for tax purposes. The county assessor will periodically perform revaluations of all properties throughout the county to ensure that there is a consistent and fair tax basis, but does not assess new taxes.

City Government

When the nation was founded, it was composed of rural communities and dispersed towns. With the exception of New York, Philadelphia, and Boston, very few cities existed. More than 90 percent of the population were farmers. Today, just the opposite is the case. Almost 80 percent of the population live in or near a metropolis (a city with at least 50,000 residents).

Some states define cities as any town or municipality (regardless of size), while other states regard large municipalities as cities, and smaller ones as boroughs, towns, or villages. Unlike counties, which are created by the state, cities are formed when a group of citizens come together and write a charter.

City Charters

For a city to be officially recognized, it must be incorporated; to be incorporated, it must first have a charter. A city charter is similar to a state constitution—it outlines the power and structure of the government, including elections and appointments. There are four types of city charters:

1. **Home rule.** The home rule is the most popular form of incorporation. It allows residents to draft a city charter, which is then put before voters for approval. Voters must also approve any amendments to the city charter. Home rule charters can be granted by the state constitution or the state legislature. When granted by the state constitution, the charter must be in accordance with the provisions of the constitution—when the two are in conflict, the state constitution wins out. When granted by the state legislature, the charter is subject to revocation at any time by the state legislature.

2. **General charter.** Under the general charter, cities are classified according to population size. This system allows for the similar treatment of both large and small cities. The general charter is the second most common form of incorporation after home rule.

3. **Optional charter.** With an optional charter, citizens can vote on one of several charters allowed by the state. It gives residents a direct voice in the incorporation process, and allows them to shape their government. Optional charters are becoming increasingly popular.

4. **Special charter.** The special charter is the oldest form of incorporation still in use, although it has fallen out of favor in recent years. Special charters are extremely time-consuming because their provisions are specific to each new city. For every new city, there must be a new charter. Moreover, any amendments to a special charter must be passed by the state legislature—an extremely cumbersome process. It's doubtful special charters will remain in use much longer.

FACT

More than half the states have provisions for home rule charters, with most coming in the West and Midwest (as well as New York). In 1875, Missouri became the first state to adopt home rule. The home rule movement didn't really catch on until the period following World War II, when a number of states passed constitutional amendments authorizing home rule.

City Government

Once a city is incorporated, it must choose a form of government. Cities have several options to choose from: mayor-council system, council-manager system, and commission system.

Mayor-Council System

Also known as the strong mayor government, the mayor-council system is the most common form of city government. In this system, both the mayor and a unicameral city council are elected. The city council is composed of either districts or at-large members. In most situations, the mayor has the authority to veto legislation passed by the city council, hire and fire city administrators and department heads, and draft a budget.

FACT

New York City is one of the best examples of the strong mayor system. In the aftermath of the September 11 terrorist attacks, New York City Mayor Rudolph Giuliani used the inherent powers of the office to lead New York through a turbulent recovery. The position of New York City mayor has often been described as the second most difficult job in the country.

Council-Manager System

Sometimes referred to as the weak mayor form of government, the council-manager system was a reformist innovation devised during the Progressive Era of the 1910s. Under this model, the city manager is a nonpolitical administrator responsible for running the daily operations of the city. He is usually appointed by the city council and provides little leadership outside of his prescribed duties. Even if the mayor is elected, the mayorship is largely a figurehead title. Consequently, the weak mayor system is popular in smaller cities, but has been rejected by larger cities, which need experienced political leaders and decisive action.

Commission System

This is the least common of the three systems—only about 100 cities nationwide use a commission. Under this scenario, an elected board of commissioners performs the operations of the city and oversees the departments and agencies. A mayor is sometimes chosen from the commissioners, though it's a largely ceremonial position. The commission system has been criticized for its lack of a single authority and reliance upon consensus. Commission systems are popular in reform-minded states. Spokane, Washington; Des Moines, Iowa; and Birmingham, Alabama, are three of the best-known commission cities. In 1960, Galveston, Texas—the birthplace of the commission system—abandoned it for a weak mayor system.

New England Town Government

In Massachusetts, Vermont, Rhode Island, New Hampshire, and Maine, a different system of government is used: the New England town hall. In this region of the country, towns consist of one or more villages and the surrounding countryside.

The New England town meeting is a vestige of the area's colonial roots. It's a form of direct democracy in which all the citizens participate equally in decision-making and governance. Essentially, an annual town meeting is held, usually sometime in March. At this meeting, the voters decide on a budget, taxes, school expenditures, and other annual matters. They also elect a school board, tax collector, and road commissions, as well as a five-person "board of advisors" that manages the town on a day-to-day basis.

In some of the larger towns, direct democracy of this nature is too unwieldy and difficult. In such cases, the townspeople elect delegates to represent them at the town meeting. Increasingly, these towns are beginning to adopt weak mayor or modified council-manager plans in order to keep up with population growth and the growing complexity of governance.

Special Districts

Government entities known as special districts carry out some municipal and county government functions. Special districts are established by state law, and are typically governed by elected boards with the help of professional staff. Special districts are single-purpose governments, meaning that their sole function is to perform one task, such as fire prevention, sewage treatment, rural irrigation, or pest control. The distinguishing characteristic of a special district is its power to impose taxes and borrow money to finance its services, as well as spend federal funds. The property tax is the most common type of levy for special districts. It is believed that California employs the most special districts, estimated to be in the tens of thousands.

School Districts

By far the most common type of special district is the school district. In 1812, New York City created the first school district, to determine where students should attend school. At one point in time, there were more than 100,000 school districts in the United States. After several decades of consolidation, that number has been reduced to about 15,000.

In 1647, Massachusetts became the first colony to pass an ordinance (the Old Deluder Satan Act) requiring towns to provide free schooling for children. By the end of the nineteenth century, mandatory education was standard in every state. At that time, school was recessed during the summer months so that children were free to help on the farms. Today, that tradition persists, even though fewer than 1 percent of the population remains in farming.

School districts are particularly common in states where the cities or counties do not administer the school systems (this occurs in about half the states). Although they come in varying sizes, school districts everywhere have one thing in common: They are run by an elected or appointed board. This board appoints a superintendent to administer the school system, and makes broad policy decisions for the district. The board also determines the district's curriculum, creates school boundaries, and makes decisions about building new schools. Board decisions are usually well publicized and highly scrutinized by district residents.

School district elections are some of the most hotly contested political contests at the state and local level. Ambitious public servants frequently use school board positions as entry points into the political system, and many school board members go on to serve in city and state government.

Regional Government

Over the past several decades, the idea of "regional government" has gained popularity in cities and towns across the United States. Regional governments are government entities that extend beyond city or town borders, but are different from county government. For example, the city of Indianapolis formed a regional government when it merged with most of its neighboring suburbs. Both Nashville, Tennessee, and Miami have formed similar regional governments with their neighboring communities.

Regional governments are attractive to city planners and politicians because they allow communities to combine resources and spend tax dollars more efficiently. There are dozens of entities that can be classified as regional governments, though only a few are commonly used:

- **City-county consolidations.** Some cities have merged with the outlying county to form a regional government. New York City and New York County serve as one governmental entity, as do Miami and Dade County, Florida. City-county consolidations are most common in large metropolitan areas.
- **Federations and voluntary associations.** These types of associations are commonly used to coordinate transportation planning in rural areas. For example, four counties in Indiana formed the Northeastern Indiana Regional Coordinating Council to provide transportation planning for the region.
- **Regional councils.** Perhaps the most popular form of regional government is the voluntary regional council. The National Association of Regional Councils estimates that there are more than 450 regional councils in the United States, and defines them as "multipurpose, multi-jurisdictional, public organizations created by local governments to respond to federal and state programs." Regional councils became

a common way for communities to implement Lyndon Johnson's Great Society programs of the mid-1960s. The Upper Minnesota Valley Regional Development Commission defines its mission as "aiding local units of government in obtaining, retaining and sustaining programs necessary for rural survival."

- **City mergers.** It's not unusual for cities to merge with or annex neighboring cities in order to create a more powerful regional authority. In some states, annexation is difficult and acrimonious. In other states, such as Texas, annexation is more common and straight-forward. Several noteworthy cities—San Diego, Tampa, Atlanta, Houston, and Phoenix—have annexed neighboring communities as part of their growth strategy.

- **Sale of services.** Many local governments contract with larger cities (and even counties) to provide basic services of government, such as police, water, sanitation, fire protection, and street maintenance. This type of arrangement is considered a regional government because it involves the shared planning of resources. Many small communities would not be able to develop were it not for this type of regional government.

- **Single-purpose entities.** Perhaps the most well-known single-purpose entity is the Port Authority of New York and New Jersey. Its mission statement is to "identify and meet the critical transportation infrastructure needs of the bi-state region's businesses, residents, and visitors." It was created in 1921 to settle harbor boundary disputes between the two states.

Local Politics

Local government serves as a basic starting point for citizens who want to enter the political process. Some citizens seek local office out of a commitment to public service. Others have a specific agenda in mind, such as rolling back property taxes, changing zoning ordinances, reassessing property values, renovating public landmarks, and so on. And still others use local government as a steppingstone to higher political office. In fact, many local leaders combine all three motives.

Local government provides a good entrance into the political process for several reasons. First, the cost of campaigning is relatively modest compared to higher office; the biggest expenditure is usually printing fliers and running local radio ads. Second, local office is rarely a full-time job, which makes campaigning less rigorous and stressful than it is for higher office. And third, candidates start off with a base of support—friends, neighbors, high-school classmates, and acquaintances. It is difficult to seek higher office without a foundation of support.

QUESTION?

What does the acronym NIMBY stand for?
NIMBY is a common expression in local government politics for "not in my back yard," and usually signifies the resistance of local residents to development—whether it's a road extension, prison, power plant, or shopping mall—in their neighborhood or town. NIMBY advocates have often been successful in banding together to defeat local development.

Some of the nation's highest officeholders began at the local level. Former California governor Pete Wilson went on to serve two terms as mayor of San Diego before he won a U.S. Senate seat in 1982. (Wilson failed in his bid to win the Republican presidential nomination in 1996.) Ohio senator George Voinovich did the opposite of Wilson, opting to run for governor after serving as the mayor of Cleveland. (Voinovich was mentioned as a possible running mate for George W. Bush in 2000.) Former vice president Hubert Humphrey, who in 1968 lost the presidency to Richard Nixon by 1 percentage point of the popular vote, began his political career as the mayor of Minneapolis.

Local government officials can best be described as citizen-politicians—most work full-time jobs during the day, and focus on local government at night and on the weekends. One of the strengths of our system of government is that the process is open to everyone, not just professional politicians and career public servants. The Founding Fathers intended for government to be the province of citizen-legislators, and at the local level this remains the case. Ⓔ

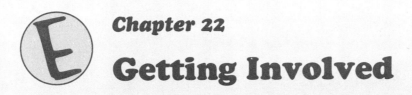

Chapter 22

Getting Involved

As you have learned throughout this book, American government works best when citizens are active participants in the process at every level and branch of government. Although today we have mostly professional legislators at the federal and state level, ample opportunities remain for ordinary citizens to become a part of the process. Voting, volunteering for campaigns, contacting elected officials, organizing at the grassroots level, submitting opinion pieces to newspapers, and running for office are just a few.

Every Vote Counts!

If any lesson was learned from the 2000 presidential election, it is that voting is among the most fundamental and important rights of every American. The next time people are heard saying, "What does it matter? My vote doesn't mean anything," they should be reminded of the Florida recount, which resulted in the presidency being decided by several hundred votes.

FACT

One of the closest Congressional elections took place in 1994, when Democrat Sam Gejdenson defeated Republican Ed Munster by two votes to capture Connecticut's 2nd Congressional District. On recount, the victory margin increased to four votes, and after a second recount it widened to twenty-one. Munster challenged Gejdenson in court, but dropped the suit the following April.

Looking Back

Voting is one of our most basic rights, and one of the easiest to perform. It is the bedrock of our republican democracy. Although today it is taken for granted that everyone has the right to vote, that has not always been the case.

The Founding Fathers created a government whereby the power to govern was established by the ballot box, not heredity—a revolutionary idea. At first, the right to vote extended only to white Protestant males who owned property. As a result, only 6 percent of the population was eligible to vote in the first presidential election.

Throughout the nineteenth century, the right to vote (the franchise, as it's sometimes called) was slowly extended to a wider segment of the population. Religious and property-owning restrictions were the first to be eliminated. By the middle of the nineteenth century, all white males were allowed to vote.

Women remained disenfranchised until the passage of the Nineteenth Amendment in 1920, which declared that voting could not be denied on the basis of gender. For African-Americans, it was a longer and more difficult struggle to obtain full franchisement. Following the Civil War, the Fifteenth Amendment established that the federal and state governments could not discriminate against voters on the basis of race, color, or the previous condition of slavery. In theory, this should have given all African-Americans the right to vote. In reality, however, it did little to bring African-Americans into the electoral process, as southern states used various tactics—literacy tests, poll taxes, and even intimidation—to keep blacks away from the polls. As a consequence, well into the twentieth century only a small percentage of African-Americans living in southern states were able to vote. It wasn't until the Twenty-fourth Amendment of 1964 and the historic Voting Rights Act of 1965 that all of these obstacles were removed.

In 1971, the Twenty-sixth Amendment was passed, which reduced the voting age from twenty-one to eighteen years. The idea behind the amendment was that anyone old enough to bear arms for his country should be eligible to vote. This was one of the few positive repercussions of the Vietnam War.

Declining Voter Turnout

Although the right to vote is our most precious right, it has been exercised with declining frequency. At the presidential level, voter turnout has witnessed a steady erosion over the past seventy years, as fewer Americans have felt connected to the political process. During the 1940s, '50s, and '60s, voter turnout regularly exceeded 60 percent of eligible voters. During the '70s and early '80s, the percentages dipped to the mid-fifties. Today presidential elections receive a 50 percent voter turnout on average. In 1996, voter turnout dropped below 50 percent for the first time in history, no doubt caused in part by the lackluster campaign between President Clinton and Senator Bob Dole.

Voter turnout during "off-year" (or nonpresidential) elections consistently averages approximately 35 percent of eligible voters, meaning that the fate of Congress is determined by only a third of the country. During primary elections, the number is even lower—in most cases, fewer than 10 percent of the eligible voters actually cast a ballot. This small band of primary voters tend to be fierce partisans and ideologically driven.

How to Vote

Although voting is a fundamental right, it is not automatic. There are still certain conditions, such as being an American citizen. Persons born in the United States are automatically given American citizenship. Persons born outside of the country must take a test in order to become a citizen.

Voter Registration

Voter registration is governed by state boards of election, and is different in every state. In every state except North Dakota, citizens must register to vote before they can cast a ballot. In most states, registration must take place at least thirty days prior to the election. In some states, such as Wisconsin, registration can take place on Election Day.

Registering to vote is easy. With the passage of the 1993 National Voter Registration Act (or Motor Voter bill), citizens are given the opportunity to register to vote as they apply for their driver's license. This has increased voter registration, particularly among young Americans. Most states' registration process requires the soon-to-be voter to select a political party (or remain independent) and provide a home address. Citizens also can register to vote at the state board of elections, post office, and at other state agencies. Registered voters are required to submit a change of address for moves within state, and re-register for moves outside of state.

FACT

In 1992, an organization called Rock the Vote was formed with the goal of increasing registration and turnout among young Americans. Over the years, Rock the Vote has partnered with popular celebrity icons, including Madonna and Kid Rock, to get the message out. In a humorous twist, it was revealed that Lenny Kravitz, one of Rock the Vote's spokespersons during the 2000 election, hadn't voted in nearly a decade.

Casting a Ballot

Elections are governed and run by state government. Every state has its own rules for carrying out the mechanics of voting. Most states use schools, firehouses, churches, and community centers as polling places. Registered voters are required to go to their assigned polling place, where they must show proper identification before casting a ballot. Some states have rules prohibiting candidates and their volunteers from distributing campaign literature within a certain distance of the polling places, while other states have no such restrictions.

The state of Oregon is unique when it comes to voting. In 1995, it adopted Voting by Mail (VBM) for statewide primary and general elections. Voters in Oregon have the option of either voting by mail or voting at polling places on Election Day. Since adopting VBM, voter turnout in Oregon has increased. A majority of Oregon residents now use VBM.

The states also determine the hours of operation on Election Day. New York offers its voters the most time to cast their votes, opening the polls at 6 A.M. and closing at 9 P.M. Most states open the polls at 8 A.M. and close at 7 P.M. New Hampshire opens the latest at 11 A.M., while Indiana, Hawaii, and Kentucky close the earliest at 6 P.M.

As we learned during the disputed Florida election in 2000, ballots come in many shapes, sizes, configurations, and levels of complexity. Some localities (most notably, Palm Beach, Florida) use the "butterfly" ballot; others use lever-booths; still others employ simple pen and paper. As a result of the 2000 election, there has been a push by both the federal and state governments to modernize and standardize the equipment and procedures for casting ballots. Many states and localities are spending millions of dollars on new machinery so as to minimize lost and defective ballots, confusion, and erroneous tabulations. Not surprisingly, the state that has spent the most on new voting machinery is Florida.

Absentee Voting

Every state allows for voters to cast their ballots from outside of the state. This is known as absentee voting, and in close elections it can sometimes make the difference between victory and defeat. In 1994, California Congresswoman Jane Harman trailed her opponent by several hundred votes on Election Day, but pulled ahead after the absentee ballots were tallied.

Military personnel, college students, and business travelers most commonly use absentee ballots. The ballots can be obtained at the local board of elections. Most states require that absentee ballots be postmarked no later than Election Day. During the disputed Florida election of 2000, absentee voting by overseas military personnel played a decisive role in providing candidate George W. Bush his razor-thin margin of victory over Vice President Gore.

Contacting Elected Officials

One of the most effective ways of voicing an opinion and making a difference is also one of the most overlooked: contacting your elected officials. Part of the role of elected officials at the national, state, and local levels is to listen to their constituents.

Members of Congress can be contacted one of several ways. Every House member has a district office where he or she has a full-time staff. Representatives from large geographic districts sometimes have multiple offices in distant corners of the district. Most members of Congress spend one or two days a week in the district, and often hold regularly scheduled "office hours" during which they meet with constituents. Speaking to your representative can be as easy as scheduling an office-hours visit! There is no better way to make your opinion known than speaking directly to your representative in Congress.

When Congress is in session, representatives and senators can be contacted at their Capitol Hill offices. Face-to-face appointments are sometimes more difficult to arrange in Washington because members keep a busy schedule, but staff is readily available to meet and discuss issues.

Citizens also can reach out to their representatives through mail and e-mail. Most elected officials are highly responsive to written correspondence, and almost always respond in kind (or at least their staffs do). Throughout history, letter-writing campaigns have been an effective tool in framing debate, shaping legislation, and changing votes on Capitol Hill. In recent years, e-mail has become a popular tool for contacting elected officials. Every member of Congress has an e-mail address. For a complete listing of these addresses, go to ✍ *www.congress.org*. Most members give e-mail correspondence the same time and consideration as traditional mail.

In most states, contacting state, county, and local officials requires only a phone call. For issues of great importance, contacting a local official is by far the most effective means of voicing an opinion and ultimately influencing public policy. Local representatives are typically amenable and highly responsive to input from their constituents, and usually treat these dialogues seriously. Too often, citizens with unique insights about pressing local issues shy away from sharing their observations with local officials because they lack either the time or disposition to speak up. We should all be reminded that local officials serve the public, and that a healthy exchange of ideas is critical to good government.

Volunteering on a Political Campaign

Volunteering on a political campaign is a great way to get involved at any level. Candidates for local, state, and national office are always in need of volunteers. Campaigns rarely turn volunteers away!

If you feel strongly about a particular issue or candidate and would like to advance the cause, contact the campaign and inquire about volunteering. Most campaigns have many volunteer positions, including the following:

- Distributing lawn signs to local residents
- Stuffing envelopes and distributing campaign literature
- Participating in phone fundraising drives
- Doing opposition research
- Calling registered voters on Election Day
- Driving voters to the poll booths on Election Day

- Coordinating fundraisers and campaign appearances
- Researching issues and clipping newspaper articles
- Attending debates and other candidate forums
- Campaigning with the candidate
- Helping with office work at headquarters
- Posting campaign fliers

Contributing money to a political candidate is another way of getting involved, but without a large time commitment. Some citizens hold fundraising events for candidates in their homes, and invite friends to contribute to the campaign. Candidates are particularly appreciative of fundraisers, and typically seek their counsel and advice on issues.

Volunteering on a political campaign is particularly valuable for citizens who have political ambitions of their own, because it illustrates the time commitment, dedication, and hard work required to run for office. Many candidates get their start in politics by volunteering on a campaign.

FACT

While the young Bill Clinton was attending law school at Yale University in Connecticut, he volunteered on Joe Lieberman's first campaign for state senate. Two years later, Clinton spent the summer with future wife Hillary working on Senator George McGovern's presidential campaign in the state of Texas. Only four years after that experience, Clinton was elected attorney general of Arkansas.

Joining an Interest Group

Interest groups aren't just for professional lobbyists and industry associations. Every year, millions of ordinary citizens join grassroots interest groups to advance a particular cause. Some are in response to national issues, others to state issues, and still others to local issues. Many local grassroots organizations form in response to NIMBY (not in my back yard) issues. For citizens who feel strongly about development projects in their town or municipality, grassroots organizing is sometimes the most effective way to make a difference.

Grassroots organizing at the local level usually begins with an initial meeting among core supporters, where an objective and strategy is agreed upon. From there, members typically expand the organization by phoning (and now e-mailing) like-minded individuals and educating them on the issue. With technologies such as cell phones, e-mail, instant messaging, and the Internet, the process of organizing an interest group is much simpler and faster than it was in years past.

Once organized, grassroots organizations can be highly effective in mobilizing citizens to contact federal, state, and local officials in order to raise concerns about the issue at hand. Well-organized and motivated grassroots groups will often stage events and rallies, hold fundraisers, run advertising, write op-ed opinion pieces, contact local officials, create newsletters, and reach out to citizens door-to-door to make their viewpoint known.

The biggest challenge facing most grassroots organizations is raising enough money to sustain the cause for a long period of time. Many local organizations use raffles, picnics, barbeques, "bakeoffs," and direct mail to raise funds. Some organizations benefit from the generosity of a wealthy benefactor committed to the cause.

Running for Office

The ultimate act of getting involved in the political process is running for office. Many a political career began as the simple exercise of responding to a local issue and trying to make a difference. As you learned in the previous chapter, the vast majority of elected positions are at the local and county level.

Deciding to Run

Running for elected office is a big step, and there are numerous factors to consider when contemplating such an undertaking. Would-be candidates typically address five questions before making a decision:

1. What do I hope to accomplish by running for office?
2. Can I make the time commitment necessary to be an effective candidate and official?
3. Which office should I seek—which would help me achieve my goals?
4. Can I articulate my point of view on the issues?
5. Does my family support this decision?

Because most elected offices are part-time positions, time commitment is usually the biggest consideration. Candidates need to juggle career, family, and political ambitions in such a way that none are neglected. Most citizens cite lack of time as the primary reason they don't seek local office.

Establishing a point of view on all the relevant issues is another important factor that weighs on a decision to run for office. Candidates must have the temperament, inclination, and ability to understand the issues and offer thoughts and solutions in order to mount an effective candidacy. Unfortunately, this consideration may be overlooked or ignored.

How to Get Started

Once a decision to pursue a candidacy has been made, the most difficult step is getting started. For novice candidates with no prior political experience, this means getting organized.

Family and close friends are usually at the center of any political campaign. It's extremely difficult to mount an effective political campaign without this solid nucleus of support. Once they're on board, the next group to reach out to are acquaintances and colleagues—not only of the candidate, but of family and friends as well. In small-town and municipal elections, the process of reaching out to friends, family, acquaintances, and colleagues can cover a good portion of the electorate. In larger districts, this circle of supporters must be expanded to the general electorate, which is where the real campaigning takes place.

Most candidates for local office do not have the resources to hire political consultants or strategists, so volunteers must do the organizing and campaigning. With limited resources for television, radio, or newspaper advertising, there are several ways for candidates to communicate their message to voters:

- **Door-to-door campaigning.** The most effective form of "retail" politics is still door-to-door campaigning. It requires no money, and allows the candidate to make a personal connection with the voters. During his first campaign for Congress, former House Majority Leader Dick Gephardt canvassed tens of thousands of homes in his St. Louis district to introduce himself to voters. The personal touch made all the difference, and allowed him to pull off a narrow upset.

- **Phone banking.** The next best thing to meeting voters in person is talking to them on the phone. Like door-to-door communicating, phone banking can be inexpensive (for local calls), and provides a personal touch. Some candidates prefer phone banking over walking the district because it allows them to reach a greater number of voters in a shorter period of time.

- **Lawn signs, posters, and fliers.** During election season, it is not unusual to see posters, lawn signs, and fliers distributed throughout the neighborhood on billboards, telephone poles, lampposts, fences, and in store windows. The strategy here is not so much to communicate a specific message (since there is limited space), but rather to create "name recognition." This strategy requires some resources, but it's not nearly as expensive as television or radio advertising.

- **Speaking and meeting opportunities.** A critical component of any political campaign is speaking before large groups of voters. This includes walking in parades, speaking before community organizations (like the American Legion, Chamber of Commerce, etc.), attending local sporting events, participating in candidate debates, and so on. Candidates must be comfortable speaking before large audiences in order to successfully communicate their ideas.

- **Free media.** As we discussed in Chapter 18, "earning" free media is one of the most important tasks of any political candidate. Attracting local press coverage requires candidates to be accessible to reporters, able to voice strong (and quotable) opinions on the issues, and creative in staging campaign events. Media coverage is particularly important in campaigns that cover a wide geographic area.

- **Word-of-mouth campaigning.** Just as good movies receive "word-of-mouth" endorsements from one moviegoer to the next, so too do political candidates. A strong performance by the candidate at a speaking engagement, campaign stop, or debate can oftentimes encourage citizens to "pass the word" to their friends and acquaintances. This type of campaigning amounts to the "buzz" that surrounds successful campaigns.

Most candidates use a combination of these strategies to run an effective campaign. Of course, even the best-laid campaigns can go awry, as skill and persistence sometimes give way to luck and chance.

Appendix A

Declaration of Independence and the Constitution of the United States

The Declaration of Independence
In Congress, July 4, 1776

THE UNANIMOUS DECLARATION of the thirteen united States of America, When in the Course of human events, it becomes necessary for one people to dissolve the political bands which have connected them with another, and to assume among the powers of the earth, the separate and equal station to which the Laws of Nature and of Nature's God entitle them, a decent respect to the opinions of mankind requires that they should declare the causes which impel them to the separation.

We hold these truths to be self-evident, that all men are created equal, that they are endowed by their Creator with certain unalienable Rights, that among these are Life, Liberty and the pursuit of Happiness. —That to secure these rights, Governments are instituted among Men, deriving their just powers from the consent of the governed, —That whenever any Form of Government becomes destructive of these ends, it is the Right of the People to alter or to abolish it, and to institute new Government, laying its foundation on such principles and organizing its powers in such form, as to them shall seem most likely to effect their Safety and Happiness. Prudence, indeed, will dictate that Governments long established should not be changed for light and transient causes; and accordingly all experience hath shewn, that mankind are more disposed to suffer, while evils are sufferable, than to right themselves by abolishing the forms to which they are accustomed. But when a long train of abuses and usurpations, pursuing invariably the same Object evinces a design to reduce them under absolute Despotism, it is their right, it is their duty, to throw off such Government, and to provide new Guards for their future security. —Such has been the patient sufferance of these Colonies; and such is now the necessity which constrains them to alter their former Systems of Government. The history of the present King of Great Britain is a history of repeated injuries and usurpations, all having in direct object the establishment of an absolute Tyranny over these States. To prove this, let Facts be submitted to a candid world.

He has refused his Assent to Laws, the most wholesome and necessary for the public good.

He has forbidden his Governors to pass Laws of immediate and pressing importance, unless suspended in their operation till his Assent should be obtained; and when so suspended, he has utterly neglected to attend to them.

He has refused to pass other Laws for the accommodation of large districts of people, unless those people would relinquish the right of Representation in the Legislature, a right inestimable to them and formidable to tyrants only.

He has called together legislative bodies at places unusual, uncomfortable, and distant from the depository of their public Records, for the sole purpose of fatiguing them into compliance with his measures.

He has dissolved Representative Houses repeatedly, for opposing with manly firmness his invasions on the rights of the people.

He has refused for a long time, after such dissolutions, to cause others to be elected; whereby the Legislative powers, incapable of Annihilation, have returned to the People at large for their exercise; the State remaining in the mean time exposed to all the dangers of invasion from without, and convulsions within.

He has endeavoured to prevent the population of these States; for that purpose obstructing the Laws for Naturalization of Foreigners; refusing to pass others to encourage their migrations hither, and raising the conditions of new Appropriations of Lands.

He has obstructed the Administration of Justice, by refusing his Assent to Laws for establishing Judiciary powers.

He has made Judges dependent on his Will alone, for the tenure of their offices, and the amount and payment of their salaries.

He has erected a multitude of New Offices, and sent hither swarms of Officers to harass our people, and eat out their substance.

He has kept among us, in times of peace, Standing Armies without the Consent of our legislatures.

He has affected to render the Military independent of and superior to the Civil power.

He has combined with others to subject us to a jurisdiction foreign to our constitution, and unacknowledged by our laws; giving his Assent to their Acts of pretended Legislation:

For quartering large bodies of armed troops among us:

For protecting them, by a mock Trial, from punishment for any Murders which they should commit on the Inhabitants of these States:

For cutting off our Trade with all parts of the world:

For imposing Taxes on us without our Consent:

For depriving us in many cases, of the benefits of Trial by Jury:

For transporting us beyond Seas to be tried for pretended offences:

For abolishing the free System of English Laws in a neighbouring Province, establishing therein an Arbitrary government, and enlarging its Boundaries so as to render it at once an example and fit instrument for introducing the same absolute rule into these Colonies:

For taking away our Charters, abolishing our most valuable Laws, and altering fundamentally the Forms of our Governments:

For suspending our own Legislatures, and declaring themselves invested with power to legislate for us in all cases whatsoever.

He has abdicated Government here, by declaring us out of his Protection and waging War against us.

He has plundered our seas, ravaged our Coasts, burnt our towns, and destroyed the lives of our people.

He is at this time transporting large Armies of foreign Mercenaries to compleat the works of death, desolation and tyranny, already begun with circumstances of Cruelty & perfidy scarcely paralleled in the most barbarous ages, and totally unworthy the Head of a civilized nation.

He has constrained our fellow Citizens taken Captive on the high Seas to bear Arms against their Country, to become the executioners of their friends and Brethren, or to fall themselves by their Hands.

He has excited domestic insurrections amongst us, and has endeavoured to bring on the inhabitants of our frontiers, the merciless Indian Savages, whose known rule of warfare, is an undistinguished destruction of all ages, sexes and conditions.

In every stage of these Oppressions We have Petitioned for Redress in the most humble terms: Our repeated Petitions have been answered only by repeated injury. A Prince whose character is thus marked by every act which may define a Tyrant, is unfit to be the ruler of a free people.

Nor have We been wanting in attentions to our British brethren. We have warned them from time to time of attempts by their legislature to extend an unwarrantable jurisdiction over us. We have reminded them of the circumstances of our emigration and settlement here. We have appealed to their native justice and magnanimity, and we have conjured them by the ties of our common kindred to disavow these usurpations, which, would inevitably interrupt our connections and correspondence. They too have been deaf to the voice of justice and of consanguinity. We must, therefore, acquiesce in the necessity, which denounces our Separation, and hold them, as we hold the rest of mankind, Enemies in War, in Peace Friends.

We, therefore, the Representatives of the united States of America, in General Congress, Assembled, appealing to the Supreme Judge of the world for the rectitude of our intentions, do, in the Name, and by Authority of the good People of these Colonies, solemnly publish and declare, That these United Colonies are, and of Right ought to be Free and Independent States, that they are Absolved from all Allegiance to the British Crown, and that all political connection between them and the State of Great Britain, is and ought to be totally dissolved; and that as Free and Independent States, they have full Power to levy War, conclude Peace, contract Alliances, establish Commerce, and to do all other Acts and Things which Independent

States may of right do. And for the support of this Declaration, with a firm reliance on the protection of divine Providence, we mutually pledge to each other our Lives, our Fortunes and our sacred Honor.

John Hancock

New Hampshire:
Josiah Bartlett, William Whipple, Matthew Thornton

Massachusetts:
John Hancock, Samuel Adams, John Adams, Robert Treat Paine, Elbridge Gerry

Rhode Island:
Stephen Hopkins, William Ellery

Connecticut:
Roger Sherman, Samuel Huntington, William Williams, Oliver Wolcott

New York:
William Floyd, Philip Livingston, Francis Lewis, Lewis Morris

New Jersey:
Richard Stockton, John Witherspoon, Francis Hopkinson, John Hart, Abraham Clark

Pennsylvania:
Robert Morris, Benjamin Rush, Benjamin Franklin, John Morton,

Pennsylvania (cont.):
George Clymer, James Smith, George Taylor, James Wilson, George Ross

Delaware:
Caesar Rodney, George Read, Thomas McKean

Maryland:
Samuel Chase, William Paca, Thomas Stone, Charles Carroll of Carrollton

Virginia:
George Wythe, Richard Henry Lee, Thomas Jefferson, Benjamin Harrison, Thomas Nelson, Jr., Francis Lightfoot Lee, Carter Braxton

North Carolina:
William Hooper, Joseph Hewes, John Penn

South Carolina:
Edward Rutledge, Thomas Heyward, Jr., Thomas Lynch, Jr., Arthur Middleton

Georgia:
Button Gwinnett, Lyman Hall, George Walton

The Constitution of the United States

WE THE PEOPLE OF THE UNITED STATES, in Order to form a more perfect Union, establish Justice, insure domestic Tranquility, provide for the common defence, promote the general Welfare, and secure the Blessings of Liberty to ourselves and our Posterity, do ordain and establish this Constitution for the United States of America.

Article I.

Section 1.

All legislative Powers herein granted shall be vested in a Congress of the United States, which shall consist of a Senate and House of Representatives.

Section 2.

Clause 1: The House of Representatives shall be composed of Members chosen every second Year by the People of the several States, and the Electors in each State shall have the Qualifications requisite for Electors of the most numerous Branch of the State Legislature.

Clause 2: No Person shall be a Representative who shall not have attained to the Age of twenty five Years, and been seven Years a Citizen of the United States, and who shall not, when elected, be an Inhabitant of that State in which he shall be chosen.

Clause 3: Representatives and direct Taxes shall be apportioned among the several States which may be included within this Union, according to their respective Numbers, which shall be determined by adding to the whole Number of free Persons, including those bound to Service for a Term of Years, and excluding Indians not taxed, three fifths of all other Persons. The actual Enumeration shall be made within three Years after the first Meeting of the Congress of the United States, and within every subsequent Term of ten Years, in such Manner as they shall by Law direct. The Number of Representatives shall not exceed one for every thirty Thousand, but each State shall have at Least one Representative; and until such enumeration shall be made, the State of New Hampshire shall be entitled to chuse three, Massachusetts eight, Rhode-Island and Providence Plantations one, Connecticut five, New-York six, New Jersey four, Pennsylvania eight, Delaware one, Maryland six, Virginia ten, North Carolina five, South Carolina five, and Georgia three.

Clause 4: When vacancies happen in the Representation from any State, the Executive Authority thereof shall issue Writs of Election to fill such Vacancies.

Clause 5: The House of Representatives shall chuse their Speaker and other Officers; and shall have the sole Power of Impeachment.

Section 3.

Clause 1: The Senate of the United States shall be composed of two Senators from each State, chosen by the Legislature thereof for six Years; and each Senator shall have one Vote.

Clause 2: Immediately after they shall be assembled in Consequence of the first Election, they shall be divided as equally as may be into three Classes. The Seats of the Senators of the first Class shall be vacated at the Expiration of the second Year, of the second Class at the Expiration of the fourth Year, and of the third Class at the Expiration of the sixth Year, so that one third may be chosen every second Year; and if Vacancies happen by Resignation, or otherwise, during the Recess of the Legislature of any State, the Executive thereof may make temporary Appointments until the next Meeting of the Legislature, which shall then fill such Vacancies.

Clause 3: No Person shall be a Senator who shall not have attained to the Age of thirty Years, and been nine Years a Citizen of the United States, and who shall not, when elected, be an Inhabitant of that State for which he shall be chosen.

Clause 4: The Vice President of the United States shall be President of the Senate, but shall have no Vote, unless they be equally divided.

Clause 5: The Senate shall chuse their other Officers, and also a President pro tempore, in the Absence of the Vice President, or when he shall exercise the Office of President of the United States.

Clause 6: The Senate shall have the sole Power to try all Impeachments. When sitting for that Purpose, they shall be on Oath or Affirmation. When the President of the United States is tried, the Chief Justice shall preside: And no Person shall be convicted without the Concurrence of two thirds of the Members present.

Clause 7: Judgment in Cases of Impeachment shall not extend further than to removal from Office, and disqualification to hold and enjoy any Office of honor, Trust or Profit under the United States: but the Party convicted shall nevertheless be liable and subject to Indictment, Trial, Judgment and Punishment, according to Law.

Section 4.

Clause 1: The Times, Places and Manner of holding Elections for Senators and Representatives, shall be prescribed in each State by the Legislature thereof; but the Congress may at any time by Law make or alter such Regulations, except as to the Places of chusing Senators.

Clause 2: The Congress shall assemble at least once in every Year, and such Meeting shall be on the first Monday in December, unless they shall by Law appoint a different Day.

Section 5.

Clause 1: Each House shall be the Judge of the Elections, Returns and Qualifications of its own Members, and a Majority of each shall constitute a Quorum to do Business; but a smaller Number may adjourn from day to day, and may be authorized to compel the Attendance of absent Members, in such Manner, and under such Penalties as each House may provide.

Clause 2: Each House may determine the Rules of its Proceedings, punish its Members for disorderly Behaviour, and, with the Concurrence of two thirds, expel a Member.

Clause 3: Each House shall keep a Journal of its Proceedings, and from time to time publish the same, excepting such Parts as may in their Judgment require Secrecy; and the Yeas and Nays of the Members of either House on any question shall, at the Desire of one fifth of those Present, be entered on the Journal.

Clause 4: Neither House, during the Session of Congress, shall, without the Consent of the other, adjourn for more than three days, nor to any other Place than that in which the two Houses shall be sitting.

Section 6.

Clause 1: The Senators and Representatives shall receive a Compensation for their Services, to be ascertained by Law, and paid out of the Treasury of the United States. They shall in all Cases, except Treason, Felony and Breach of the Peace, be privileged from Arrest during their Attendance at the Session of their respective Houses, and in going to and returning from the same; and for any Speech or Debate in either House, they shall not be questioned in any other Place.

Clause 2: No Senator or Representative shall, during the Time for which he was elected, be appointed to any civil Office under the Authority of the United States, which shall have been created, or the Emoluments whereof shall have been encreased during such time; and no Person holding any Office under the United States, shall be a Member of either House during his Continuance in Office.

Section 7.

Clause 1: All Bills for raising Revenue shall originate in the House of Representatives; but the Senate may propose or concur with Amendments as on other Bills.

Clause 2: Every Bill which shall have passed the House of Representatives and the Senate, shall, before it become a Law, be presented to the President of the United States: If he approve he shall sign it, but if not he shall return it, with his Objections to that House in which it shall have originated, who shall enter the Objections at large on their Journal, and proceed to reconsider it. If after such Reconsideration two thirds of that House shall agree to pass the Bill, it shall be sent, together with the Objections, to the other House, by which it shall likewise be reconsidered, and if approved by two thirds of that House, it shall become a Law. But in all such Cases the Votes of both Houses shall be determined by yeas and Nays, and the Names of the Persons voting for and against the Bill shall be entered on the Journal of each House respectively. If any Bill shall not be returned by the President within ten Days (Sundays excepted) after it shall have been presented to him, the Same shall be a Law, in like Manner as if he had signed it, unless the Congress by their

Adjournment prevent its Return, in which Case it shall not be a Law.

Clause 3: Every Order, Resolution, or Vote to which the Concurrence of the Senate and House of Representatives may be necessary (except on a question of Adjournment) shall be presented to the President of the United States; and before the Same shall take Effect, shall be approved by him, or being disapproved by him, shall be repassed by two thirds of the Senate and House of Representatives, according to the Rules and Limitations prescribed in the Case of a Bill.

Section 8.

Clause 1: The Congress shall have Power To lay and collect Taxes, Duties, Imposts and Excises, to pay the Debts and provide for the common Defence and general Welfare of the United States; but all Duties, Imposts and Excises shall be uniform throughout the United States;

Clause 2: To borrow Money on the credit of the United States;

Clause 3: To regulate Commerce with foreign Nations, and among the several States, and with the Indian Tribes;

Clause 4: To establish an uniform Rule of Naturalization, and uniform Laws on the subject of Bankruptcies throughout the United States;

Clause 5: To coin Money, regulate the Value thereof, and of foreign Coin, and fix the Standard of Weights and Measures;

Clause 6: To provide for the Punishment of counterfeiting the Securities and current Coin of the United States;

Clause 7: To establish Post Offices and post Roads;

Clause 8: To promote the Progress of Science and useful Arts, by securing for limited Times to Authors and Inventors the exclusive Right to their respective Writings and Discoveries;

Clause 9: To constitute Tribunals inferior to the supreme Court;

Clause 10: To define and punish Piracies and Felonies committed on the high Seas, and Offences against the Law of Nations;

Clause 11: To declare War, grant Letters of Marque and Reprisal, and make Rules concerning Captures on Land and Water;

Clause 12: To raise and support Armies, but no Appropriation of Money to that Use shall be for a longer Term than two Years;

Clause 13: To provide and maintain a Navy;

Clause 14: To make Rules for the Government and Regulation of the land and naval Forces;

Clause 15: To provide for calling forth the Militia to execute the Laws of the Union, suppress Insurrections and repel Invasions;

Clause 16: To provide for organizing, arming, and disciplining, the Militia, and for governing such Part of them as may be employed in the Service of the United States, reserving to the States respectively, the Appointment of the Officers, and the Authority of training the Militia according to the discipline prescribed by Congress;

Clause 17: To exercise exclusive Legislation in all Cases whatsoever, over such District (not exceeding ten Miles square) as may, by Cession of particular States, and the Acceptance of

Congress, become the Seat of the Government of the United States, and to exercise like Authority over all Places purchased by the Consent of the Legislature of the State in which the Same shall be, for the Erection of Forts, Magazines, Arsenals, dock-Yards, and other needful Buildings;—And

Clause 18: To make all Laws which shall be necessary and proper for carrying into Execution the foregoing Powers, and all other Powers vested by this Constitution in the Government of the United States, or in any Department or Officer thereof.

Section 9.

Clause 1: The Migration or Importation of such Persons as any of the States now existing shall think proper to admit, shall not be prohibited by the Congress prior to the Year one thousand eight hundred and eight, but a Tax or duty may be imposed on such Importation, not exceeding ten dollars for each Person.

Clause 2: The Privilege of the Writ of Habeas Corpus shall not be suspended, unless when in Cases of Rebellion or Invasion the public Safety may require it.

Clause 3: No Bill of Attainder or ex post facto Law shall be passed.

Clause 4: No Capitation, or other direct, Tax shall be laid, unless in Proportion to the Census or enumeration herein before directed to be taken.

Clause 5: No Tax or Duty shall be laid on Articles exported from any State.

Clause 6: No Preference shall be given by any Regulation of Commerce or Revenue to the Ports of one State over those of another: nor shall Vessels bound to, or from, one State, be obliged to enter, clear, or pay Duties in another.

Clause 7: No Money shall be drawn from the Treasury, but in Consequence of Appropriations made by Law; and a regular Statement and Account of the Receipts and Expenditures of all public Money shall be published from time to time.

Clause 8: No Title of Nobility shall be granted by the United States: And no Person holding any Office of Profit or Trust under them, shall, without the Consent of the Congress, accept of any present, Emolument, Office, or Title, of any kind whatever, from any King, Prince, or foreign State.

Section 10.

Clause 1: No State shall enter into any Treaty, Alliance, or Confederation; grant Letters of Marque and Reprisal; coin Money; emit Bills of Credit; make any Thing but gold and silver Coin a Tender in Payment of Debts; pass any Bill of Attainder, ex post facto Law, or Law impairing the Obligation of Contracts, or grant any Title of Nobility.

Clause 2: No State shall, without the Consent of the Congress, lay any Imposts or Duties on Imports or Exports, except what may be absolutely necessary for executing its inspection Laws: and the net Produce of all Duties and Imposts, laid by any State on Imports or Exports, shall be for the Use of the Treasury of the United States; and all such Laws shall be subject to the Revision and Control of the Congress.

Clause 3: No State shall, without the Consent of Congress, lay any Duty of Tonnage, keep Troops, or Ships of War in time of Peace, enter into any Agreement or Compact with another State, or with a foreign Power, or engage in War, unless actually invaded, or in such imminent Danger as will not admit of delay.

Article II.

Section 1.

Clause 1: The executive Power shall be vested in a President of the United States of America. He shall hold his Office during the Term of four Years, and, together with the Vice President, chosen for the same Term, be elected, as follows:

Clause 2: Each State shall appoint, in such Manner as the Legislature thereof may direct, a Number of Electors, equal to the whole Number of Senators and Representatives to which the State may be entitled in the Congress: but no Senator or Representative, or Person holding an Office of Trust or Profit under the United States, shall be appointed an Elector.

Clause 3: The Electors shall meet in their respective States, and vote by Ballot for two Persons, of whom one at least shall not be an Inhabitant of the same State with themselves. And they shall make a List of all the Persons voted for, and of the Number of Votes for each; which List they shall sign and certify, and transmit sealed to the Seat of the Government of the United States, directed to the President of the Senate. The President of the Senate shall, in the Presence of the Senate and House of Representatives, open all the Certificates, and the Votes shall then be counted. The Person having the greatest Number of Votes shall be the President, if such Number be a Majority of the whole Number of Electors appointed; and if there be more than one who have such Majority, and have an equal Number of Votes, then the House of Representatives shall immediately chuse by Ballot one of them for President; and if no Person have a Majority, then from the five highest on the List the said House shall in like Manner chuse the President. But in chusing the President, the Votes shall be taken by States, the Representation from each State having one Vote; A quorum for this Purpose shall consist of a Member or Members from two thirds of the States, and a Majority of all the States shall be necessary to a Choice. In every Case, after the Choice of the President, the Person having the greatest Number of Votes of the Electors shall be the Vice President. But if there should remain two or more who have equal Votes, the Senate shall chuse from them by Ballot the Vice President.

Clause 4: The Congress may determine the Time of chusing the Electors, and the Day on which they shall give their Votes; which Day shall be the same throughout the United States.

Clause 5: No Person except a natural born Citizen, or a Citizen of the United States, at the time of the Adoption of this Constitution, shall be eligible to the Office of President; neither shall any Person be eligible to that Office who shall not have attained to the Age of thirty five Years, and been fourteen Years a Resident within the United States.

Clause 6: In Case of the Removal of the President from Office, or of his Death, Resignation, or Inability to discharge the Powers and Duties of the said Office, the Same shall devolve on the Vice President, and the Congress may by Law provide for the Case of Removal, Death, Resignation or Inability, both of the President and Vice President, declaring what Officer shall then act as President, and such Officer shall act accordingly, until the Disability be removed, or a President shall be elected.

Clause 7: The President shall, at stated Times, receive for his Services, a Compensation, which shall neither be increased nor diminished during the Period for which he shall have been elected, and he shall not receive within that Period any other Emolument from the United States, or any of them.

Clause 8: Before he enter on the Execution of his Office, he shall take the following Oath or Affirmation:—"I do solemnly swear (or affirm) that I will faithfully execute the Office of President of the United States, and will to the best of my Ability, preserve, protect and defend the Constitution of the United States."

Section 2.
Clause 1: The President shall be Commander in Chief of the Army and Navy of the United States, and of the Militia of the several States, when called into the actual Service of the United States; he may require the Opinion, in writing, of the principal Officer in each of the executive Departments, upon any Subject relating to the Duties of their respective Offices, and he shall have Power to grant Reprieves and Pardons for Offences against the United States, except in Cases of Impeachment.

Clause 2: He shall have Power, by and with the Advice and Consent of the Senate, to make Treaties, provided two thirds of the Senators present concur; and he shall nominate, and by and with the Advice and Consent of the Senate, shall appoint Ambassadors, other public Ministers and Consuls, Judges of the supreme Court, and all other Officers of the United States, whose Appointments are not herein otherwise provided for, and which shall be established by Law: but the Congress may by Law vest the Appointment of such inferior Officers, as they think proper, in the President alone, in the Courts of Law, or in the Heads of Departments.

Clause 3: The President shall have Power to fill up all Vacancies that may happen during the Recess of the Senate, by granting Commissions which shall expire at the End of their next Session.

Section 3.
He shall from time to time give to the Congress Information of the State of the Union, and recommend to their Consideration such Measures as he shall judge necessary and expedient; he may, on extraordinary Occasions, convene both Houses, or either of them, and in Case of Disagreement between them, with Respect to the Time of Adjournment, he may adjourn them to such Time as

he shall think proper; he shall receive Ambassadors and other public Ministers; he shall take Care that the Laws be faithfully executed, and shall Commission all the Officers of the United States.

Section 4.

The President, Vice President and all civil Officers of the United States, shall be removed from Office on Impeachment for, and Conviction of, Treason, Bribery, or other high Crimes and Misdemeanors.

Article III.

Section 1.

The judicial Power of the United States, shall be vested in one supreme Court, and in such inferior Courts as the Congress may from time to time ordain and establish. The Judges, both of the supreme and inferior Courts, shall hold their Offices during good Behaviour, and shall, at stated Times, receive for their Services a Compensation, which shall not be diminished during their Continuance in Office.

Section 2.

Clause 1: The judicial Power shall extend to all Cases, in Law and Equity, arising under this Constitution, the Laws of the United States, and Treaties made, or which shall be made, under their Authority;—to all Cases affecting Ambassadors, other public Ministers and Consuls;—to all Cases of admiralty and maritime Jurisdiction;—to Controversies to which the United States shall be a Party;—to Controversies between two or more States;—

between a State and Citizens of another State;—between Citizens of different States;—between Citizens of the same State claiming Lands under Grants of different States, and between a State, or the Citizens thereof, and foreign States, Citizens or Subjects.

Clause 2: In all Cases affecting Ambassadors, other public Ministers and Consuls, and those in which a State shall be Party, the supreme Court shall have original Jurisdiction. In all the other Cases before mentioned, the supreme Court shall have appellate Jurisdiction, both as to Law and Fact, with such Exceptions, and under such Regulations as the Congress shall make.

Clause 3: The Trial of all Crimes, except in Cases of Impeachment, shall be by Jury; and such Trial shall be held in the State where the said Crimes shall have been committed; but when not committed within any State, the Trial shall be at such Place or Places as the Congress may by Law have directed.

Section 3.

Clause 1: Treason against the United States, shall consist only in levying War against them, or in adhering to their Enemies, giving them Aid and Comfort. No Person shall be convicted of Treason unless on the Testimony of two Witnesses to the same overt Act, or on Confession in open Court.

Clause 2: The Congress shall have Power to declare the Punishment of Treason, but no Attainder of Treason shall work Corruption of Blood, or Forfeiture except during the Life of the Person attainted.

Article IV.

Section 1.

Full Faith and Credit shall be given in each State to the public Acts, Records, and judicial Proceedings of every other State. And the Congress may by general Laws prescribe the Manner in which such Acts, Records and Proceedings shall be proved, and the Effect thereof.

Section 2.

Clause 1: The Citizens of each State shall be entitled to all Privileges and Immunities of Citizens in the several States.

Clause 2: A Person charged in any State with Treason, Felony, or other Crime, who shall flee from Justice, and be found in another State, shall on Demand of the executive Authority of the State from which he fled, be delivered up, to be removed to the State having Jurisdiction of the Crime.

Clause 3: No Person held to Service or Labour in one State, under the Laws thereof, escaping into another, shall, in Consequence of any Law or Regulation therein, be discharged from such Service or Labour, but shall be delivered up on Claim of the Party to whom such Service or Labour may be due.

Section 3.

Clause 1: New States may be admitted by the Congress into this Union; but no new State shall be formed or erected within the Jurisdiction of any other State; nor any State be formed by the Junction of two or more States, or Parts of States, without the Consent of the Legislatures of the States concerned as well as of the Congress.

Clause 2: The Congress shall have Power to dispose of and make all needful Rules and Regulations respecting the Territory or other Property belonging to the United States; and nothing in this Constitution shall be so construed as to Prejudice any Claims of the United States, or of any particular State.

Section 4.

The United States shall guarantee to every State in this Union a Republican Form of Government, and shall protect each of them against Invasion; and on Application of the Legislature, or of the Executive (when the Legislature cannot be convened), against domestic Violence.

Article V.

The Congress, whenever two thirds of both Houses shall deem it necessary, shall propose Amendments to this Constitution, or, on the Application of the Legislatures of two thirds of the several States, shall call a Convention for proposing Amendments, which, in either Case, shall be valid to all Intents and Purposes, as Part of this Constitution, when ratified by the Legislatures of three fourths of the several States, or by Conventions in three fourths thereof, as the one or the other Mode of Ratification may be proposed by the Congress; Provided that no Amendment which may be made prior to the Year One thousand eight hundred and eight shall in any Manner affect the first and fourth Clauses in the Ninth Section of the first Article; and that no State, without its Consent, shall be deprived of its equal Suffrage in the Senate.

Article VI.

Clause 1: All Debts contracted and Engagements entered into, before the Adoption of this Constitution, shall be as valid against the United States under this Constitution, as under the Confederation.

Clause 2: This Constitution, and the Laws of the United States which shall be made in Pursuance thereof; and all Treaties made, or which shall be made, under the Authority of the United States, shall be the supreme Law of the Land; and the Judges in every State shall be bound thereby, any Thing in the Constitution or Laws of any State to the Contrary notwithstanding.

Clause 3: The Senators and Representatives before mentioned, and the Members of the several State Legislatures, and all executive and judicial Officers, both of the United States and of the several States, shall be bound by Oath or Affirmation, to support this Constitution; but no religious Test shall ever be required as a Qualification to any Office or public Trust under the United States.

Article VII.

The Ratification of the Conventions of nine States, shall be sufficient for the Establishment of this Constitution between the States so ratifying the Same.

Done in Convention by the Unanimous Consent of the States present the Seventeenth Day of September in the Year of our Lord one thousand seven hundred and Eighty seven and of the Independence of the United States of America the Twelfth In witness whereof We have hereunto subscribed our Names,

G. Washington, President and deputy from Virginia

Delaware:	North Carolina:	New Hampshire:	New Jersey:
Geo: Read	Wm. Blount	John Langdon	Wil: Livingston
Gunning Bedford jun	Richd. Dobbs Spaight	Nicholas Gilman	David Brearley
John Dickinson	Hu Williamson	Massachusetts:	Wm. Paterson
Richard Bassett	South Carolina:	Nathaniel Gorham	Jona: Dayton
Jaco: Broom	J. Rutledge	Rufus King	Pennsylvania:
Maryland:	Charles Cotesworth Pinckney	Connecticut:	B Franklin
James McHenry	Charles Pinckney	Wm. Saml. Johnson	Thomas Mifflin
Dan of St Thos. Jenifer	Pierce Butler	Roger Sherman	Robt. Morris
Danl. Carroll	Georgia:	New York:	Geo. Clymer
Virginia:	William Few	Alexander Hamilton	Thos. FitzSimons
John Blair	Abr Baldwin		Jared Ingersoll
James Madison Jr.			James Wilson
			Gouv Morris

Bill of Rights (Amendments 1–10)

Amendment I

Congress shall make no law respecting an establishment of religion, or prohibiting the free exercise thereof; or abridging the freedom of speech, or of the press; or the right of the people peaceably to assemble, and to petition the Government for a redress of grievances.

Amendment II

A well regulated Militia, being necessary to the security of a free State, the right of the people to keep and bear Arms, shall not be infringed.

Amendment III

No Soldier shall, in time of peace be quartered in any house, without the consent of the Owner, nor in time of war, but in a manner to be prescribed by law.

Amendment IV

The right of the people to be secure in their persons, houses, papers, and effects, against unreasonable searches and seizures, shall not be violated, and no Warrants shall issue, but upon probable cause, supported by Oath or affirmation, and particularly describing the place to be searched, and the persons or things to be seized.

Amendment V

No person shall be held to answer for a capital, or otherwise infamous crime, unless on a presentment or indictment of a Grand Jury, except in cases arising in the land or naval forces, or in the Militia, when in actual service in time of War or public danger; nor shall any person be subject for the same offence to be twice put in jeopardy of life or limb; nor shall be compelled in any criminal case to be a witness against himself, nor be deprived of life, liberty, or property, without due process of law; nor shall private property be taken for public use, without just compensation.

Amendment VI

In all criminal prosecutions, the accused shall enjoy the right to a speedy and public trial, by an impartial jury of the State and district wherein the crime shall have been committed, which district shall have been previously ascertained by law, and to be informed of the nature and cause of the accusation; to be confronted with the witnesses against him; to have compulsory process for obtaining witnesses in his favor, and to have the Assistance of Counsel for his defence.

Amendment VII

In suits at common law, where the value in controversy shall exceed twenty dollars, the right of trial by jury shall be preserved, and no fact tried by a jury, shall be otherwise reexamined in any Court of the United States, than according to the rules of the common law.

Amendment VIII

Excessive bail shall not be required, nor excessive fines imposed, nor cruel and unusual punishments inflicted.

Amendment IX

The enumeration in the Constitution, of certain rights, shall not be construed to deny or disparage others retained by the people.

Amendment X

The powers not delegated to the United States by the Constitution, nor prohibited by it to the States, are reserved to the States respectively, or to the people.

Amendments 11–27

Amendment XI

The judicial power of the United States shall not be construed to extend to any suit in law or equity, commenced or prosecuted against one of the United States by Citizens of another State, or by Citizens or Subjects of any Foreign State.

Amendment XII

The Electors shall meet in their respective states and vote by ballot for President and Vice-President, one of whom, at least, shall not be an inhabitant of the same state with themselves; they shall name in their ballots the person voted for as President, and in distinct ballots the person voted for as Vice-President, and they shall make distinct lists of all persons voted for as President, and of all persons voted for as Vice-President, and of the number

of votes for each, which lists they shall sign and certify, and transmit sealed to the seat of the government of the United States, directed to the President of the Senate;—The President of the Senate shall, in the presence of the Senate and House of Representatives, open all the certificates and the votes shall then be counted;—the person having the greatest number of votes for President, shall be the President, if such number be a majority of the whole number of Electors appointed; and if no person have such majority, then from the persons having the highest numbers not exceeding three on the list of those voted for as President, the House of Representatives shall choose immediately, by ballot, the President. But in choosing the President, the votes shall be taken by states, the representation from each state having one vote; a quorum for this purpose shall consist of a member or members from two-thirds of the states, and a majority of all the states shall be necessary to a choice. And if the House of Representatives shall not choose a President whenever the right of choice shall devolve upon them, before the fourth day of March next following, then the Vice-President shall act as President, as in the case of the death or other constitutional disability of the President. The person having the greatest number of votes as Vice-President, shall be the Vice-President, if such number be a majority of the whole number of electors appointed, and if no person have a majority, then from the two highest numbers on the list, the Senate shall choose the Vice-President; a quorum for the purpose shall consist of two-thirds of the whole number of Senators, and a majority of the whole number shall be necessary to a choice. But no person constitutionally ineligible to the office of President shall be eligible to that of Vice-President of the United States.

Amendment XIII

Section 1.

Neither slavery nor involuntary servitude, except as a punishment for crime whereof the party shall have been duly convicted, shall exist within the United States, or any place subject to their jurisdiction.

Section 2.

Congress shall have power to enforce this article by appropriate legislation.

Amendment XIV

Section 1.

All persons born or naturalized in the United States, and subject to the jurisdiction thereof, are citizens of the United States and of the State wherein they reside. No State shall make or enforce any law which shall abridge the privileges or immunities of citizens of the United States; nor shall any State deprive any person of life, liberty, or property, without due process of law; nor deny to any person within its jurisdiction the equal protection of the laws.

Section 2.

Representatives shall be apportioned among the several States according to their respective numbers, counting the whole number of persons in each State, excluding Indians not taxed. But when the right to vote at any election for the choice of electors for President and Vice-President of the United States, Representatives in Congress, the Executive and Judicial officers of a State, or the members of the Legislature thereof, is denied to any of the male inhabitants of such State, being twenty-one years of age, and citizens of the United States, or in any way abridged, except for participation in rebellion, or other crime, the basis of representation therein shall be reduced in the proportion which the number of such male citizens shall bear to the whole number of male citizens twenty-one years of age in such State.

Section 3.

No person shall be a Senator or Representative in Congress, or elector of President and Vice-President, or hold any office, civil or military, under the United States, or under any State, who, having previously taken an oath, as a member of Congress, or as an officer of the United States, or as a member of any State legislature, or as an executive or judicial officer of any State, to support the Constitution of the United States, shall have engaged in insurrection or rebellion against the same, or given aid or comfort to the enemies thereof. But Congress may by a vote of two-thirds of each House, remove such disability.

Section 4.

The validity of the public debt of the United States, authorized by law, including debts incurred for payment of pensions and bounties for services in suppressing insurrection or rebellion, shall not be questioned. But neither the United States nor any State shall assume or pay any debt or obligation incurred in aid of insurrection or rebellion against the United States, or any claim for the loss or emancipation of any slave; but all such debts, obligations and claims shall be held illegal and void.

Section 5.

The Congress shall have power to enforce, by appropriate legislation, the provisions of this article.

Amendment XV

Section 1.

The right of citizens of the United States to vote shall not be denied or abridged by the United States or by any State on account of race, color, or previous condition of servitude.

Section 2.

The Congress shall have power to enforce this article by appropriate legislation.

Amendment XVI

The Congress shall have power to lay and collect taxes on incomes, from whatever source derived, without apportionment among the several States, and without regard to any census or enumeration.

Amendment XVII

The Senate of the United States shall be composed of two Senators from each State, elected by the people thereof, for six years; and each Senator shall have one vote. The electors in each State shall have the qualifications requisite for electors of the most numerous branch of the State legislatures.

When vacancies happen in the representation of any State in the Senate, the executive authority of such State shall issue writs of election to fill such vacancies: *Provided,* That the legislature of any State may empower the executive thereof to make temporary appointments until the people fill the vacancies by election as the legislature may direct.

This amendment shall not be so construed as to affect the election or term of any Senator chosen before it becomes valid as part of the Constitution.

Amendment XVIII

Section 1.
After one year from the ratification of this article the manufacture, sale, or transportation of intoxicating liquors within, the importation thereof into, or the exportation thereof from the United States and all territory subject to the jurisdiction thereof for beverage purposes is hereby prohibited.

Section 2.
The Congress and the several States shall have concurrent power to enforce this article by appropriate legislation.

Section 3.
This article shall be inoperative unless it shall have been ratified as an amendment to the Constitution by the legislatures of the several States, as provided in the Constitution, within seven years from the date of the submission hereof to the States by the Congress.

Amendment XIX

The right of citizens of the United States to vote shall not be denied or abridged by the United States or by any State on account of sex.

Congress shall have power to enforce this article by appropriate legislation.

Amendment XX

Section 1.
The terms of the President and Vice President shall end at noon on the 20th day of January, and the terms of Senators and Representatives at noon on the 3d day of January, of the years in which such terms would have ended if this article had not been ratified; and the terms of their successors shall then begin.

Section 2.
The Congress shall assemble at least once in every year, and such meeting shall begin at noon on the 3d day of January, unless they shall by law appoint a different day.

Section 3.
If, at the time fixed for the beginning of the term of the President, the President elect shall have died, the Vice President elect shall become President. If a President shall not have been chosen before the time fixed for the beginning of his term, or if the President elect shall have failed to qualify, then the Vice President elect shall act as President until a President shall have qualified; and the Congress may by law provide for the case wherein neither a President elect nor a Vice President elect shall have qualified, declaring who shall then act as President, or the manner in which one who is to act shall be selected, and such person shall act accordingly until a President or Vice President shall have qualified.

Section 4.

The Congress may by law provide for the case of the death of any of the persons from whom the House of Representatives may choose a President whenever the right of choice shall have devolved upon them, and for the case of the death of any of the persons from whom the Senate may choose a Vice President whenever the right of choice shall have devolved upon them.

Section 5.

Sections 1 and 2 shall take effect on the 15th day of October following the ratification of this article.

Section 6.

This article shall be inoperative unless it shall have been ratified as an amendment to the Constitution by the legislatures of three-fourths of the several States within seven years from the date of its submission.

Amendment XXI

Section 1.

The eighteenth article of amendment to the Constitution of the United States is hereby repealed.

Section 2.

The transportation or importation into any State, Territory, or Possession of the United States for delivery or use therein of intoxicating liquors, in violation of the laws thereof, is hereby prohibited.

Section 3.

This article shall be inoperative unless it shall have been ratified as an amendment to the Constitution by conventions in the several States, as provided in the Constitution, within seven years from the date of the submission hereof to the States by the Congress.

Amendment XXII

Section 1.

No person shall be elected to the office of the President more than twice, and no person who has held the office of President, or acted as President, for more than two years of a term to which some other person was elected President shall be elected to the office of the President more than once. But this Article shall not apply to any person holding the office of President when this Article was proposed by the Congress, and shall not prevent any person who may be holding the office of President, or acting as President, during the term within which this Article becomes operative from holding the office of President or acting as President during the remainder of such term.

Section 2.

This article shall be inoperative unless it shall have been ratified as an amendment to the Constitution by the legislatures of three-fourths of the several States within seven years from the date of its submission to the States by the Congress.

Amendment XXIII

Section 1.

The District constituting the seat of Government of the United States shall appoint in such manner as Congress may direct:

A number of electors of President and Vice President equal to the whole number of Senators and Representatives in Congress to which the District would be entitled if it were a State, but in no event more than the least populous State; they shall be in addition to those appointed by the States, but they shall be considered, for the purposes of the election of President and Vice President, to be electors appointed by a State; and they shall meet in the District and perform such duties as provided by the twelfth article of amendment.

Section 2.

The Congress shall have power to enforce this article by appropriate legislation.

Amendment XXIV

Section 1.

The right of citizens of the United States to vote in any primary or other election for President or Vice President, for electors for President or Vice President, or for Senator or Representative in Congress, shall not be denied or abridged by the United States or any State by reason of failure to pay any poll tax or other tax.

Section 2.

The Congress shall have power to enforce this article by appropriate legislation.

Amendment XXV

Section 1.

In case of the removal of the President from office or of his death or resignation, the Vice President shall become President.

Section 2.

Whenever there is a vacancy in the office of the Vice President, the President shall nominate a Vice President who shall take office upon confirmation by a majority vote of both Houses of Congress.

Section 3.

Whenever the President transmits to the President pro tempore of the Senate and the Speaker of the House of Representatives his written declaration that he is unable to discharge the powers and duties of his office, and until he transmits to them a written declaration to the contrary, such powers and duties shall be discharged by the Vice President as Acting President.

Section 4.

Whenever the Vice President and a majority of either the principal officers of the executive departments or of such other body as Congress may by law provide, transmit to the President pro tempore of the Senate and the Speaker of the House of Representatives their written declaration that the President is unable to discharge the powers and duties of his office, the Vice President shall immediately assume the powers and duties of the office as Acting President.

Thereafter, when the President transmits to the President pro tempore of the Senate and the Speaker of the House of Representatives his written declaration that no inability exists, he shall resume the powers and duties of his office unless the Vice President and a majority of either the principal officers of the executive department or of such other body as Congress may by law provide, transmit within four days to the President pro tempore of the Senate and the Speaker of the House of Representatives their written declaration that the President is unable to discharge the powers and duties of his office. Thereupon Congress shall decide the issue, assembling within forty-eight hours for that purpose if not in session. If the Congress, within twenty-one days after receipt of the latter written declaration, or, if Congress is not in session, within twenty-one days after Congress is required to assemble, determines by two-thirds vote of both Houses that the President is unable to discharge the powers and duties of his office,

the Vice President shall continue to discharge the same as Acting President; otherwise, the President shall resume the powers and duties of his office.

Amendment XXVI

Section 1.
The right of citizens of the United States, who are eighteen years of age or older, to vote shall not be denied or abridged by the United States or by any State on account of age.

Section 2.
The Congress shall have the power to enforce this article by appropriate legislation.

Amendment XXVII

No law, varying the compensation for the services of the Senators and Representatives, shall take effect, until an election of representatives shall have intervened.

Appendix B

Timeline of Events

1787 The Constitution of the United States is drafted and signed; Federalist Papers are published

1789 Constitution is ratified; George Washington is elected as first president; Judiciary Act passes

1791 Bill of Rights is adopted

1794 Whiskey Rebellion is put down

1795 Eleventh Amendment, prohibiting lawsuits against states in federal court, is ratified

1798 Alien and Sedition Acts are passed

1800 Capital moves from Philadelphia to Washington, D.C.

1803 Thomas Jefferson approves Louisiana Purchase, doubling the size of the United States; Supreme Court establishes doctrine of judicial review

1804 Lewis and Clark begin exploration of the Northwest Territories

1804 The Twelfth Amendment, altering presidential elections, is ratified

1808 Slave trade is banned

1810 United States annexes west Florida

1814 During the War of 1812 with England, Francis Scott Key writes the words to "The Star-Spangled Banner"; Treaty of Ghent is signed, ending the war of 1812

1817 New York Stock Exchange is founded

1819 Spain cedes Florida to the United States

1820 Missouri Compromise outlaws slavery in states north of latitude 36° 30'

1823 President James Monroe warns European countries not to interfere in the diplomacy of the Western Hemisphere, establishing the Monroe Doctrine

1830 President Jackson signs the Indian Removal Act, forcing all Native Americans to move west of the Mississippi

1841 President William Henry Harrison is inaugurated on March 4, and dies from pneumonia on April 4, having served what today is still the shortest presidential term in American history

1848 United States accepts Republic of Texas into the Union after winning Mexican-American War

1849 California gold rush gets underway

1854 Kansas-Nebraska act is signed, admitting the two states to the Union and repealing the Missouri Compromise; Republican Party is formed

1857 In the Dred Scott case, the Supreme Court rules that Congress cannot ban slavery and that slaves aren't citizens

1860 Abraham Lincoln is elected president

1861 Civil War begins when Confederacy attacks Ft. Sumter in South Carolina

1863 President Lincoln signs the Emancipation Proclamation, freeing the Southern slaves; delivers Gettysburg Address

1865 Civil War ends; President Lincoln is assassinated by John Wilkes Booth; Thirteenth Amendment, prohibiting slavery, is ratified

1867 United States purchases Alaska from Russia

1868 Fourteenth Amendment is ratified, creating due process and equal protection of the law for all Americans; President Andrew Johnson is impeached by the House and acquitted by one vote in the Senate

1869 Transcontinental railroad is completed

1870 Fifteenth Amendment gives all male Americans the right to vote

1878 President Rutherford B. Hayes installs first telephone in the White House

1883 Pendleton Act establishes federal civil service

1886 American Federation of Labor (AFL) is organized

1890 Sherman Anti-Trust Act is passed

1896 In *Plessy v. Ferguson*, Supreme Court declares that segregation is legal so long as it's "separate but equal," paving the way for Jim Crow in the South

1898   United States annexes Hawaii

1901   Following the assassination of William McKinley, Theodore Roosevelt becomes president

1909   NAACP is formed

1913   Federal Reserve system is created; Sixteenth Amendment gives Congress the right to levy an income tax; Seventeenth Amendment puts into effect the direct election of U.S. senators

1914   Panama Canal opens, linking the Atlantic and Pacific oceans

1917   United States enters World War I

1919   Eighteenth Amendment prohibits the consumption of alcohol; Senate rejects the Treaty of Versailles

1920   Nineteenth Amendment gives women the right to vote

1929   Stock market crashes; beginning of Great Depression

1933   Franklin Roosevelt is inaugurated as president; Twentieth Amendment moves the presidential inauguration date from March 4 to January 20; Twenty-first Amendment repeals prohibition

1935   Social Security Act is passed

1937   President Roosevelt's plan to "pack" the Supreme Court is rebuffed by Congress

1941   Japan attacks Pearl Harbor; United States enters World War II

1944   D-Day liberation of Western Europe

1945   Allied forces defeat Germany; atomic bombs are dropped on Hiroshima and Nagasaki; Japan surrenders; United Nations is established

1948   Congress passes the Marshall Plan to rebuild Western Europe; Truman Doctrine of "containing" communism is established

1949   North American Treaty Organization (NATO) is created; Soviet Union acquires atomic bomb

1950   United States enters Korean War

1951   Twenty-second Amendment limits president's tenure to two terms

1953   Korean War ends

1954 Supreme Court outlaws school segregation in *Brown v. Board of Education*; Wisconsin Senator Joseph McCarthy is censured by the Senate

1959 Hawaii and Alaska become the last two states to join the United States

1961 Twenty-third Amendment gives residents of the District of Columbia the right to vote in presidential elections

1963 President John F. Kennedy is assassinated

1964 Congress authorizes use of force in Vietnam; Civil Rights Act is passed; Twenty-fourth Amendment eliminates poll taxes as an obstacle to voting

1965 Medicare is established as part of Lyndon Johnson's Great Society program

1967 Thurgood Marshall is appointed first African-American justice to the Supreme Court; Twenty-fifth Amendment outlines presidential and vice presidential succession

1968 Martin Luther King Jr. is assassinated

1969 Neil Armstrong and Edwin (Buzz) Aldrin Jr. walk on the moon

1971 Twenty-sixth Amendment gives eighteen-year-olds the right to vote

1973 War Powers Act is passed; Supreme Court legalizes abortion in *Roe v. Wade*

1974 President Nixon is impeached and resigns from office

1981 U.S. hostages in Iran are released after 444 days in captivity; Sandra Day O'Connor becomes first woman Supreme Court justice

1986 President Reagan overhauls federal tax code

1989 End of the cold war

1990 Americans with Disabilities Act is passed

1992 Twenty-seventh Amendment alters the process for congressional pay raises

1994 NAFTA agreement is passed

1996 President Clinton signs welfare reform legislation

1998 President Clinton is impeached by the House of Representatives and acquitted the following year

2001 Terrorist attacks on the World Trade Towers and Pentagon kill over 3,000 people

2002 Department of Homeland Security created

Index

O

Office of Management and Budget (OMB), 128, 169–70
Office of Personnel Management (OPM), 136
Off-the-record conversations, 212
OMB (Office of Management and Budget), 128, 169–70
Omnibus bills, 68
Opinion journalism, 210–11
OPM (Office of Personnel Management), 136
O'Rourke, Andrew, 247

P

PACs (Political action committees), 199–200
Paine, Thomas, 4–5
Pardons, 95–96
Parties (political), 177–90
  advocating political issues, 189
  current issue positions, 182–84
  duality of issues and, 185
  organization structure of, 189–90
  organizing government, 188
  overview, 177
  raising money, 188
  recruiting candidates, 187–88
  roles of, 187–89
  supporting campaigns, 188
  third parties today, 186–87
  two-party system, 178–81, 184–85
  winner-takes-all system and, 184–85
  See also specific party names
Party affiliation, 59
  caucuses/coalitions/alliances and, 42–43
  House leadership and, 38–39
  House rules and, 42
  majority leaders and, 38, 50
  minority leaders and, 38–39, 50
  presidential nomination confirmations and, 47–48
  Senate leadership and, 50
  Speaker of the House and, 37–38
  whips and, 39

Pataki, George, 238
Patterson, William, 9
Peace Corps, 132
Pell, Claiborne, 69
Pelosi, Nancy, 39
Penn, William, 24
Penumbral rights, 31
People for the Ethical Treatment of Animals (PETA), 192
The People's House, 36
Perkins, Frances, 126
Perot, H. Ross, 88, 186, 227
PETA (People for the Ethical Treatment of Animals), 192
Philadelphiensis, 12
Pierce, Franklin, 82, 107, 108
PIRG (Public Interest Research Groups), 197
Plessy v. Ferguson, 155
Plymouth (MA), 2
Political action committees (PACs), 199–200
Political parties. See Parties (political); Party affiliation; specific party names
Polk, James K., 82
Pool reporting, 216
Pork-barrel spending, 44, 60, 174–75
Powell, Colin, 88, 126
PPF (Putting People First), 192
Preamble (Constitution), 14
Presidency, 79–92
  Article II and, 17–20, 278–80
  bureaucracy and, 63
  caretaker era, 82
  congressional relations and, 38, 61–62
  evolution of, 82–84
  George Washington shaping, 80–82
  media and, 214–16, 226–27
  overview, 79
  paths to, 54, 87–88
  requirements for, 87
  running mate considerations, 113–14
  shortest tenure of, 89
  uniqueness of, 80
  See also Presidential powers/roles; Presidents
Presidential elections
  campaign, 225–28
  campaign consultants for, 219

debates for, 227
Election Day, 18, 228
Electoral College and. See Electoral College
history of, 10–11, 18
issue stances and, 225–26
media coverage, 226–27
nominating conventions and, 224–25
preparation for, 218–20
process, 218
raising money for, 218–19
state campaigns, 219–20
volunteering for, 263–64
See also Presidential primaries
Presidential powers/roles, 19–20, 93–104
  appointments, 19, 33, 47–48, 94–95
  checking Supreme Court, 163–64
  chief diplomat, 99–101
  chief executive, 94–96
  "comforter-in-chief", 104
  commander in chief, 19, 97–99
  diplomatic recognition authorization, 101
  expansion of, 19–20
  granting pardons/reprieves, 95–96
  head of state, 96–97
  legislator in chief, 102–3
  party leadership, 103–4
  treaty authorization, 19, 99–100
  vetoing legislation, 78, 102–3
  See also Presidency; Presidents
Presidential primaries
  campaign consultants for, 219
  caucuses for, 221–22
  debates for, 220–21
  frontloading, 223–24
  Iowa Caucus, 222
  New Hampshire Primary, 222–23
  preparation for, 218–20
  raising money for, 218–19
  regional, 223–24
  state campaigns, 219–20
  straw polls, 221
  types of, 224
  volunteering for, 263–64
  winning nomination, 221–24
  See also Presidential elections
Presidential succession, 37, 88–90, 110–12, 287–88, 289–90
Presidential Succession Act (1947), 89

THE EVERYTHING SERIES!

BUSINESS

Everything® **Business Planning Book**
Everything® **Coaching and Mentoring Book**
Everything® **Fundraising Book**
Everything® **Home-Based Business Book**
Everything® **Leadership Book**
Everything® **Managing People Book**
Everything® **Network Marketing Book**
Everything® **Online Business Book**
Everything® **Project Management Book**
Everything® **Selling Book**
Everything® **Start Your Own Business Book**
Everything® **Time Management Book**

COMPUTERS

Everything® **Build Your Own Home Page Book**
Everything® **Computer Book**
Everything® **Internet Book**
Everything® **Microsoft® Word 2000 Book**

COOKBOOKS

Everything® **Barbecue Cookbook**
Everything® **Bartender's Book, $9.95**
Everything® **Chinese Cookbook**
Everything® **Chocolate Cookbook**
Everything® **Cookbook**
Everything® **Dessert Cookbook**
Everything® **Diabetes Cookbook**
Everything® **Indian Cookbook**
Everything® **Low-Carb Cookbook**
Everything® **Low-Fat High-Flavor Cookbook**

Everything® **Low-Salt Cookbook**
Everything® **Mediterranean Cookbook**
Everything® **Mexican Cookbook**
Everything® **One-Pot Cookbook**
Everything® **Pasta Book**
Everything® **Quick Meals Cookbook**
Everything® **Slow Cooker Cookbook**
Everything® **Soup Cookbook**
Everything® **Thai Cookbook**
Everything® **Vegetarian Cookbook**
Everything® **Wine Book**

HEALTH

Everything® **Alzheimer's Book**
Everything® **Anti-Aging Book**
Everything® **Diabetes Book**
Everything® **Dieting Book**
Everything® **Herbal Remedies Book**
Everything® **Hypnosis Book**
Everything® **Massage Book**
Everything® **Menopause Book**
Everything® **Nutrition Book**
Everything® **Reflexology Book**
Everything® **Reiki Book**
Everything® **Stress Management Book**
Everything® **Vitamins, Minerals, and Nutritional Supplements Book**

HISTORY

Everything® **American Government Book**
Everything® **American History Book**
Everything® **Civil War Book**
Everything® **Irish History & Heritage Book**

Everything® **Mafia Book**
Everything® **Middle East Book**
Everything® **World War II Book**

HOBBIES & GAMES

Everything® **Bridge Book**
Everything® **Candlemaking Book**
Everything® **Casino Gambling Book**
Everything® **Chess Basics Book**
Everything® **Collectibles Book**
Everything® **Crossword and Puzzle Book**
Everything® **Digital Photography Book**
Everything® **Easy Crosswords Book**
Everything® **Family Tree Book**
Everything® **Games Book**
Everything® **Knitting Book**
Everything® **Magic Book**
Everything® **Motorcycle Book**
Everything® **Online Genealogy Book**
Everything® **Photography Book**
Everything® **Pool & Billiards Book**
Everything® **Quilting Book**
Everything® **Scrapbooking Book**
Everything® **Sewing Book**
Everything® **Soapmaking Book**

HOME IMPROVEMENT

Everything® **Feng Shui Book**
Everything® **Feng Shui Decluttering Book, $9.95 (15.95 CAN)**
Everything® **Fix-It Book**
Everything® **Gardening Book**
Everything® **Homebuilding Book**

All Everything® books are priced at $12.95 or $14.95, unless otherwise stated. Prices subject to change without notice.
Canadian prices range from $11.95–$31.95, and are subject to change without notice.

Everything® **Home Decorating Book**
Everything® **Landscaping Book**
Everything® **Lawn Care Book**
Everything® **Organize Your Home Book**

EVERYTHING® *KIDS'* BOOKS

All titles are $6.95

Everything® **Kids' Baseball Book, 3rd Ed. ($10.95 CAN)**
Everything® **Kids' Bible Trivia Book** ($10.95 CAN)
Everything® **Kids' Bugs Book** ($10.95 CAN)
Everything® **Kids' Christmas Puzzle & Activity Book** ($10.95 CAN)
Everything® **Kids' Cookbook** ($10.95 CAN)
Everything® **Kids' Halloween Puzzle & Activity Book** ($10.95 CAN)
Everything® **Kids' Joke Book** ($10.95 CAN)
Everything® **Kids' Math Puzzles Book** ($10.95 CAN)
Everything® **Kids' Mazes Book** ($10.95 CAN)
Everything® **Kids' Money Book** ($11.95 CAN)
Everything® **Kids' Monsters Book** ($10.95 CAN)
Everything® **Kids' Nature Book** ($11.95 CAN)
Everything® **Kids' Puzzle Book** ($10.95 CAN)
Everything® **Kids' Riddles & Brain Teasers Book** ($10.95 CAN)
Everything® **Kids' Science Experiments Book** ($10.95 CAN)
Everything® **Kids' Soccer Book** ($10.95 CAN)
Everything® **Kids' Travel Activity Book** ($10.95 CAN)

KIDS' STORY BOOKS

Everything® **Bedtime Story Book**
Everything® **Bible Stories Book**
Everything® **Fairy Tales Book**
Everything® **Mother Goose Book**

LANGUAGE

Everything® **Inglés Book**
Everything® **Learning French Book**
Everything® **Learning German Book**
Everything® **Learning Italian Book**
Everything® **Learning Latin Book**
Everything® **Learning Spanish Book**
Everything® **Sign Language Book**
Everything® **Spanish Phrase Book, $9.95 ($15.95 CAN)**

MUSIC

Everything® **Drums Book (with CD), $19.95 ($31.95 CAN)**
Everything® **Guitar Book**
Everything® **Playing Piano and Keyboards Book**
Everything® **Rock & Blues Guitar Book (with CD), $19.95 ($31.95 CAN)**
Everything® **Songwriting Book**

NEW AGE

Everything® **Astrology Book**
Everything® **Divining the Future Book**
Everything® **Dreams Book**
Everything® **Ghost Book**
Everything® **Love Signs Book, $9.95 ($15.95 CAN)**
Everything® **Meditation Book**
Everything® **Numerology Book**
Everything® **Palmistry Book**
Everything® **Psychic Book**
Everything® **Spells & Charms Book**
Everything® **Tarot Book**
Everything® **Wicca and Witchcraft Book**

PARENTING

Everything® **Baby Names Book**
Everything® **Baby Shower Book**
Everything® **Baby's First Food Book**
Everything® **Baby's First Year Book**
Everything® **Breastfeeding Book**

Everything® **Father-to-Be Book**
Everything® **Get Ready for Baby Book**
Everything® **Getting Pregnant Book**
Everything® **Homeschooling Book**
Everything® **Parent's Guide to Children with Autism**
Everything® **Parent's Guide to Positive Discipline**
Everything® **Parent's Guide to Raising a Successful Child**
Everything® **Parenting a Teenager Book**
Everything® **Potty Training Book, $9.95 ($15.95 CAN)**
Everything® **Pregnancy Book, 2nd Ed.**
Everything® **Pregnancy Fitness Book**
Everything® **Pregnancy Organizer, $15.00 ($22.95 CAN)**
Everything® **Toddler Book**
Everything® **Tween Book**

PERSONAL FINANCE

Everything® **Budgeting Book**
Everything® **Get Out of Debt Book**
Everything® **Get Rich Book**
Everything® **Homebuying Book, 2nd Ed.**
Everything® **Homeselling Book**
Everything® **Investing Book**
Everything® **Money Book**
Everything® **Mutual Funds Book**
Everything® **Online Investing Book**
Everything® **Personal Finance Book**
Everything® **Personal Finance in Your 20s & 30s Book**
Everything® **Wills & Estate Planning Book**

PETS

Everything® **Cat Book**
Everything® **Dog Book**
Everything® **Dog Training and Tricks Book**
Everything® **Golden Retriever Book**
Everything® **Horse Book**
Everything® **Labrador Retriever Book**
Everything® **Puppy Book**
Everything® **Tropical Fish Book**

All Everything® books are priced at $12.95 or $14.95, unless otherwise stated. Prices subject to change without notice.
Canadian prices range from $11.95–$31.95, and are subject to change without notice.

REFERENCE

Everything® **Astronomy Book**
Everything® **Car Care Book**
Everything® **Christmas Book, $15.00**
    ($21.95 CAN)
Everything® **Classical Mythology Book**
Everything® **Einstein Book**
Everything® **Etiquette Book**
Everything® **Great Thinkers Book**
Everything® **Philosophy Book**
Everything® **Psychology Book**
Everything® **Shakespeare Book**
Everything® **Tall Tales, Legends, &**
    Other Outrageous
    Lies Book
Everything® **Toasts Book**
Everything® **Trivia Book**
Everything® **Weather Book**

RELIGION

Everything® **Angels Book**
Everything® **Bible Book**
Everything® **Buddhism Book**
Everything® **Catholicism Book**
Everything® **Christianity Book**
Everything® **Jewish History &**
    Heritage Book
Everything® **Judaism Book**
Everything® **Prayer Book**
Everything® **Saints Book**
Everything® **Understanding Islam**
    Book
Everything® **World's Religions Book**
Everything® **Zen Book**

SCHOOL & CAREERS

Everything® **After College Book**
Everything® **Alternative Careers Book**
Everything® **College Survival Book**
Everything® **Cover Letter Book**
Everything® **Get-a-Job Book**
Everything® **Hot Careers Book**

Everything® **Job Interview Book**
Everything® **New Teacher Book**
Everything® **Online Job Search Book**
Everything® **Resume Book, 2nd Ed.**
Everything® **Study Book**

SELF-HELP/ RELATIONSHIPS

Everything® **Dating Book**
Everything® **Divorce Book**
Everything® **Great Marriage Book**
Everything® **Great Sex Book**
Everything® **Kama Sutra Book**
Everything® **Romance Book**
Everything® **Self-Esteem Book**
Everything® **Success Book**

SPORTS & FITNESS

Everything® **Body Shaping Book**
Everything® **Fishing Book**
Everything® **Fly-Fishing Book**
Everything® **Golf Book**
Everything® **Golf Instruction Book**
Everything® **Knots Book**
Everything® **Pilates Book**
Everything® **Running Book**
Everything® **Sailing Book, 2nd Ed.**
Everything® **T'ai Chi and QiGong Book**
Everything® **Total Fitness Book**
Everything® **Weight Training Book**
Everything® **Yoga Book**

TRAVEL

Everything® **Family Guide to Hawaii**
Everything® **Guide to Las Vegas**
Everything® **Guide to New England**
Everything® **Guide to New York City**
Everything® **Guide to Washington D.C.**
Everything® **Travel Guide to The Dis-**
    neyland Resort®, Cali-
    fornia Adventure®,

Universal Studios®, and
the Anaheim Area
Everything® **Travel Guide to the Walt**
    Disney World Resort®, Uni-
    versal Studios®, and
    Greater Orlando, 3rd Ed.

WEDDINGS

Everything® **Bachelorette Party Book,**
    $9.95 ($15.95 CAN)
Everything® **Bridesmaid Book, $9.95**
    ($15.95 CAN)
Everything® **Creative Wedding Ideas**
    Book
Everything® **Elopement Book, $9.95**
    ($15.95 CAN)
Everything® **Groom Book**
Everything® **Jewish Wedding Book**
Everything® **Wedding Book, 2nd Ed.**
Everything® **Wedding Checklist,**
    $7.95 ($11.95 CAN)
Everything® **Wedding Etiquette Book,**
    $7.95 ($11.95 CAN)
Everything® **Wedding Organizer,**
    $15.00 ($22.95 CAN)
Everything® **Wedding Shower Book,**
    $7.95 ($12.95 CAN)
Everything® **Wedding Vows Book,**
    $7.95 ($11.95 CAN)
Everything® **Weddings on a Budget**
    Book, $9.95 ($15.95 CAN)

WRITING

Everything® **Creative Writing Book**
Everything® **Get Published Book**
Everything® **Grammar and Style Book**
Everything® **Grant Writing Book**
Everything® **Guide to Writing Chil-**
    dren's Books
Everything® **Screenwriting Book**
Everything® **Writing Well Book**

Available wherever books are sold!
To order, call 800-872-5627, or visit us at everything.com

Everything® and everything.com® are registered trademarks of F+W Publications, Inc.